# Mornings *with* JESUS 2014

DAILY ENCOURAGEMENT *for your* SOUL

**365** DEVOTIONS

RENEE ANDREWS

SUSANNA FOTH AUGHTMON

GWEN FORD FAULKENBERRY

GRACE FOX

TRICIA GOYER

SHARON HINCK

REBECCA BARLOW JORDAN

ERIN KEELEY MARSHALL

DIANNE NEAL MATTHEWS

CYNTHIA RUCHTI

**Guideposts**

New York

*Mornings with Jesus 2014*

Published by Guideposts
16 East 34th Street
New York, New York 10016
Guideposts.org

## Acknowledgments

Every attempt has been made to credit the sources of copyrighted material used in this book. If any such acknowledgment has been inadvertently omitted or miscredited, receipt of such information would be appreciated.

"Joyfully" by Ed Cash, Mia Fieldes and Kari Jobe copyright © 2009 SHOUT! Music Publishing (APRA) Gateway Create Publishing (BMI) (Adm. at EMICMGPublishing.com)/Wondrously Made Songs (BMI). All rights reserved. Used by permission. International copyright secured. All rights reserved. Used by permission.

Scripture quotations marked (AMP) are taken from *The Amplified Bible*, © 1954, 1958, 1962, 1964, 1965, 1987 by The Lockman Foundation. Used by permission. www.Lockman.org

Scripture quotations marked (CEB) are taken from *Common English Bible*. Copyright © 2011 Common English Bible.

Scripture quotations marked (ESV) are taken from the Holy Bible, English Standard Version, copyright © 2001 by Crossway Bibles, a division of Good News Publishers. Used by permission. All rights reserved.

Scripture quotations marked (GNT) are taken from *Good News Translation*. Copyright © 1992 by American Bible Society.

Scripture quotations marked (GW) are taken from *God's Word Translation*. Copyright © 1995 by God's Word to the Nations. Used by permission of Baker Publishing Group.

Scripture quotations marked (HCS) are taken from the Holman Christian Standard Bible. Copyright © 1999, 2000, 2002, 2003 by Holman Bible Publishers, Nashville, Tennessee. All rights reserved.

Scripture quotations marked (KJV) are taken from *The King James Version of the Bible*.

Scripture quotations marked (MSG) are taken from *The Message*. Copyright © 1993, 1994, 1995, 1996, 2000, 2001, 2002 by Eugene H. Peterson.

Scripture quotations marked (NAS) are taken from the *New American Standard Bible*, copyright © 1960, 1962, 1963, 1968, 1971, 1972, 1973, 1975, 1977, 1995 by the Lockman Foundation. Used by permission. www.Lockman.org

Scripture quotations marked (NCV) are taken from the *New Century Version*. Copyright © 2005 by Thomas Nelson, Inc. Used by permission. All rights reserved.

Scripture quotations marked (NIV) are taken from two editions: *The Holy Bible, New International Version, NIV*. Copyright © 1973, 1978, 1984, 2011 by Biblica. All rights reserved worldwide. *The Holy Bible, New International Version*. Copyright © 1973, 1978, 1984 International Bible Society. Used by permission of Zondervan Bible Publishers.

Scripture quotations marked (NKJV) are taken from *The Holy Bible, New King James Version*. Copyright © 1997, 1990, 1985, 1983 by Thomas Nelson, Inc.

Scripture quotations marked (NLT) are taken from the *Holy Bible*, New Living Translation. Copyright © 1996. Used by permission of Tyndale House Publishers, Inc., Wheaton, Illinois 60189. All rights reserved.

Scripture quotations marked (NRSV) are taken from the *New Revised Standard Version Bible*. Copyright © 1989 by the Division of Christian Education of the National Council of the Churches of Christ in the U.S.A. Used by permission. All rights reserved.

Scripture quotations marked (RSV) are taken from the *Revised Standard Version of the Bible*, copyright © 1946, 1952, and 1971 the Division of Christian Education of the National Council of the Churches of Christ in the United States of America. Used by permission. All rights reserved.

Scripture quotations marked (VOICE) are taken from *The Voice Bible*. Copyright © 2012 Thomas Nelson, Inc. The Voice™ translation © 2012 Ecclesia Bible Society. All rights reserved.

Cover and interior design by Müllerhaus
Cover photo by Shutterstock
Indexed by Indexing Research
Typeset by Aptara, Inc.

Printed and bound in the United States of America
10 9 8 7 6 5 4 3 2 1

# INTRODUCTION

WHO AMONG US HASN'T STRUGGLED with the difficulties of being with God and the anointed one, Jesus, with all our hearts, all our minds, and all our actions? We know what is expected of us, and yet, Jesus's stillness occasionally escapes us. But His words to us are clear: "I myself am the Way—I am Truth, and I am Life. No one comes to Abba God, but through me" (John 14:6, TIB).

Jesus makes a point of inviting us to be with Him—to sit with Him, to pray with Him, to love Him, and to be like Him. We are told to give all of our cares to God—*all of them* (1 Peter 5:7). We are reassured that as long as we come to Jesus, we will never be without Him or His love (John 6:37).

In the spirit of that Scripture, what better, more genuine way to live Jesus's words than to spend our time in His presence, in thoughtful and loving prayer and devotion, drinking from the springs of His never-ending compassion and feasting on His joy (John 6:53–58). All of us come to understand, through prayer, worship, and study, that knowing Jesus is knowing truth (John 8:31–32). The night comes and the day begins, and we arise anew in His grace.

We titled this devotional *Mornings with Jesus* because, regardless of when you have time, the morning—with all of its fresh beginnings, new hopes, and dazzling light—seems to best edify Jesus's radiant love.

It is our sincerest hope that in the pages of *Mornings with Jesus 2014*, you'll find inspiration to lay aside anxiety and, instead, seek the kingdom of God. You will recognize the easy-to-use format of this book. There is a one-page reading for every day of the year. It starts with a Bible verse, followed by a devotion by one of ten specially selected contributors who connect the Scripture to a moment in their lives, sharing their wisdom and insights with the hope of encouraging you. "Faith Step" ends each day's reading; it's a practical way to apply what you've read to your life and to continue thinking about the day's lesson. Faith Steps will challenge you to look at Scripture in a new way, ask a question that will help you make a change in your life, or simply encourage you to praise and thank Jesus.

### *Mornings with Jesus* in Your In-box

Now you can enjoy the daily encouragement of *Mornings with Jesus 2014* wherever you are! Receive each day's devotion on your computer, tablet, or smartphone. Visit MorningswithJesus.org/MWJ2014 and enter this code: MWJ2014.

Sign up for the *Mornings with Jesus* online newsletter through Guideposts .org. Each week you'll receive an encouraging devotion or personal thoughts from an author about her own devotional time, prayer life, what it was like to write her devotions, how focusing on Jesus affected her relationship with Him, and more!

# WEDNESDAY, JANUARY 1

*Later Jesus found him at the temple and said to him,
"See, you are well again. Stop sinning or something
worse may happen to you." John 5:14 (NIV)*

MY HUSBAND AND I HAVE an annual miniretreat each New Year's Day. This year instead of praying about goals for the year, we decided to invite the Holy Spirit to convict us, guiding us to repent of bad habits and confess sins that were His priority for us to change.

Along with our daughter who was home from college for the holidays, we spent time in prayer, writing down insights that came to mind. After we filled our pages, we prayed and asked Jesus to grant us forgiveness and also to change us through His power.

A large pillar candle was burning in the middle of the table, and its center was guttered down, creating a perfect vessel to symbolically burn our papers full of sins.

We folded up our papers and tucked them down by the wick, feeling grateful as we watched them burn. Unfortunately, the extra flames from the paper caused the wax sides of the candle to melt rapidly. Soon liquid wax poured over the coffee table and dripped onto the floor. We scrambled to put out the flame and clean up the mess.

The experience helped me make sense of this verse. Although forgiveness is a free gift and we are completely absolved of guilt through Christ, there are often natural consequences to persisting in sin. I'm grateful for Jesus's forgiveness, but also reminded of the damage my poor choices can cause. All the more reason to ask for His grace to work in me each day.

**FAITH STEP:** *Have you noticed the effects of poor choices spilling into your life or the lives of others? If so, in what ways? Receive the forgiveness of Jesus, and ask Him for strength to stop sinning.*

—*Sharon Hinck*

# THURSDAY, JANUARY 2

*So faith comes from hearing, that is, hearing
the Good News about Christ. Romans 10:17 (NLT)*

I HAD NO BOYFRIEND, NO friends. I was a big mess. But as I lay there—seventeen, pregnant, and depressed—I thought back to days long ago when I'd attended Sunday school. Words . . . God's Word . . . filtered through my mind:

"For God so loved the world, that he gave his only begotten Son, that whosoever believeth in him should not perish, but have everlasting life" (John 3:16, KJV).

I thought back to the stories I heard as a child about a God who would never leave me, would never forsake me. Then I prayed the first prayer I'd prayed in years. It wasn't eloquent, but it was real.

"I've really messed up this time, God. If You can do better, please do." That was my moment of change. The moment when heaven met my heart. And God has indeed done better. I had led myself down a dark path, but through God I had found a silver lining.

I discovered that no matter what I had done in my life, through the forgiveness of Jesus Christ, I was a new creation. I can't say at that moment I realized fully how special I was to God or that I knew then that God had big plans for me. But over time, as I continued to read His Word, I grew in my relationship with Him. And this path started with the simplest Scripture verse of all.

Faith comes when we hear the Good News of Jesus and believe it. We don't need to know the whole Bible well to start our faith journey. We just need to believe and accept what we do know—believe it with all of our hearts. Once I took my life and placed it in Jesus's hands, our relationship grew.

Every relationship has a first step before there is a next step. What step of faith is God asking you to take today?

**FAITH STEP:** *Write down some of the Scripture verses that you have memorized. Is there any truth in them that you need to accept today in a way that you haven't accepted before?*

—*Tricia Goyer*

# FRIDAY, JANUARY 3

---

*When we heard of it, our hearts melted in fear and everyone's courage failed because of you, for the Lord your God is God in heaven above and on the earth below. Joshua 2:11 (NIV)*

---

JOSHUA, THE ISRAELITES' NEWLY APPOINTED leader, was about to cross the Jordan River into God's "promised land." He sent in two spies to look over the area, especially the city of Jericho. The two spies took refuge in the home of a prostitute named Rahab, a rather questionable place to hide for two God-believers.

But Rahab was different. She, along with the people around her, had heard of God's miraculous intervention: God enabled one million-plus Israelites to cross the mighty Red Sea after they had spent over four hundred years as Egyptian slaves.

Wait! That event had occurred forty years earlier. Rahab still remembered—if she was even born then. Or her family and those around her had passed on the remarkable story, along with recent news. God's name and authority made a lasting impression on that pagan community! Rahab chose to believe in the "God in heaven above and on the earth below." She hid the spies, and God spared her life.

On the other hand, the Hebrew children of Israel experienced short-term memory loss—often. The Bible records them forgetting about their miraculous crossing. They began grumbling three days after their feet hit dry land (Exodus 15:22–24).

When I read those passages recently, I wondered which kind of faith I've mirrored the most through the years: the reverential fear that remembers God's faithfulness or the fickle faith of the Israelites.

Instead of my forgetfulness, I pray I'll focus daily on God's long-term faithfulness—extravagantly poured out through the greatest miracle of all, Jesus.

---

FAITH STEP: *Review the Israelites' miraculous crossing of the Red Sea in Exodus 14. What impossible things will you believe in Jesus for this year?*

*—Rebecca Barlow Jordan*

# SATURDAY, JANUARY 4

*Then He said to them all, "If anyone wants to come with Me, he must deny himself, take up his cross daily, and follow Me." LUKE 9:23 (HCS)*

I FELT POSITIVELY VIRTUOUS AS I went about my morning. This time I would really stick with my commitment to eat a healthier diet. For breakfast, I had enjoyed Greek yogurt with homemade granola. *See,* I told myself, *it's not so hard.* Then I opened a kitchen drawer and found myself staring at a paper-wrapped rectangular object with my name written all over it. Drat that Ikea for selling such creamy chocolate bars with crunchy hazelnuts! And for giving a special price when you buy three giant bars at once. By midmorning, I no longer felt virtuous. And I didn't have any chocolate left to share with my husband.

Self-denial is not a popular concept in our culture, which promotes self-absorption. We demand instant gratification and the freedom to make lots of personal choices. Jesus taught that being His follower means taking on a different mind-set. Going against our human nature, which seeks our personal desires above all else. Relinquishing control of our lives in order to follow His leading. Dying to self so we can live for Him.

When it comes to chocolate or desserts, I can have a real problem with self-denial. And while there are times when I'm willing to subjugate my own desires for a greater good or for the benefit of a loved one, I have to admit that dying to self is an ongoing battle. It certainly doesn't come naturally.

Taking up my cross to follow Jesus means making a conscious decision every day, moment by moment. It also means believing that if Jesus calls me to give up something that I *think* I want, it's only so that I can receive what He knows will truly satisfy me.

**FAITH STEP:** *Is Jesus asking you to give up something you want in order to follow Him more fully? Do you trust Him enough to believe that He has a reason for doing so?*

*—Dianne Neal Matthews*

# SUNDAY, JANUARY 5

*For God made Christ, who never sinned, to be the offering for our sin, so that
we could be made right with God through Christ. 2 Corinthians 5:21 (NLT)*

I'VE ONLY BEEN TO NEW York City a few times, but each time I go, I've seen
something that I haven't seen before. One night I saw something so bizarre I
doubt I will ever forget the image.

We had just finished seeing a Broadway show and were walking back to
our hotel when we saw a large group of elegantly dressed men and women
Dumpster-diving. Yes, you're reading that correctly. They were in evening
wear, fancy dresses, suits, and tuxedos . . . and leaning over a large Dumpster
to pull things out of the trash. As we neared, we saw what the fuss was about.
The Dumpster had apparently been brought in by a large publishing company, and they had filled it with brand-new hardcover books. These weren't
just any ol' books. They were by best-selling authors, several of whom were
on the *New York Times* best-seller list. I know because the crowd would cheer
the name of the coveted author when they hauled out another book.

That group was willing to do something they normally would never do in
order to gain the prize of a best-selling author's books (or in this case, a *lot* of
authors' books). In spite of how beautifully they were dressed and their prob-
able affluent lifestyles, they dove in to the trash to gain the prize.

Christ dove into the trash once, too, didn't He? When He left his beautiful
sin-free realm of Heaven to come to earth and take on our sin. Christ, like
that group that night, was willing to dive into the trash, because He found
the prize worthy. He found *us* worthy!

**FAITH STEP:** *When you put something in the trash today, push the item down into the
can. Think about your hand, surrounded by that muck. Then imagine surrounding your
pristine soul with sin. That's what Christ did. Now, wash your hand and praise Him for
washing your sin away.*

—*Renee Andrews*

# MONDAY, JANUARY 6

*Therefore, imitate God like dearly loved children. Live your life with love, following the example of Christ, who loved us and gave himself for us. Ephesians 5:1–2 (CEB)*

DIGITAL CAMERAS AND CAMERA PHONES have ushered in dramatic changes in our culture. We take more photos than ever before. Even amateur photographers can produce an artistic image. We don't stand at the photo counter mourning an entire roll of film that came out looking like the interior of a coal mine on a moonless night, or bleached-out reddish brown from overexposure. We no longer save shoe boxes full of photo duplicates or hang on to images that can be deleted.

We may not waste film anymore, as we once did. We may not shoot pictures that aren't worth taking. But we may waste focus.

I remember being awed by my then ten-year-old granddaughter as she took random photos while on a field trip. When asked why she photographed those particular individuals, she answered, "I'm taking pictures of *kind* people."

What a photo album that will make!

Jesus asked us to imitate Him, to imprint His image on our lives, and to focus on the good and worthy and honorable. Is that where my lens is focused? Do I point my mind's camera at those who act like Jesus, show kindness like He did, love as He did, sacrifice like He did, give generously like He did?

If others are focused on the same, how often will I show up in someone's "looks like Jesus" shot?

FAITH STEP: *The pictures we think worth taking tell a lot about us and where our attention is focused. Take a moment today to skim through the images on your camera. Do you see a theme? Beauty, nature, family, friends, acts of kindness? Or are there coarse, unkind, immature, greed-revealing images ready for the Delete button?*

*—Cynthia Ruchti*

# TUESDAY, JANUARY 7

*You have turned for me my mourning into dancing; You have loosed my sackcloth and girded me with gladness; That my soul may sing praise to You, and not be silent. O Lord my God, I will give thanks to You forever. Psalm 30:11–12 (NAS)*

TONIGHT I TUCKED THREE LITTLE ones into bed, and their prayers went something like this. "Dear Jesus, thank You for our dog, Jake, and our beds, and the ladder on the bunk bed, and our curtains. Thank You for Mommy, Daddy, our books, and toys. Thank You for popcorn and . . ." (You get the idea.)

Sometimes I want to give my kids a limit. "Okay, only pick ten things each to be thankful for tonight." Yet, even as I considered that, I felt a gentle stirring in my soul. Maybe I need to be more like them. Maybe I need my list to be longer, rather than their list be shorter.

When do we outgrow thankfulness? When do we come to the age when we only thank God for the big things? This is one of those times that Isaiah 11:6 (NLT) talks about: "a little child will lead them all."

Do you want to be more thankful in your life? As you're going through the day washing laundry, driving to work, or chasing around kids, make it a habit to thank God for the little things around you that may seem commonplace—your ability to use a washing machine, the radio in your car, the sunshine outside. I try to remember to thank God for my family members as I'm folding my family's clothes. As I fold my husband's shirts I thank God for his arms of support. As I fold little socks I thank God that my children are healthy and able to run and play.

Finally, thank God for all the ways He's turned your mourning into dancing. The way He's taken away your heaviness and filled you with gladness. The moments I'm most thankful are when I look back to where I was in times of sadness and pain, and see where God has brought me to now!

**FAITH STEP:** *Buy a yearly calendar to use as a thanksgiving journal. For each day write down one thing that you're thankful for. It'll be a wonderful keepsake!*

—*Tricia Goyer*

# WEDNESDAY, JANUARY 8

---

*"Abide in Me, and I in you. As the branch cannot bear fruit of itself, unless it abides in the vine, neither can you, unless you abide in Me." John 15:4 (NKJV)*

---

"IT'S A NEW YEAR! WHAT are you planning to do this year? Start a diet, exercise more, read the Bible more, organize your closets?" We usually ask each other the same questions every year. But those endless projects usually share one common factor: "doing." And there's nothing wrong with that.

But as I took a closer look at the life of Jesus, I discovered He seems more interested in who I am, rather than what I do. In other words, Jesus cares more about my character than He does my activity.

Yes, He gave active instructions to the disciples: "Go...teach...baptize... make disciples...." And we are to follow those same teachings. But how many of Jesus's parables involved showing mercy, forgiveness, grace, and love—all the qualities of Jesus's own life? Paul echoed this principle in Colossians 3:12 (NKJV): "put on tender mercies, kindness, humility, meekness, longsuffering."

Even James, the half brother of Jesus, emphasized character development. In fact, he offered the right balance between both "being" and "doing": "Show me your faith without deeds, and I will show you my faith by what I do" (James 2:18, NIV). Both are important, but one is impossible without the other.

The disciples asked Jesus, "'What must we do to do the works God requires?' Jesus answered, 'The work of God is this: to believe in the one he has sent'" (John 6:29, NIV). In other words, *abide*. It's all about relationship. Stay connected to Jesus so the actions will flow naturally from the character of Jesus growing within.

I shortened my New Year's list this year: "Stay close to Jesus. Abide in Him." Because when the character grows, the right actions will follow.

---

FAITH STEP: *What character qualities would you like Jesus to develop in you this year?*

—*Rebecca Barlow Jordan*

# THURSDAY, JANUARY 9

*"Whatever you have said in the dark will be heard in the light, and what you have whispered behind closed doors will be shouted from the housetops for all to hear!" Luke 12:3 (NLT)*

HAVE YOU SUCCUMBED TO THE Twitter world yet? I've given in a little, not much, but there's a push in the publishing world to utilize social media to build a network and a following for books. I have a love-hate relationship with it, to be honest. Part of me is intrigued by the idea that I can send out any message I want to the world; the other part of me finds that horrifying because I know I'm not always wise, not even part of the time. I'm a work in progress, and sometimes I need quite a bit more work.

Anyway, a couple of months ago I retweeted a link about an Iranian pastor who was on trial. Christians around the world were praying for him, that justice would reign and God's truth would win. Somehow that tweet automatically set up my account to retweet updates from that link every day or so. I feel like my private world keeps whispering in the invisible world of cyberspace. Feels powerful in a way.

Actually, much of the Christian world whispers its faith in the dark. Yet no matter how their governments try to control and destroy them, their faith is anchored powerfully in the Lord of the universe, King Jesus, who reigns over time and nations and all the evil that threatens the world.

Someday Jesus will free His whole network of followers to worship Him in public, shouting His truths from the rooftops. In the meantime, He still is not limited by His enemies. Every silent—or retweeted—prayer from every believer is like a shouted battle cry for His kingdom.

Shout His praises from your heart today.

**FAITH STEP:** *Commit to pray for persecuted Christians worldwide. Visit the Web site for Voice of the Martyrs at www.persecution.com.*

—*Erin Keeley Marshall*

# FRIDAY, JANUARY 10

*Pray without ceasing. 1 Thessalonians 5:17 (KJV)*

MY BROTHER-IN-LAW NEEDED A PLACE to stay. Our simple life in the country offered the kind of reflection time he craved while he waited for the sentence that would change his life dramatically for the next seven years.

So my husband and I took him in for two months and adapted to his habits as he did to ours. We quickly became accustomed to his peanut M&M addiction.

When he left our house to begin serving his court-ordered sentence, we held on to the ever-present bowl of peanut M&M's and turned it from addiction to a prayer ministry. Guests and family who knew the story were told, "You're welcome to the M&M's, but if you take one, use it as a reminder to pray."

The grandkids were especially interested in a prayer ministry connected with a big bowl of M&M's. "Who are you praying for now, Josh?" I asked as he swiped another from the bowl.

"The whole world."

"Oh. Okay." Can't fault a child for knowing the whole world needs prayer.

Five-year-old Andy grabbed a chocolate-covered peanut, bowed his head and leaned it against the buffet on which the bowl rested, ate the peanut, then promptly grabbed another and bowed his head again.

What had we started?

When I'd caught Josh with his hand in the bowl too many times one afternoon, I asked, "Now, be honest with Grammie. Who were you praying for just now?"

"I was just telling Jesus how much I love Him."

"Um…carry on."

FAITH STEP: *How many quick but deeply meaningful "Jesus, I love You so much!" prayers pepper your day and mine? I have to believe He's at least as pleased to hear it as I am to know my grandsons—whatever the motivation—are faithful to say it.*

—*Cynthia Ruchti*

# SATURDAY, JANUARY 11

*Since, then, you have been raised with Christ, set your hearts on things above, where Christ is seated at the right hand of God. Set your minds on things above, not on earthly things. Colossians 3:1–2 (NIV)*

I PULLED MY CHAIR UP to my desk. To meet my deadline, I needed to write several pages in the next few hours. As my file opened on the computer, I noticed the desktop seemed dusty. I left the office to grab cleaning supplies. In the hallway, I noticed the entryway rugs looked grimy. I opened the door to shake out the rugs and saw that the front flower boxes looked dry. If I didn't water them now, I'd forget to do it later. There were sure a lot of weeds springing up. Maybe I should . . .

No, no, no. Time to get serious about the day's writing. I went back inside and saw my voice message light blinking. My manuscript waited on my computer, ignored and neglected as I returned the call.

If anyone had asked me whether my writing work was a top priority for me, I would have answered with a resounding, "Yes!" But my actions sure didn't show it. I wasn't focusing. My attention flitted to each new thing that caught my eye.

As a follower of Jesus, if anyone asked me if He is my priority, I'd also answer with a resounding, "Yes!" But my actions often don't show it. My focus drifts quickly to earthly things. A stack of bills can send my worries into a tailspin, a hurtful comment from a friend can make my thoughts dwell on my emotional needs, a big sale can stir cravings for unimportant things I don't really need.

My theme for this year is, "Focus." Each time I feel the distracting pull of earthly things, I want to use that as a reminder to set my heart and mind on Jesus.

FAITH STEP: *Which earthly things tend to draw your attention? Consciously steer your thoughts toward Jesus instead.*

—*Sharon Hinck*

# SUNDAY, JANUARY 12

---

*The life I now live in the body, I live by faith in the Son of God, who loved me and gave himself for me.* Galatians 2:20 (NIV)

---

ONE THING I ENJOY ABOUT my little grandson is that he loves to hear me sing. As he grows older, he'll become more discriminating in his musical tastes. I'm sure my voice will lose its charm. But for now, he's happy to hear hymns, standards like "The Wheels on the Bus," and songs that I make up on the spot. This comes in handy when he needs to be soothed or when I'm trying to change the diaper on his squirming bottom.

As I took care of him one week, I added a classic Joe Cocker song to my repertoire; however, I never made it past the first line. "You are so beautiful . . . ." I would sing. Every single time, before I could get the words "to me" out, Roman looked up and declared, "I *am* beautiful." He spoke these words in complete innocence, free of pride, embarrassment, or egotism. Just a simple agreement with my own words.

Roman believes that he's beautiful because his Nana tells him so. He knows he is loved because his family tells him in words and actions. But I couldn't help wondering if Roman's self-esteem will erode as he gets close to the teen years. I remembered my own struggle with a negative self-image, how I let my worth be determined by others' comments or opinions.

Sometimes I have a hard time believing what Jesus says about me. In His eyes, I'm a dearly loved child of God, forgiven, a co-heir to a glorious inheritance. But playing the comparison game can make me feel inferior. And my shortcomings and failures can convince me that I will never measure up. During those moments, I need to remember that Jesus sees me as someone worth dying for. Then I can also say with confidence, "I *am* beautiful."

---

FAITH STEP: *Each time you have a negative thought about yourself today, stop and ask Jesus to remind you how He sees you.*

—*Dianne Neal Matthews*

# MONDAY, JANUARY 13

*You are precious in my eyes, and honored, and I love you. Isaiah 43:4 (ESV)*

THE OTHER DAY I WAS shopping at our local grocery store. There was a promotion that week, and the cashier stamped my card and then scratched it with a quarter to find the hidden message. Her face lit up like a flashing sale sign.

"You're a winner!"

She rang a deafening bell, proclaiming my newly discovered greatness to the entire store over the loud speaker. Someone emerged from the front office to take a picture and give me my five-dollar reward. The photo, I was told, would be displayed on a poster with all of the other winners.

When I arrived home with enough food to feed my little army, I told them of my fame.

"I'm a winner!"

My family looked at me like I was crazy, as they often do.

"It's true! The lady at CV's told me so!"

It was fun being a winner for the rest of the evening. The next day, however, in spite of their best efforts, my daughter's team lost a ball game. According to the scoreboard, Grace was a loser, and so was I, as her biggest fan.

We were on the way back up later in the week when Harper won the spelling bee at school. But that excitement only lasted till afternoon recess, when he was called into the principal's office for breaking someone's glasses (by accident, of course).

If we place our value in the hands of others, life will always be like the weather in Arkansas—up and down and all around. The opinions of people can be as unpredictable as our performance on a given day. But Jesus's love never changes. No matter what anyone else says, He says you're to die for. And He should know.

FAITH STEP: *When assessing your value, to whose voices do you listen? Take a moment to hear from the One Who died for you. You are precious. Honored. I love you—forever.*

—*Gwen Ford Faulkenberry*

# TUESDAY, JANUARY 14

*Then call on me when you are in trouble,*
*and I will rescue you, and you will give me glory.*
Psalm 50:15 (NLT)

THE BEST MARKETING SLOGAN OF all time has to be, "Would you like fries with that?" How many billions of dollars have been made with one question . . . one suggestion? The offer of French fries comes at the perfect time: The need is there. The customer is hungry. The price is right too. What's another dollar? What's a few more calories? And by responding positively, the diner turns a mere sandwich into a meal.

In our everyday lives we too often miss the opportunity to greatly impact others—whether they are a family member, a friend, or a new acquaintance. One of the most underused phrases in our Christian walk can do more for Jesus's name than anything else, but we haven't understood its power. What's the phrase? "Can I pray with you about that right now?"

It's a question, but also an offer. It's offering your words and suggesting Who is the solution. The need is there. The "customer" is hungry for peace, or help, or hope. The price is even better than a medium fry. It's free. And Psalm 107:13 (NLT) is a good example of what will happen: "'Lord, help!' they cried in their trouble, and he saved them from their distress."

What will stopping for a moment to pray cost you? It'll take paying attention. It'll mean stepping out of your comfort zone. It might even bring you embarrassment once or twice. But what's a bit of nervousness when it means you're bringing the needs of another person before Jesus? When the other person responds positively, your prayers will feed his or her soul. More than that, you're reminding that person to Whom to turn when the next need arises.

FAITH STEP: *The next time someone brings a need for prayer before you, pause right there and ask, "Can I pray with you about that right now?"*

*—Tricia Goyer*

# WEDNESDAY, JANUARY 15

---

*"I am the Alpha and the Omega," says the Lord God, "who is,
and who was, and who is to come, the Almighty." Revelation 1:8 (NIV)*

---

YESTERDAY MORNING, MY SIX-YEAR-OLD, ADDISON, came and crawled in bed next to me. We were snuggly and warm and neither of us really wanted to get up. But breakfast was calling, so Addie and I decided to play a round of rock-paper-scissors to see who would get out of bed first.

Round 1: rock vs. rock. Round 2: Addie waited until I put out rock and he put out paper. "Hey, you can't wait until I do rock and then put out paper!" He giggled. Round 3: scissors vs. gun. "What is that?" "A laser." "A laser? Since when does rock-paper-scissors have a laser?" "It's extreme rock-paper-scissors." Round 4: one index finger pointing up versus arms spread wide as if holding a giant ball. "What is that?" Addie asked of my finger pointing to the sky. "A stick of dynamite." I said grinning, excited by my own creativity. "What do your arms mean?" I asked. Addie grinned bigger, "God." "God? If you are God, then you win every time!" Bigger grin. "Yep."

Addie went holy on me. There was no way I could top it. When it comes to Jesus, you just can't get any bigger or better than that. I got up and made breakfast.

---

FAITH STEP: *Spread your arms out wide as far as you can. Remind yourself that Jesus is the Alpha and Omega, the beginning and the end. He is powerful and holy. Speak out the above verse and believe it, knowing that He can do anything!*

*—Susanna Foth Aughtmon*

# THURSDAY, JANUARY 16

*"Woe to you, teachers of the law and Pharisees, you hypocrites! You are like whitewashed tombs, which look beautiful on the outside but on the inside are full of the bones of the dead and everything unclean. In the same way, on the outside you appear to people as righteous but on the inside you are full of hypocrisy and wickedness." Matthew 23:27–28 (NIV)*

AMONG MY FRIENDS WITH CHRONIC illness, we often discuss the difficulty of having an "invisible illness." We use that term because although we suffer pain, weakness, and large challenges to daily life, our outward appearance isn't hugely affected. In fact, we often hear the perky comment from friends, "But you look fine!"

The Pharisees also looked fine from the outside. They followed all the obvious rules. But Jesus saw beyond the show. Inside, the invisible illness of sin was eating away at their souls.

The "woe to you" chapter of Matthew 23 isn't my favorite of Jesus's sermons. But as I reread it today, I could hear His compassion behind the rebuke. We can waste our lives trying to spruce up our appearance and miss His grace.

Just as medical scans and tests can sometimes help pinpoint the damage that doesn't show on the outside, Jesus reveals what is going on in our hearts—hidden from view. He points out how lost we are apart from Him. But He doesn't leave us there. He offers His own suffering and death to bring us the cure.

FAITH STEP: *Today, let's confess to Jesus any way we've tried to whitewash our souls, and admit our inability to get at the root problem on our own. Then let's thank Him for seeing beyond the façade and providing forgiveness and love.*

*—Sharon Hinck*

# FRIDAY, JANUARY 17

*Weeping may last through the night, but joy comes with the morning.*
Psalm 30:5 (NLT)

CANCER STRUCK MORE THAN THIRTY friends and family members in a three-year period. Most returned to health, but several succumbed to the disease. Also during that time my dad, mother-in-law, and father-in-law died. Then came the shock of our kids' youth pastor abandoning his family.

Quite honestly, I hope we never experience another season like that again. The darkness of discouragement threatened to overtake us at times, and I wondered if the night would ever end.

The secret to perseverance, I found, was remembering Scripture's promises to give strength, hope, and peace. It helped to recall Jesus's commands not to fear, and the reminders of His presence. It also helped to know that, contrary to whatever my emotions said, this night would not last forever.

As surely as the sun rises every day, so morning follows the dark night of grief. Wounds heal. We learn to breathe and, yes, to laugh again.

Perhaps the darkness of discouragement surrounds you. The night's been a long one, and you doubt whether tomorrow's dawn will ever come. Be encouraged, my friend. Morning's on its way, and it brings joy.

FAITH STEP: *Turn Isaiah 61:3 into a prayer—"Father, thank You for promising to comfort me when I mourn. You will give beauty for ashes, joy instead of mourning, and praise instead of despair. Use my difficult situation to plant me like a strong and graceful oak for Your own glory. In Jesus's name, amen."*

—*Grace Fox*

# SATURDAY, JANUARY 18

*When you look for me, you will find me. When you wholeheartedly seek me,
I will let you find me, declares the Lord. Jeremiah 29:13–14 (GW)*

As I'M WRITING THIS, THE Sundance Film Festival is taking place about an hour from my home. Each January, this ten-day event features screenings of independent films and programs showcasing producers, directors, and actors. For each of those days, crowds of people swarm to the Park City area. Even if they don't have tickets for an event, many people are willing to spend long periods of time standing in bitter cold, hoping just to catch a glimpse of a star.

I've never been the type of person to get starstruck, but I do get excited about what I call "Jesus Sightings" in the Old Testament. These are verses or passages that picture the Messiah and His future ministry. In Genesis He's the promised descendant of Eve who will crush the serpent's head. In Exodus every object in the tabernacle portrays some aspect of Jesus. The book of Ruth shows how Jesus would fulfill the role of our Kinsman-Redeemer.

Many verses in Psalms offer details about Jesus's life; chapter 22 describes what He would endure on the cross. Isaiah foretells His virgin birth, Micah pinpoints an obscure village as His birthplace, and Zechariah describes His riding into Jerusalem on a donkey. More than three hundred prophecies portray Jesus before we get to the four gospel accounts of His life.

On more than one occasion the Jewish leaders looked for Jesus to have Him arrested. But He slipped from their notice because the right time had not come. Jesus never hides from those who love Him. We don't have to drive around hoping to snag a glimpse of Him before He darts off. We can see Him pictured throughout the Bible; more importantly we can see His presence and working in our own life. And that's the most exciting "sighting" we will ever get.

FAITH STEP: *Do you need a fresh glimpse of Jesus? Ask Him to reveal Himself to you today and then keep your eyes open.*

*—Dianne Neal Matthews*

# SUNDAY, JANUARY 19

*And he said to them all, If any man will come after me, let him deny himself, and take up his cross daily, and follow me. Luke 9:23 (KJV)*

WHEN MY BROTHER HAD AN appendectomy and had to stay in the hospital overnight, my sister-in-law and mother stayed with him. It was my job to stay home with the kids. After I fed them pizza and macaroni-and-cheese, my niece Madeline crawled up in my lap. Her blue eyes seemed as big as dinner plates.

"My daddy had to get his independence out."

I nodded soberly, stroking her blonde hair and trying to restrain a snicker.

"What's an independence?"

I showed her a drawing of the vermiform appendix and explained, as best as I could, about how it got sick and hurt her daddy, so it had to come out.

"He won't miss it, though. We don't even need it!"

If only there was a procedure to remove our independence, once and for all. I'd have it done. My worst struggles as a Christian always get back to my stubborn insistence on my own way. But such "independence" never leads to peace.

Instead, when we belong to Jesus, the only path to peace is our total dependence on Him. It's a daily—and if you're like me, sometimes moment-by-moment—decision.

FAITH STEP: *What do you need to lay down today in order to pick up your cross and follow Jesus? Resolve to do it. You need Him more than your independence.*

—*Gwen Ford Faulkenberry*

# MONDAY, JANUARY 20

*Gold there is, and rubies in abundance, but lips that speak knowledge are a rare jewel. Proverbs 20:15 (NIV)*

I BENT TO PICK UP the colorful plastic "gems" scattered over the carpet. Dropping them into my kids' pirate treasure chests, I couldn't help but smile. How they loved their role-playing games.

Though both children were upstairs sleeping, echoes of "*Argh!*" and "Ahoy matey!" still filtered around me. Fit words for a pirate or a young child in the land of daydreams, but those expressions don't often show up in normal conversation. In fact, I think the only ones who utter them at all are people working with kids and actors playing pirates. They just don't serve much purpose for good or bad.

Yet as I finished straightening up at the end of a busy day, I got to wondering about the phrases I do hear and say frequently, terms I probably shouldn't let slip. Got any of those in your verbal closet, anything that a child would correct you for talking naughty?

I've never had much of a potty mouth, but sometimes I am guilty of failing to show wisdom in my tone of voice, in my "pithy" (aka sarcastic) comments that really would be better off left unsaid.

Generations after King Solomon (the wisest man born) wrote today's verse, Jesus lived out its message. One reading of John 8 shows Jesus's speech and tone embodying wisdom as He talked graciously with the woman caught in adultery (verses 1–11), humbly when He stated that His authority came from God, His Father (verse 8), authoritatively when He clarified that He is the One to believe in (verse 24), and honestly throughout the chapter as He dealt with the Pharisees' twisted teachings.

I pray that my speech and tone will echo the rare treasures of Jesus's wisdom.

**FAITH STEP:** *Ask Jesus to open your ears to the quality of your speech and tighten your lips to allow only words of wisdom to pass through them.*

*—Erin Keeley Marshall*

# TUESDAY, JANUARY 21

*"The people living in darkness have seen a great light;*
*on those living in the land of the shadow of death a light has dawned."*
Matthew 4:16 (NIV)

WHERE I LIVE IN THE suburbs, appearances are kept up. Life seems bright and sunshine-y. No one really knows when their neighbor is struggling. Addictions are secret. Problems are buried. People suffer in silence and pretend they have their lives in order. There is the general attitude of: *If we are educated and rich and politically correct, do we really need God?*

I told my cousin Gretchen last week, "I keep forgetting we are in a battle." Because it is a different kind of battle. This creeping coldness that hardens hearts and turns minds inward. The gray thinking that sin isn't actually sin if we don't want it to be a sin. The rampant belief that evil doesn't actually exist.

Maybe this is the worst kind of darkness there is. Because the truth is, suburbs or not, we need the light of the world to come with His clarity and hope and vision and growth and warmth and salvation.

We need the dawn of His love to break over us, warm and vibrant. We need the piercing light of His rightness to show us the path He has for us. We need the brilliance of who He is to heal us and transform us. I have had the thought that I need to climb up on my roof here to get close to the sun and remind myself how much I need His light. However, I am not agile and that could be disastrous, so I'm keeping to the patio.

But I am sending a high prayer to the heavens this morning, a petition to the Bright and Morning Star, and it is simply this, "Lord, please bring Your light!" And I believe He is.

FAITH STEP: *Go outside and sit in the sun. Close your eyes and ask Jesus to fill you with His light from the inside out, to give you clarity and direction as you follow Him today.*

—Susanna Foth Aughtmon

# WEDNESDAY, JANUARY 22

---

*While Jesus was still speaking, some men came from the house of Jairus,
the synagogue ruler. "Your daughter is dead," they said. "Why bother the teacher
any more?" Ignoring what they said, Jesus told the synagogue ruler,
"Don't be afraid; just believe." Mark 5:35–36* (NIV)

---

JAIRUS MUST HAVE BEEN ON an emotional roller coaster. Relief flooded his heart when Jesus agreed to go to his house and heal his dying daughter. But then Jesus stopped to have a conversation with a woman in the crowd. Jairus was forced to wait, knowing that each minute's delay put his little girl in greater danger. Then, just as Jesus finished his business with the woman, messengers brought the news Jairus dreaded to hear. His daughter had died.

I can only imagine how the devoted father's heart clenched in his chest when he saw the men approaching. Did he have time to think, *Too late! It was all for nothing?* Jesus turned to Jairus as though He hadn't heard what the men said. "Don't be afraid. Just believe." Soon, Jairus saw his longing fulfilled. He got his daughter back.

It's exciting to read the gospel accounts of Jesus restoring life to people who had died. But today He still works as the Life-giver in the lives of believers. He raises dead hopes, resurrects old dreams, and brings life to relationships that seem to have died. He wants to breathe new life into us in all sorts of ways. But He wants us to understand that miracles are tied to faith.

Our circumstances may seem hopeless. Other people may tell us that it's no use. That person will never come to faith. That relationship will never work. You'll never pull it off. "Why bother the Teacher anymore?"

Jesus says otherwise. He asks us to ignore what seems obvious and to trust Him to work in our life. Against all odds, He asks us to *just believe*.

---

FAITH STEP: *Do you have a situation in your life that makes you feel all hope is lost? Ask Jesus to give you the courage to "just believe."*

—*Dianne Neal Matthews*

# THURSDAY, JANUARY 23

*My heart says of you, "Seek his face!" Your face, Lord, I will seek. Psalm 27:8 (NIV)*

ARE YOU DISCOURAGED TODAY? Is your to-do list long enough to wrap around the state of Montana five times? Our discouragement always comes from chasing something—chasing order, chasing enough money to get a little bit ahead, or chasing a sense of accomplishment. We may chase accomplishments, or peace, or the dream life we've always wanted, but the thing is, in this life we'll never catch what we're chasing. Ask any actor if he's had enough fame. Ask any billionaire if he's content with his bank account. Ask any model if she's happy with her body just the way it is.

Our souls are made for eternity, for heaven, and for a relationship with Jesus. Our heart wants to connect with the One Who will make all the difference, yet the lures of this world draw us away. Author Jennie Allen says, "God is the only thing we will chase that doesn't make us feel more empty."

Pause for a moment and consider heaven. Think of the gates of pearl, the choirs of angels, and the throne where the Almighty sits. Can you picture the splendor and glory? It's awe-inspiring, isn't it? Then consider that what you imagine doesn't come even close to the real thing.

Now think about what this world tells us to seek. The shiniest car on earth pales to the roads we'll walk on in eternity. The finest meal looks like a sack lunch compared to Jesus's banqueting table. The largest house on earth is a shack compared to Jesus's home. And any praise you can receive will be like grumbling and mumbling when you think about Jesus's eye meeting yours and His voice raising, "Well done, good and faithful servant!"

What can you chase on earth that will bring you happiness? Jesus alone.

**FAITH STEP:** *Write a list of things you'd like to have and do on earth. Look over your list and then cross every item out, writing at the top: "Lord, Your face will I seek."*

—*Tricia Goyer*

# FRIDAY, JANUARY 24

---

*Jesus replied, "Your mistake is that you don't know the Scriptures, and you don't know the power of God." Matthew 22:29 (NLT)*

---

THE FURNACE WAS ACTING UP. A metallic rattle made us jump every time the furnace kicked in. And it didn't seem to push warmed air into the house, which is pretty much the only function of a furnace.

Before long, a heating and air-conditioning truck sat in our driveway and a repairman stood in our basement, removing parts, inspecting, and tromping upstairs to the family room to offer his diagnosis.

"Your furnace will never work right like that. Not efficient. Not getting enough air. There's your problem."

The people to whom Jesus ministered were often confused about why things weren't working out well in their lives, their relationships, their faith. They asked Him what must have seemed ridiculously tangled questions, like to whom a woman belonged in heaven if she was married and widowed seven times, outliving those seven brothers. Sounds like a soap opera plot.

In Matthew 22:29 Jesus quickly diagnosed the heart of the issue: "Your mistake is that you don't know the Scriptures, and you don't know the power of God."

How easily and quickly Jesus got to the heart of the problem. "You wouldn't be confused, you wouldn't be asking these irrelevant questions, if you really knew God's Word and understood God's power and His purpose."

The next time I'm rattling around, making too much noise, operating inefficiently or not at all, I think I'll call in the Expert. I already know what He'll say. "Here's your problem, right here, lady."

---

FAITH STEP: *What are you doing to keep your spiritual life well maintained? And what ridiculously tangled questions have you asked that fall away in light of knowing God's Word and His power? Write down the first thing(s) that came to mind. Stick that slip of paper in the spot in your Bible where you find God makes the answer clear.*

—*Cynthia Ruchti*

# SATURDAY, JANUARY 25

*A twinkle in the eye means joy in the heart,*
*And good news makes you feel fit as a fiddle. Proverbs 15:30* (MSG)

MY HOUSE WAS A COMPLETE wreck, like my body. At forty years old, I'd just had my fourth child, and although the whole experience had been completely exhausting for me, my new baby didn't seem to require much sleep. At least not at night. Tensions in the family were running pretty high—as high as my energy level was low.

One day my niece Sophia came over to visit. She has perpetually sparkly enormous blue eyes, but on this day I noticed what seemed like an extra measure of twinkle. She ran right up to where I was folding clothes, bursting with the news: "I have a loose tooth!" Then she proceeded to take my index finger in her small hand, and navigated it toward her mouth, where, indeed, one of her top central incisors wiggled when I touched it.

"I can't believe it!" Sophia continued. "I'm going to lose my first tooth! Can you believe it?"

Actually, it was not totally surprising to me. She was in kindergarten, after all. Many children lose their first tooth in kindergarten. But for Sophia, this was big.

Putting down my husband's shirt, I looked into her eyes, surrendering to the moment. I began to share the excitement of her news. And as I fully appreciated the magnitude of her joy, a cool thing happened. Some of it spilled over into my heart, refreshing my mind and reviving my spirit.

Of course it was about six months till I got a good night's sleep, but God kept sending me opportunities for joy—glimpses of Jesus's loving care in my life—just like He does today.

FAITH STEP: *Thank the Lord for good news, however small. How can you celebrate the glimpses of Jesus's love—and good news—in your life today? Pray that Jesus would make you a joy-bringer in the lives of others, spreading the good news of Jesus's love wherever you go.*

*—Gwen Ford Faulkenberry*

# SUNDAY, JANUARY 26

*Joyful are those who obey his laws and search for him
with all their hearts. Psalm 119:2 (NLT)*

A WOMAN I KNOW EXPERIENCED the heartache of spousal infidelity and divorce. She remarried but divorced again. And again. And again. Her search for love and happiness led her to a dead end. Why? She looked in the wrong place.

Everyone yearns for happiness. Some women think they'll find it in marriage, while others seek it outside their marriage.

Some think they'll discover happiness in a career. Others count the days until retirement.

Some believe happiness comes with having children. Others can hardly wait for the kids to leave home.

We invest time, energy, and resources seeking happiness, but it eludes us. Perhaps that's because our human desires overrule what matters most—an intimate relationship with Jesus Christ.

The psalmist understood this. He wrote, "Make me walk along the path of your commands, for that is where my happiness is found...I reflect at night on who are you, O Lord, therefore I obey your instructions. This is how I spend my life: obeying your commandments" (Psalm 119:35, 55–56, NLT).

True happiness flows from knowing Jesus and obeying Him as a result. When we walk according to His ways, He protects us from making unwise choices and guards us from the fallout of misplaced priorities. When our relationship with Him is in order, everything else falls into place.

Today and always, pursue knowing Christ and embrace His ways. Therein lies the key to happiness.

FAITH STEP: *Memorize Psalm 119:2.*

*—Grace Fox*

# MONDAY, JANUARY 27

*Then Jesus told him, "Because you have seen me, you have believed; blessed are those who have not seen and yet have believed." John 20:29 (NIV)*

A CHURCH BOOK GROUP IN Atlanta asked me to speak at their annual retreat. Since travel is difficult for me, we decided to set up a live connection via computers. We tested it out the day before, and I had a lovely chat with the retreat coordinator. Everything worked great. I could see the room of empty chairs where the women would be, and they had a big-screen television where they would see me.

However, the next day, we had trouble getting the connection to work. Finally, they were able to see and hear me, but I couldn't see them, and couldn't hear much except some garbled background sounds. I launched into my talk, and shared from my heart, staring at the little green dot of my computer camera. When I speak, I love to make eye contact with people in the audience, to notice when something I've said coaxes a smile or a laugh or a nod of agreement. It was difficult to keep talking, hoping my themes resonated with the women at the retreat, but getting no feedback. At one point it occurred to me that perhaps we'd completely lost the connection and I'd been talking animatedly to myself in an empty room for the past half hour.

Later, a friend from Atlanta who had attended the retreat told me the talk had been very well received. Although I couldn't see it, they were taking notes, engaged, and later talked about new ideas they had gleaned.

The experience reminded me that often we have to step forward in trust, unable to see if we are fulfilling the purpose Jesus has in mind. Unable to see *Him* in the tangible way we long to. Jesus gave Thomas a vibrant visual aid: "Put your finger here; see My hands." But He also calls us to believe during those times when we can't see.

FAITH STEP: *Close your eyes and think about all the items nearby that you know are there, even though you can't see them. Ask Jesus to strengthen your faith to believe He is active in your life, even where you can't see it yet.*

—*Sharon Hinck*

# TUESDAY, JANUARY 28

*Jesus answered, "I am the way and the truth and the life.
No one comes to the Father except through me." John 14:6 (NIV)*

"WHICH DO YOU WANT FIRST, the good news or the bad?"

Have you ever been asked that popular question? I have, and I'm typically a bad news first kind of person. I want to get the bad over with, so I can end with the good.

The Bible is filled with good news and bad news. In the beginning, we get the good news first. God's glorious creation is described in beautiful detail. But soon after, we get the bad news when sin enters the world.

In Romans 3:23, we're told the bad news first. "For all have sinned and fall short of the glory of God." But then in the very next verse, Romans 3:24 bellows the good news, "And all are justified freely by his grace through the redemption that came by Christ Jesus." Likewise, 2 Corinthians 4:16 says that "though outwardly we are wasting away, inwardly we are being renewed day by day." And Romans 5:19 spells it out clearly: Because one person (Adam) disobeyed God, many became sinners. But because one other person (Christ) obeyed God, many will be made righteous.

Isn't it wonderful when you end with good news? Isn't it powerful that we know we can end with good news, when we follow our Lord and Savior and enter His kingdom for eternity?

FAITH STEP: *Share the real Good News, God's Word, with someone today.*

—*Renee Andrews*

# WEDNESDAY, JANUARY 29

*Have I been stingy with my food and refused to share it with orphans?*
*No, from childhood I have cared for orphans like a father, and all my life*
*I have cared for widows. Job 31:17–18 (NLT)*

AS A MOM OF A toddler I rarely have trouble sleeping. Usually when my head hits the pillow I'm out for good. But there was one night—just a few weeks ago—when I tossed and turned. The next day we would be opening our home to a sibling group from the foster care system. It was the first step into making them part of our home—our forever family.

My husband and I knew God had called us to care for the orphans . . . but were these the two orphans He'd planned for us? The next morning we prayed for peace. As we talked and read God's Word, our worried thoughts settled. As my husband and I talked over the decision, we reminded each other of God's call, God's provision, and God's strength. Surely if He could form the mountains and oceans with His voice, He could help us as we grew our family, right?

After our talk, John and I sat down to read our Bible, and we opened to the book of James—the next book in our reading schedule. My husband's voice quivered as we came to the last verse for the day, James 1:27: "Pure and genuine religion in the sight of God the Father means caring for orphans and widows in their distress and refusing to let the world corrupt you." Tears came next—both his and mine.

We hadn't asked God for a neon sign, yet that verse became one for us. It was a confirmation that we were doing the right thing, at the right time. God had children who needed a home, and He wanted it to be ours.

---

FAITH STEP: *Do you know any orphans and widows in need? Consider an older woman from church. Or maybe children in your neighborhood who are being raised by a family member or don't have a father at home. Pray and ask God to show you one way you can express "pure religion" by reaching out to them.*

*—Tricia Goyer*

# THURSDAY, JANUARY 30

---

*Pray without ceasing…for this is God's will for you in Christ Jesus.*
*1 Thessalonians 5:17–18 (NAS)*

---

IF YOU MISSED THE YOUTUBE video of Sweet Brown being interviewed on the news in Oklahoma City after her apartment building caught on fire, stop reading this right now and go Google it. It's one of the funniest things I have ever seen.

A lady named Sweet Brown—and that's her real name—gives this account: "When I woke up to go get me a cold pop…I thought somebody was barbecuing! I said, 'Lord Jesus! It's a fire!' Then I ran. I didn't grab no shoes or nothin', Jesus, I ran for my life!"

She goes on to describe her bout with bronchitis, caused by smoke inhalation. The line that caused the whole thing to go viral is this: "Ain't nobody got time for that!"

I love this lady. She showed so much spirit and personality in that interview that she's now being courted for her own television show. But what I love, besides how she makes me laugh till I cry, is the spiritual principle she also demonstrates to the world.

The presence of Jesus is apparently such a reality in her life that He fills her conversation. Her first reaction to the smell of smoke is to pray. And as she runs for her life, it's as if Jesus is right beside her and she's talking to Him. Which He is, no doubt.

I want to be like that. I want to live every moment with the keen awareness that He is near me, not just as a spiritual force who guides my heart and mind, but one whose presence is my reality.

---

FAITH STEP: *Don't let your devotional time end with the last word on this page. Instead, meditate on the nearness of Jesus. Think of it as a conversation with your Best Friend that goes on all day!*

—*Gwen Ford Faulkenberry*

# FRIDAY, JANUARY 31

---

*With God all things are possible. Matthew 19:26 (NAS)*

---

MIRACLES ARE THOSE BIBLICAL GOD-THINGS of the past, right? That's what some people believe. While we may or may not experience the "mountain-moving" kind of miracles in our lifetime—the kind that leave your mouth gaping, your heart throbbing, and your doctor scratching his head in disbelief—does that negate Jesus's power to accomplish them? Absolutely not!

As a Christian I've witnessed Jesus's miracles in my own life. I'm sure you have too. But at times I may overlook the hidden ones. Jesus may send a God-thing on the wings of pain or interruption. Sometimes He sandwiches miracles into an ordinary day like the filling of an Oreo cookie. What a sweet, creamy surprise when we receive it as a gift from Him!

One problem in not recognizing miracles may be our shortsighted, earthly perspective. We pray for change in someone's life, for them to know Jesus. But could God be using a sudden painful illness to miraculously answer that prayer? We pray for a raise or new job as a cure for our financial troubles and see no answer. But do we fail to connect the dots when repairs, doctor bills, and other usual expenses mysteriously disappear the next year? Sometimes the miracle may even arrive through God's formation of Christ-like character in our own lives.

Jesus still does the impossible. Even He prayed for a miracle—some other way for His Father to accomplish salvation besides Jesus's death (see Luke 22:42). But God controlled the power of life and death and planned a greater miracle: Jesus's death and subsequent resurrection.

We ask and we wait…and then, like Jesus, we whisper that miracle prayer, "But if not…Thy will be done." Sometimes God gives us a knowing word. However, trusting God's sovereignty is perhaps one of the hardest parts of the Christian life. Yet it's truly where miracles begin.

---

FAITH STEP: *As you think back over the past year in your own life, what are some God-things you recognize as miracles? What are you trusting God for this year?*

—*Rebecca Barlow Jordan*

# SATURDAY, FEBRUARY 1

*When the Sabbath came, he began to teach in the synagogue, and many who heard him were amazed. "Where did this man get these things?" they asked. "What's this wisdom that has been given him, that he even does miracles!" Mark 6:2 (NIV)*

LIFE IS ALWAYS SURPRISING. SOMETIMES the things you think are going to happen don't happen at all. Sometimes the things that you think will never happen do. And sometimes miracles happen. Small ones. Medium ones. Miracles, nonetheless.

For the last eight months my friend Shelly has been fighting ovarian cancer. These last couple of weeks have been difficult ones. She has been in the hospital, in pain, enduring tests and procedures. It looked doubtful that she would be able to go home any time soon.

But Shelly's home church declared this past week a 24–7 prayer week. Around the clock people took hour time slots to pray for Shelly. While praying, I asked God, "Don't You hear us? All of us? All of these prayers for Shelly?" Then I had the thought, *What would be happening if we* weren't *praying for Shelly?* I think Jesus was urging us to prayer at exactly the right time.

Because when the week ended, Ben, Shelly's husband, texted us that Shelly was coming home. I shouted out loud, "Praise the Lord!" And did a happy dance. I think Jesus was reminding me that He hears each and every word we utter. He is the God of Red Sea partings. The God who walks on water. The God who raises people from the dead. He is the Magnificent…the Conqueror…the Healer.

I took Shelly's coming home as a sign of hope. A sign of things to come. I, for one, can't wait to see what the next miracle is going to be.

FAITH STEP: *Sometimes we forget that Jesus is a miraculous God. Take out your journal and write a list of the miracles He has performed in your life, big and small, and remind yourself that you serve a God that does the impossible.*

—*Susanna Foth Aughtmon*

# SUNDAY, FEBRUARY 2

*"There is more than enough room in my Father's home. If this were not so, would I have told you that I am going to prepare a place for you? When everything is ready, I will come and get you, so that you will always be with me where I am." John 14:2–3 (NLT)*

WHEN MY HUSBAND ACCEPTED A job in Utah, he moved west before I did to start his new position. I stayed behind in Illinois to get our house ready to go on the market and then to keep it ready to show potential buyers, as well as tie up loose ends there. Over the next several months, I flew out to Salt Lake City three times to look at houses. Finally, we decided to buy a lot and build.

Since the realty company hadn't found a buyer for our house, we sold it to the relocation company, at a price below the appraisal value. A few days after Thanksgiving, a moving company came to pack up our possessions. Our new home wouldn't be ready for two months, so our stuff would go into storage while we lived in an apartment. We racked our brains trying to figure out what we needed to take with us in the car on the final drive out to Utah, and what we could do without for a couple of months. In the meantime, I wished the moving process could be simpler.

I find great comfort in Jesus's assurance that my final relocation will go much more smoothly. He has gone on ahead to take care of all the preparations. Someday He will come to get me and I won't have to worry about a single detail. No bags to pack or decisions to make. No sorrow over things left behind. Just an immediate transfer from this earthly life to my perfect home with Jesus. What could be simpler than that?

FAITH STEP: *Spend a few minutes thinking about your future home and thanking Jesus for all He has done to make that possible.*

—*Dianne Neal Matthews*

# MONDAY, FEBRUARY 3

---

*"You intended to harm me, but God intended it all for good. He brought me to this position so I could save the lives of many people." Genesis 50:20 (NLT)*

---

DURING WINTER MY HANDS ARE chronically dry, itchy, and cracking. Because I wash them frequently, I'm hard pressed to keep lotion on to make a healing difference. Even when my skin isn't dry enough to hurt, my fingertips often feel like sandpaper because they're healed only halfway.

Take a look at Joseph in the Old Testament. Talk about a wounded past. His jealous brothers hated him so much that they threw him in a well, then sold him to foreigners. The Lord raised him to a high place as a servant, but his employer's wife wrongly accused him of attacking her. He went to prison but again earned respect and a position as second-in-command of Egypt.

We read this story in a couple of minutes, but victimization, stolen freedom, and lost dreams plagued Joseph's life. As minutes became days then months and years, his hope surely wavered that he'd ever regain his life.

Yet the end of Genesis describes an emotional reunion that reveals how thoroughly the Lord healed Joseph. Joseph was whole enough to take the high road and reassure the very brothers who instigated his life of heartache. *He* reassured *them* of the Lord's sovereign goodness that reigned over their horrific actions. That kind of forgiveness and grace can happen only through the Lord's healing.

Hundreds of years after Joseph experienced healing, Jesus also showed grace toward those who hated Him.

Remember Joseph's story. Your Creator included it in His love letter to you as a gift of hope and promise to be your Healer.

---

FAITH STEP: *Take your heartache to Jesus and, in faith, tell Him you're expecting His thorough healing.*

*—Erin Keeley Marshall*

# TUESDAY, FEBRUARY 4

*"Come to me, all you who are weary and burdened, and I will give you rest.
Take my yoke upon you and learn from me, for I am gentle and humble in heart,
and you will find rest for your souls. For my yoke is easy and my burden is light."*
Matthew 11:28–30 (NIV)

SUN SPARKLED ON FRESH SNOW as if someone had scattered glitter across the vacant lot. The cold air pinched my nose and numbed my toes, and I settled my cross-country skis into the path I'd created the day before, eager to get moving. Two smooth channels, hip width apart, were carved into the snow, and I dug in my poles and glided smoothly around the outer edges of the lot.

After a few laps, the allure of untouched snow enticed me. I left the path and cut across the middle of the lot. Deep snow piled against my boots and resisted my skis. Soon sweat trickled down my back from the effort of shuffling forward.

When I embrace Jesus's yoke and follow the path He's already prepared, life can have the lightness and ease of gliding on packed snow. But when I pull away from Him, each step becomes a heavy effort. Sometimes I pull toward a path of selfish ambition, focusing on winning the approval or admiration of others. Sometimes I indulge in self-pity, comparing my struggles to the supposed ease of others. Sometimes I veer into worry about the future and try to control too many circumstances around me. Whenever I set out in a way that leaves the path of Jesus, I'm soon emotionally and spiritually bogged down.

Life gives us plenty of opportunities to feel weary and burdened. When we feel as if we're dragging through deep snow, we can ask Jesus to show us if we are tugging against His yoke and making our path more difficult than it needs to be.

FAITH STEP: *What situation in life is feeling the most heavy and difficult today? Ask Jesus to ease the load and guide you in His path.*

—*Sharon Hinck*

# WEDNESDAY, FEBRUARY 5

*Surely goodness and mercy shall follow me all the days of my life; and I will dwell in the house of the Lord forever. Psalm 23:6 (NKJV)*

WE HAVE ALWAYS BEEN A dog family. Ever since I can remember, even as a child, a fur-legged, tail-wagging creature would greet us each morning with affection. Almost without exception through the years, our differing breeds had one thing in common. They loved to get away. And for the most part, that love of adventure got them in lots of trouble.

Except for Brandy. We adopted this temperamental cocker spaniel from our daughter who was in college at the time. Brandy became *my* dog. Wherever I went, Brandy followed me. When I would write at the computer, she slept near my feet. When I cooked, she would sit or lie with her head propped on the kitchen windowsill, following every movement outside. She rarely left my side.

Brandy died several years ago, and I've never replaced her. Even in her testy moments, Brandy remained my favorite dog. I still miss her.

Jesus reminded me recently that a couple of constant "companions" follow me day after day. They sleep by my bed. They watch while I eat or work. They travel with me faithfully, no matter where I go or what I do.

The truth is, all of God's children know these two companions: goodness and mercy. "All the days of my life" means every day, every night, until I draw my last breath. Jesus's goodness, immeasurable and unfailing, and His mercy, extravagant and undeserving, is better than any four-legged canine's companionship.

Even our closest human relationships can't offer the same soul-satisfying joy as Jesus's own presence—and those faithful godly companions: goodness and mercy.

FAITH STEP: *Thank Jesus for your loyal companions, goodness and mercy. Take time today to remember the experiences when those two have consciously made a difference in your life.*

—*Rebecca Barlow Jordan*

# THURSDAY, FEBRUARY 6

*Follow God's example, therefore, as dearly loved children and walk in the way of love, just as Christ loved us and gave himself up for us as a fragrant offering and sacrifice to God. Ephesians 5:1–2 (NIV)*

LAST FEBRUARY, OUR OLDEST SON, Rene, proposed to a wonderful young woman named Ariel Tingle. Rene had been traveling across the country with the Bearing Witness ministry and hadn't told Ariel that he'd returned home early so he could ask her to be his wife.

Friends and family gathered for the surprise, which made the event even more meaningful and precious. But what touched my heart the most were these words in his proposal...

"If you will let me, I will spend my whole life doing my best to love you as Christ loved the church."

His statement brings up this question: How did Christ love the church?

The answer is simple, really. He loved us, His church, enough to give the ultimate sacrifice, to leave the glory of Heaven and suffer on Earth for our sake—to die for our souls. He left a multitude of angels for a few disciples. *That's* how Christ loved the church, and Rene couldn't have expressed how much he loves Ariel more than with this example. Ephesians 5:25 tells husbands to love their wives as Christ loved the church. That's exactly what our son plans to do, and we couldn't be more pleased.

**FAITH STEP:** *If you have children, pray for their future spouses and for them to love each other as Christ loved the church. If you are looking for that special person, ask God to lead you to someone who will help you grow stronger spiritually. And if you've found the one you love, tell that person today how you plan to love them as Christ loved the church. Wholly. Completely. That's the kind of love that will stand the test of time, and the kind that will last for eternity.*

—*Renee Andrews*

# FRIDAY, FEBRUARY 7

*Arise, shine, for your light has come, and the glory of the Lord rises upon you.*
Isaiah 60:1 (NIV)

WINTER HAS BEEN COLD AND dark this year. It is as though I am living in the Arctic Circle instead of in the moderate climate of California.

The sky is black until seven, and there is frost on the ground and dusting the trees. It is the perfect time to snuggle down and dream of hot chocolate and crackling fires. If you venture outside, you can see your breath hang in the air like small puffs of fog. It is more than a little chilly. The last thing I want to do is hop out of bed and face the day. I want to stay hunkered down in the dark under the covers.

Life can feel cold and dark sometimes, just like a frigid winter morning. But Jesus is not so interested in our staying curled up in the dark. He has plans for us. He wants us to get up and embrace the life He has set before us.

In Isaiah it says, "Arise, shine, for your light has come." In all of His grace and mercy, Jesus has made a way for us to be the person He created us to be. But it's only when we get up and start moving, engaging with those around us, and invite the light of Jesus into our lives that His life and love begin to show through us.

I think it's time to get up and start shining.

FAITH STEP: *Turn off all of the lights in your room before you go to bed. Place candles around your room and light them. Notice the difference just one candle makes in the dark. Spend some time in the candlelight praising Jesus for the warmth and light He has brought into your life.*

—*Susanna Foth Aughtmon*

# SATURDAY, FEBRUARY 8

*"I am the Lord; there is no other God. I have equipped you for battle, though you don't even know me." Isaiah 45:5 (NLT)*

MY SON STARTED KINDERGARTEN LAST fall. He's doing great. Deep down I thought he would be fine, but you know, a mother's heart and all. I can breathe a sigh that he has adjusted well in the big world of school and strangers outside our home. It's the job of parents to equip our kids with what they need to succeed. They trust us because they know us.

When I think about how much I pour my heart into my children, the people who need me most in the world, I'm caught a bit off guard by today's verse. To think that the Lord equipped me for life's battles before I even knew Him . . . it amazes me. He bears the biggest responsibility for my life, all the while giving me room to make decisions of my own free will.

Jesus spent His life preparing people for His death, as well as for their own lives and deaths. His purpose in coming to earth was to ready us to know the high cost of choosing not to follow Him and the vast rewards of accepting all He came to give us.

*Before* we even knew Him. *Before* we experienced our first memorable heartache or dream come true, *before* we made the decisions that led to our most recent regret or success.

Think about how He woos your heart right now, this moment, before the rest of the day hits you. Before tomorrow's unexpected joys and sorrows, He's already there, readying you.

FAITH STEP: *Think back through your life's highs and lows. Spend a while journaling about those memories, and see them in a new light, knowing God sent Jesus to prepare your way before you were born. He's still preparing you for today and your future.*

—*Erin Keeley Marshall*

# SUNDAY, FEBRUARY 9

*If we are faithless, he remains faithful—for he cannot deny himself.*
2 Timothy 2:13 (NRSV)

I HAVE A GOOD FRIEND whose heart was broken by her husband's infidelity, yet because he repented, she chose to stay in the marriage and try to rebuild trust. She sought counsel from a professional and also read a lot of books in her efforts to deal with the problem in a healthy way. One thing she told me she read over and over was a word of caution. Apparently wives who face this kind of rejection are prone to seek revenge, or at least comfort, in another man's arms. All of the writers she read said the same thing—that countering her husband's unfaithfulness with an affair of her own would not help, but only bring her more heartache in the long run.

I asked her if she had been tempted to be unfaithful herself.

"Yes, but because of my relationship with Jesus, it's never been a real option. I know it is wrong."

Pretty simple, yet pretty amazing.

My friend's story is one of true oneness with Christ. While she had every reason—every right—to retaliate with the same infidelity she'd experienced, she listened to a higher call. Even though her husband was faithless, she remained faithful, because of the nature of Jesus, who lives within her. He remains faithful no matter what, because He cannot deny Himself.

FAITH STEP: *Praise the Lord that Jesus is faithful to us, no matter how we fail Him. Decide today to let His faithfulness motivate you to greater faithfulness to Him and others.*

*—Gwen Ford Faulkenberry*

# MONDAY, FEBRUARY 10

*"So in everything, do to others what you would have them do to you, for this sums up the Law and the Prophets." Matthew 7:12 (NIV)*

I HAD A DIFFICULT TIME with my first pregnancy. At one point, I ended up in the emergency room and a doctor told me he was sorry but there was nothing he could do to save our child. However, Rene continued to fight the odds, and though he came a month early, he was perfectly healthy.

During the pregnancy, because I wouldn't stop hemorrhaging, I was put on bed rest and only allowed up to go to the bathroom. Our church in New Orleans announced my situation, and instantly the women of the congregation signed up to bring meals every other day to me and my husband.

One of the meals I received was homemade lasagna from Dena Doom. Dena lived near to us and never failed to check on me through my days in bed or to bring us anything we needed. The lasagna was so amazing I asked for the recipe, and she brought it, handwritten on an index card that I still use when I make lasagna. The "from the kitchen of Dena Doom" at the top of the note reminds me of the lady who cared for me when I couldn't care for myself.

Christ said that we should do to others as we would have them do to us, and Dena truly did. She showed Christ-like love when she took the time and effort to cook that lasagna for us. And after I made the dish myself, I learned that this is no "throw together" type of meal. It takes time and love, things that Christ expects from us and things that He expects us to provide to each other...as Dena did.

FAITH STEP: *Find your favorite lasagna recipe and double it, making an extra lasagna that you can share with a neighbor, a family member, or a friend. If you don't have a favorite recipe, send me an e-mail and I'll send you Dena's amazing recipe. (renee@ reneeandrews.com)*

—*Renee Andrews*

# TUESDAY, FEBRUARY 11

*Therefore do not let anyone judge you by what you eat or drink,*
*or with regard to a religious festival, a New Moon celebration, or a Sabbath day.*
*These are a shadow of the things that were to come; the reality,*
*however, is found in Christ. Colossians 2:16–17 (NIV)*

WE LIVE CLOSE TO A large mall that includes a lot of attractions. One month, a new feature opened that sounded like fun—a mirror maze. My husband and I decided to try it out. After paying our entrance fee, we were given gloves, since the maze was so disorienting, we'd need to walk with our hands in front of us, and often touch the mirrors to find real open walkways among the many illusions.

At one point, just as we turned to our left to try a new path, I looked down a hall that seemed to stretch into infinity. Far at the end I saw two figures turning and moving to the right. As I looked closer, I realized those figures were my husband and me. The strange configuration of mirrors created an illusion of ourselves, but with reversed direction.

I grabbed my husband's arm, reassuring myself that we were the real people among all the mirrored images.

When I read this verse in Colossians, I remembered that maze and all the reflections. Sometimes I'm so intent on spiritual practices—singing certain songs, a specific order to worship, holiday customs—that I focus on these shadow elements more than Jesus. Religious traditions can be wonderful symbols, helpful images to give our hearts and minds fuller understanding of Jesus. But they fail us if they become substitutes for the real thing.

FAITH STEP: *Are you focusing on shadows or the reality of Christ? Ask Jesus to show you any traditions that may have become a distraction from Him. Try worshipping Him in a new way today.*

—*Sharon Hinck*

# WEDNESDAY, FEBRUARY 12

*Then, when our dying bodies have been transformed into bodies that will never die, this Scripture will be fulfilled: "Death is swallowed up in victory." 1 Corinthians 15:54 (NLT)*

IN MY PERSONAL LIFE AND as a minister's wife, I've walked away from numerous funerals wanting to speak out loud the whisper in my heart: "Why?" Viewing twin, shoe box–sized caskets, the body of a seventeen-year-old dynamic Christian, a young father ripped away from his wife and small children prematurely—it's those seemingly "senseless" deaths that seize your heart and beg for an audience with a sovereign God. We feel the loss, especially when that loss is someone close to us, and we struggle to make sense of the unexplainable. And we also fear the things we don't understand, especially death—perhaps even more when we're younger.

The older I get, the more I realize that death doesn't have to be a mystery to those who love the Lord. On the other side of death is the other side of life. A "place" awaits us—a place being prepared for us by Jesus Himself (see John 14:1–3). It's a place where all needs are met, where time stands still, where we will finally have complete understanding: a safe place filled with the presence of love and the absence of hate, the presence of joy and the absence of sorrow, the presence of peace, and the absence of turmoil.

On the other side of death is the other side of life—full, purposeful, complete—life for which we were created, life that begins now and never ends. And it's all because of Jesus's death, burial, and resurrection. Death has been "swallowed up in victory."

No matter how incomplete our understanding or how much we ache for those who have gone before us, there's no place like our home, eternal, sweet home—because Jesus lives there.

FAITH STEP: *Spend some time today thanking Jesus for making death a victory. List all the things you are looking forward to "on the other side of death."*

—*Rebecca Barlow Jordan*

# THURSDAY, FEBRUARY 13

*Jesus spoke to the people again, saying, "I am the light of the world. Whoever follows me won't walk in darkness but will have the light of life." John 8:12 (CEB)*

ALL I DID WAS GET a new lamp for my office. Inexpensive, but it throws a warm glow over an area that had one of two looks prior—glaring overhead light or shadowy darkness.

The glow from my computer screen shows I'm working. But it's not what one would call an atmosphere-enhancing light.

Now I have a just-the-right-size lamp with a rubbed bronze finish and a linen-like shade. How can a simple, demure lamp make such a difference? I don't know. But in the evenings, it's less chore-like to retreat to my shadowy office to put in a few more hours' work…because of my lamp. The glow it throws is warm, inviting. "Come, let's make literature together!" it seems to call.

Some writers have to have a cat on their lap when they write. Some need chocolate. Some have a cat on the lap, chocolate in hand, and a dog at their feet. I just want my lamp.

No wonder things—even dark things—are better with Jesus around. He is the Light of the world. In Him is no darkness at all.

Does that verse resonate with you? No darkness *at all.*

It's said that the kind of light that illuminates heaven—from God the Father and His Son—eliminates the possibility of shadows.

I pray I never try to write a word without the Light of the world by my side. Write or speak or give or love or walk or run or work or move…

FAITH STEP: *What in your life needs to have a little light thrown on it? Make it your prayer to ask, "Light of the world, shine here, and here, and here. Let me see this clearly, well-lit by You."*

—*Cynthia Ruchti*

# FRIDAY, FEBRUARY 14

*Love is patient, love is kind.* 1 Corinthians 13:4 (NIV)

MY GRANDFATHER'S BIRTHDAY IS COMING up in a few weeks. He died in 1999, but you'd never know it's been that long. My grandmother still talks about the great times they had together. At least once a month I hear about when they met, when they bought their first house, and when they welcomed each of their three daughters. You'd think by listening to her that they had a perfect marriage. They didn't. There were many hard times, and they didn't become Christians until later in life. Yet she chooses to focus her memories and words on the good times. Witnessing their fifty-year marriage was a testimony to love. Hearing her words now is an added testimony.

Every married person must come to the place where they choose love. Where they choose patient love, kind love.

"Love in a Scriptural sense is not a soft, sentimental emotion," writes Phillip Keller. "It is a deliberate act of my will. It means that I am willing to lay down my life, lay myself out, put myself out on behalf of another."

For many years I had a hard time being patient or kind. I'm thankful John stuck with me. There are even days I'm still not very patient or very kind . . . but love covers it all. To will oneself to be loving isn't easy. My husband does it, and I do it too. But I'm looking forward to making that fifty-year mark, by doing what I witnessed my grandparents doing—focusing on the good and being patient and kind about the rest.

Find that hard? Turn to God to help you. Ask Him to give you a love from Him, and be willing to lay down yourself for another person just as Jesus laid down Himself for you. As 1 John 4:19 (NLT) says, "We love each other because he loved us first." We all can love better because of that!

FAITH STEP: *Ask a friend or family member who has been married for a while for their best marriage advice.*

—*Tricia Goyer*

# SATURDAY, FEBRUARY 15

*I will walk in freedom, for I have devoted myself to your commandments.*
*Psalm 119:45 (NLT)*

A YOUNG WOMAN WITH THREE young kids in tow approached the neighborhood playground. Suddenly one tyke yanked his hand from hers and dashed toward a swing occupied by an older child.

"Stop!" yelled the woman. "You're going to get…"

*Smack!* The youngster, eager to taste freedom, fell backward and cried. Everyone watching knew the accident could easily have been prevented if he'd trusted his guardian's care.

The scene provided a great reminder of what happens when we insist on doing life our way rather than trusting our heavenly Father's care. Sometimes we feel His commands restrict our freedom: Marry believers only? Reserve sex for marriage? Give up my rights lest I offend a weaker believer?

We see others seemingly have a good time and feel like we're being restrained. What do we do? We yank our hand from the Father's and dash headlong into danger.

"Stop!" the Holy Spirit warns. But we're bent on doing our own thing. *Smack!*

Know what I'm talking about? The psalmist did. He wrote, "I will walk in freedom, for I have devoted myself to your commandments" (Psalm 119:45, NLT). He knew the key to personal freedom lies not in doing our own thing but in embracing God's commands, written to protect us and preserve our well-being.

Do you feel restrained? Tempted to do your own thing? Think twice. True freedom lies in trusting God's wisdom and instruction for how to do life.

**FAITH STEP:** *Do you feel God's restricting your freedom? If so, ask yourself what you feel you're missing and why you want it so badly. Ask God to change your heart and to help you cling to, not pull away from Him.*

—*Grace Fox*

# SUNDAY, FEBRUARY 16

*Do not be overcome by evil, but overcome evil with good.*
*Romans 12:21 (NKJV)*

I KNOW SOMEONE WHO IS a recovering porn addict. Introduced to pornography as a child by his father, his habit of over thirty years almost cost him everything—family, job, reputation—before he finally got help. His treatment requires a complete overhaul of his mind. It involves weekly therapy, Celebrate Recovery meetings, and accountability partners who call him and meet with him, asking him questions that necessitate total transparency.

He was talking one day about how this period of intense treatment won't go on forever, but some parts of it, like CR and the accountability, will always be in his life. "I have to break the addiction, and then keep it from controlling me ever again. I'm learning how to do that in a thousand little ways."

When it comes to addiction, he says it's not really the big stuff that ensnares you. It's those little decisions we make over and over until habits are formed. Where to click the mouse. Whether to answer a text. "White lies" told here and there until your soul becomes as black as death.

Gandalf, from Tolkien's *Lord of the Rings* trilogy, said, "Some believe it is only great power that can hold evil in check. But that is not what I have found. I have found that it is the small everyday deeds of ordinary folk that keep the darkness at bay. Small acts of kindness and love." That's as true here as it is in Middle Earth. Jesus came to help us in all things—big and small. He is the mighty Hero who can give us victory over big things like addiction, and He is the One Who walks beside us in our small everyday deeds. He gives us the strength and discernment to hold evil at bay with our choices, and to overcome it, moment by ordinary moment, with good.

FAITH STEP: *What little things about your day might Jesus want to change in order to give you overcoming life? Be sensitive to His Spirit as He gently guides you into the good.*

—*Gwen Ford Faulkenberry*

# MONDAY, FEBRUARY 17

*Because of the Lord's great love we are not consumed, for his compassions never fail.*
*They are new every morning; great is your faithfulness.* Lamentations 3:22–23 (NIV)

LAST NIGHT I CRAWLED INTO bed and snuggled down under my comforter. I lay awake for a long time even though I was exhausted.

Sometimes I have a hard time falling asleep. My mind races with the events of the day. I replay conversations and what I would or should have said if my brain was quicker than it is. I think about my boys and my interactions with them. I think about issues in our family and the problem-solving that I do with my husband, Scott.

It is no small miracle when my thoughts finally fade into oblivion and I can actually drift off to sleep. The mind is curious that way. It is always working, planning, rethinking, and sometimes, regretting.

But there is one absolutely lovely thing about falling asleep. I get to wake up to a new day. New chances. New choices. New opportunities. And according to the Scriptures, new compassions. *New compassions.* What a truly hope-giving thought.

Because of Jesus's faithfulness, His love is inexhaustible. It doesn't run out or run dry. Jesus's character never changes. He *is* love. When the sun cracks the sky, I get to awaken to a new day full of His constant and consistent compassions.

I am thankful for a good night's sleep. But mostly I am thankful for new mornings full of Jesus.

FAITH STEP: *Find a chalkboard or whiteboard. Write down the things that you have been regretting lately. Take an eraser and wipe them clean. With Jesus we have a new day full of His compassion.*

—*Susanna Foth Aughtmon*

# TUESDAY, FEBRUARY 18

*"Can all your worries add a single moment to your life?" Matthew 6:27 (NLT)*

AS I UNPACKED MY SUITCASE, I mentally reviewed the past five days. This had only been my second time to teach at a writers' conference, the first time at one I'd never attended. The week had been energizing and productive. And not a single one of the things I'd worried about had come to pass. My flights had been on time. I'd had no trouble finding the shuttle that went to the somewhat remote conference center. My luggage arrived the same time I did.

Plenty of people had shown up for my workshops, and I found that I hadn't forgotten to bring any of my notes or visual aids. My mind never blanked out, and I didn't run out of material way before time for the class to end. I even received positive comments, both verbally and written on the evaluation forms. True, that button did pop off my waistband minutes before one class started, but with a safety pin, it all worked out. All my pre-conference worrying had been a big waste of time.

After I got home, I read an article about how research links anxiety and worry to diseases that can shorten our lives. But Jesus already knew that a couple of thousand years ago. When He spoke to a crowd one day, He pointed out the futility of worrying. Jesus promised to provide everything we need if we concentrate on loving Him and doing His will above all else.

I'm so glad that Jesus understands my propensity to worry about every little thing. And I'm grateful that He has given me the remedy to break this harmful habit. Philippians 4:6 advises me to talk to God about everything that concerns me. A heartfelt, ongoing conversation with Jesus beats indulging in worry any day.

**FAITH STEP:** *Do you have a problem with worrying? Ask Jesus to help you replace your anxiety with trust. Write out Philippians 4:6 on a note card and keep it in your wallet so you can read it whenever you're tempted to worry.*

—*Dianne Neal Matthews*

# WEDNESDAY, FEBRUARY 19

*But Christ has indeed been raised from the dead, the firstfruits*
*of those who have fallen asleep. For since death came through a man,*
*the resurrection of the dead comes also through a man. For as in Adam all die,*
*so in Christ all will be made alive. 1 Corinthians 15:20–22 (NIV)*

ANOTHER BUSINESS HAD CLOSED AT the strip mall a few blocks from our home. With the poor economy, we'd watched a number of stores come and go. Now we wondered what new business would move in next to the café.

One day I drove by and burst into laughter. Next to the restaurant called Health and Happiness, a large sign announced the new business, Caskets and More.

I often giggled at the irony of those two names side by side. But each time I drove by, it reminded me of a truth I try to ignore. Although we scramble after a bit of health and happiness in this life, we will all face the reality of death. Death is right next door during all of our mortal life. If it weren't for Jesus, death would cast a shadow of fear and despair over our brief life here on earth.

But Jesus has conquered death. Because of Him, when I attend a funeral, I know the story isn't finished yet. When a friend gets a dreaded diagnosis, I know her life is secure in Him. When I see reminders of my own time flying past—like a casket storefront or a graveyard—I thank Jesus for the reassurance in this verse that through Him, we will all be made alive.

FAITH STEP: *Next time you drive past a cemetery, praise and thank Jesus for conquering death, and ask Him to strengthen your faith to face the future with confidence.*

—*Sharon Hinck*

# THURSDAY, FEBRUARY 20

*"The Lord gave and the Lord has taken away; may the name of the Lord be praised."*
*In all this, Job did not sin by charging God with wrongdoing. Job 1:21–22 (NIV)*

SOMEONE SAID OUR FAITH IS often strengthened at the place of disappointment. That growth happens when we respond to the disappointment by choosing to trust and worship even when it hurts.

Job set the ultimate example when he fell to the ground in worship after losing his ten children and all his earthly possessions. He experienced more hurt than most of us will know in a lifetime, and yet he chose to trust. An extraordinary response, yes?

I watched my husband's faith grow when he faced the greatest disappointment of his life to date. Three days after a friend received the job Gene had applied for, he said, "I believe God wants me to worship Him in the midst of this."

Gene praised God daily for His wisdom, sovereignty, and faithfulness. He thanked Him for closing that door and for promising to guide our future. He learned to nestle rather than wrestle, even though he couldn't understand God's ways. And he mentored the fellow who got the job until God opened a different door eighteen months later.

Gene's faith grew as he embraced his place of disappointment as an opportunity to seek God and trust Him unconditionally. May this be true of us, too, when disappointment comes.

---

**FAITH STEP:** *Are there any disappointments you're currently experiencing? If so, pray that God will help you nestle in Him and trust Him to accomplish His purposes. And worship Him from that place of disappointment.*

*—Grace Fox*

# FRIDAY, FEBRUARY 21

---

*"And if you give even a cup of cold water to one of the least of my followers, you will surely be rewarded." Matthew 10:42 (NLT)*

---

WHEN PEOPLE ASK ABOUT MY ministry in the local church, I have to smile. Yes, there were times I've led a Bible study or I've spoken at women's events, but the majority of my service has been focused on children. I've worn funny costumes, put a puppet on my hand, and I've gotten on my knees and acted like a little kid. For many, many years I've given my best to Jesus by serving those under three feet tall. The same is true in my home.

I was a single mom of a toddler boy when I met and married my husband. We had two more children, and then, years later, God put adoption on our hearts. We first adopted a baby girl through a private adoption, and currently we are in the process of adopting a sibling group from the foster care system. In addition to three young adults we currently have three children five years old and under!

There are days when I wear fuzzy pajama pants all day, where I have who-knows-what smeared on the front of my shirt, and streaks of peanut butter in my hair. (Highlights anyone?)

Jesus tells us that if we offer even a cup of water to the least of His followers then we will be rewarded. I smile at this because I'm pretty sure this includes sippy cups. Children are considered "least" in so many ways. And in every-day life the rewards are not as noticeable. Children don't show you the same appreciation as Bible study ladies. (No candles and homemade cookies at Christmas!) Instead, you serve them and they turn up their nose at their lunch…or throw it on the floor. Yet I'm thankful that God reminds me where my true reward is . . . in His hands! What better place could it be than that?

---

**FAITH STEP:** *Even if you're not a parent, Jesus calls you to bless His children. To whom can you offer "a cup of cold water" today? Ask Him to bring someone in your path!*

—*Tricia Goyer*

# SATURDAY, FEBRUARY 22

*I pray that out of his glorious riches he may strengthen you with power
through his Spirit in your inner being, so that Christ may dwell in your
hearts through faith. And I pray that you, being rooted and established in love,
may have power, together with all the Lord's holy people, to grasp how wide
and long and high and deep is the love of Christ, and to know this love
that surpasses knowledge—that you may be filled to the measure of
all the fullness of God. Ephesians 3:16–19 (NIV)*

YESTERDAY AFTERNOON WHILE WE WERE walking through the Target parking
lot, Jack, our eleven-year-old, turned to me and said, "Mom, do you know
what I want more than anything when I get to college?" I pondered. "Love
and money?" What more could a college student want?

Jack grinned. "I was thinking more like a laptop and a minifridge. Could
you get me that when I go to college?" I had to laugh. "Consider it done."

I'm going to remind him when he's eighteen that that is all he requires of
me. But sometimes I think I live life with an eleven-year-old's perspective.
Here I am, thinking that all I need for a good life is an Internet connection
and an endless supply of chilled snack foods.

What I really need is a full indwelling of Jesus's incomprehensible love. It
is easy to settle for less in this life and miss out on Jesus's boundless supply of
love, grace, and knowledge. But I don't want to settle. I want my life planted
deep in the soil of His love so I can experience the fullness of God in my life.

I am praying this for Jack, too, as he grows into the young man God designed him to be. That he will experience the goodness and richness of God's
love in his own life too—with or without a minifridge.

FAITH STEP: *Think back over this past year. Are there any areas in your life where you
have settled for less than Jesus is offering you? Ask Him to show you how you can live more
in the fullness of His love.*

—*Susanna Foth Aughtmon*

# SUNDAY, FEBRUARY 23

*My heart has heard you say, "Come and talk with me." And my heart responds,*
*"Lord, I am coming." Psalm 27:8 (NLT)*

SINCE MOVING SO FAR AWAY, I don't get to see my children very often. That makes phone calls especially important. It's not as good as a face-to-face conversation, but it's better than nothing—and better than texting, which they often prefer. I have a need to hear their voices and know that they're doing okay. When they don't return my call right away, my imagination kicks in. I think of worst-case scenarios that might explain why I haven't heard back. What a relief when I see their number pop up on my cell phone.

My maternal need to hear from my children is nothing compared with Jesus's longing to communicate with us. In Luke 10 we see how it pleased Jesus that Mary chose to sit at His feet, drinking in His every word. In Revelation 3:20 Jesus pictures Himself as knocking on our door, hoping we will invite Him to come in and fellowship with us.

I'm ashamed to admit it, but sometimes my prayers resemble a quick text more than a deep conversation with the One Who died for me. *Help this dental procedure go okay. Please protect my loved ones. Where did I put those keys?* Those kinds of prayers don't exactly throw the door open wide and invite Him in.

Jesus wants to have intimate fellowship and conversation with me because He loves me so deeply. And because He knows how much I need Him. Spending time talking things over with Jesus gives me exactly what I need to see me through my day, whether wisdom and guidance, comfort and encouragement, or a sense of peace and security. When the Lover of my soul wants me to talk with Him, how can I answer anything other than, "Lord, I am coming"?

FAITH STEP: *The next time you're tempted to skip your daily prayer time, picture Jesus holding out His arms and saying, "Come and talk with Me." How will you choose to respond?*

—*Dianne Neal Matthews*

# MONDAY, FEBRUARY 24

*"Come now, let's settle this," says the Lord. "Though your sins are like scarlet,
I will make them as white as snow. Though they are red like crimson,
I will make them as white as wool." Isaiah 1:18 (NLT)*

I LOOKED OUT THE WINDOW at the winter wonderland of white that blanketed the previously barren ground. There's something about the whiteness, the purity, and the dazzling brightness that sucks my breath away and fills me with a sense of awe.

A flash of red darted in between the trees of our backyard and landed on one of the sturdy limbs. A beautiful cardinal had come to visit. Maybe he was looking for breakfast or just lighting on a dry place. But the bright scarlet color gave such a vivid contrast to the surrounding white.

That entire picture reminded me of a familiar Scripture from Isaiah. God had spoken some powerful encouragement to His prophet regarding the nation of Judah at that time. The wealthy lorded their power over the poor; morality had fled, and their religion offered only lip service, not true obedience to God. So He initiated an invitation to the nation.

In the middle of that sordid picture God flashed a glorious wonder: Their sins, like scarlet, would soon be covered. In this prophetic declaration, Jesus's own blood—and death—would provide the actual covering. It was a word to us, as well. For those who looked to Him in obedience and acceptance would feel and sense the wonder of His purity.

Because of Jesus, God would now view our sins—once red like scarlet—as white as snow. The once-barren ground of our lives would become a scene of rare beauty.

FAITH STEP: *Take a blank, white sheet of paper and write the words of Isaiah 1:18 across it, thanking Jesus for His snow-white covering.*

*—Rebecca Barlow Jordan*

# TUESDAY, FEBRUARY 25

*"Which of you fathers, if your son asks for a fish, will give him
a snake instead? Or if he asks for an egg, will give him a scorpion?
If you then, though you are evil, know how to give good gifts to your
children, how much more will your Father in heaven give the
Holy Spirit to those who ask him!" Luke 11:11–13 (NIV)*

A GROUP OF FRIENDS FROM church were gathering for a luncheon and time to catch up with each other's lives. I'd been looking forward to it for weeks, and prayed I'd be able to attend, even though health issues often keep me homebound. However, the day of the get-together, I was in the midst of a bad setback. I sent a quick e-mail to the group letting them know I couldn't make it, and dragged myself back to bed, battling disappointment at yet another activity snatched away from me by illness.

About the time the lunch was scheduled to start, the phone rang. My son, who is so busy he sometimes goes weeks without communicating, wanted to chat. Not only that, he was facing a large decision and wanted to talk it over with me. Hearing his voice was a precious gift. If I'd been at the luncheon, the moment would have been missed.

In this Scripture, Jesus reminds us that our heavenly Father gives us better gifts than we even know to ask for. We all feel disappointed when a prayer is answered with a "no," or a "not yet." It's often hard to find the blessing beyond the disappointment. But this instance of seeing a direct gift that God brought about through something frustrating, encouraged me to trust for the times I can't see.

**FAITH STEP:** *Ask Jesus for the gift of His Holy Spirit, and ask Him to open your eyes to see a blessing from His hand that has come through something that looked like a disappointment.*

—*Sharon Hinck*

# WEDNESDAY, FEBRUARY 26

*If it is possible, as far as it depends on you, live at peace with everyone.*
*Romans 12:18 (NIV)*

I WATCHED A PASSING NEWS report about a reality television star being startled by her own show. As she watched herself, she noted how dramatic she was . . . and how she jumped into other people's issues, leaving behind a trail of tears. As a mentor to teenage mothers, I see this type of drama lived out every week. With witty, but often hurtful, words slung around on television shows—reality television and sitcoms—it's no wonder that a generation is being raised to live their lives with the same level of drama they see on the screen. Young people today don't understand peace. They lash out with words that wound others, and they find themselves wounded in the same way.

When I first became a follower of Christ, I struggled with being peaceful. It's easy to speak without thinking. Harder is to hold your tongue, to lift another up in prayer, and to display the love of Jesus Christ. After trying to "be peaceful" on my own and failing, I discovered one way to succeed. To be peaceful like Jesus, I needed to let Jesus fill me. When I turned to Him daily in prayer and Scripture reading—and when I asked Him to fill me and direct my heart—my actions didn't stem from my own efforts, but rather God's work in me.

Are you tired of the drama? As Romans 14:19 (NIV) says, "Let us therefore make every effort to do what leads to peace and to mutual edification."

Want to be peaceful? Ask Jesus to be peaceful through you. Lift up prayers before you jump into the situation. In a world that is filled with drama, your gentleness will shine. And instead of leaving a trail of tears behind, you'll leave a fragrance of joy as others experience God through you.

FAITH STEP: *Next time you feel like jumping in and stating your opinion, pause and pray. Ask God to show you how to respond.*

—*Tricia Goyer*

# THURSDAY, FEBRUARY 27

---

*"Suppose a woman has ten silver coins and loses one.*
*Won't she light a lamp and sweep the entire house and search*
*carefully until she finds it?" Luke 15:8 (NLT)*

---

MY HUSBAND IS ONE OF the hardest workers I know, and he's a dreamer to boot. He will work to his limits in pursuit of a dream, and he loves watching that drive in others, as well. Throughout the week he anticipates watching *Gold Rush* on Friday night. The mystique of buried treasure, the increasing interest in precious metals, the nuggets of reward that the miners give their all for, these are captivating reasons to watch.

The woman in the above verse obviously valued her coin enough to upend her home to reclaim it; she would not stop until she found it. Throughout the Bible we see examples of people who were not only willing to be detoured from the common lifestyle, but who acted on that willingness. Abraham moved from home in obedience to God. If that weren't loyalty enough, he obeyed God's direction to sacrifice his son, Isaac; surely he collapsed in relief when God stopped his hand in time. But he was in the process of acting on his willingness.

What will you never give up pursuing? Love? Peace? Security? Financial freedom? Worthwhile pursuits. How about the salvation of others, both from their troubles on earth as well as for eternity?

Jesus came to show us abundant life beyond any pursuit we could chase on our own. He thinks we're worth giving His all for, because that's exactly what He did. We are that prize coin, that treasured golden nugget, that child He literally brought back from the dead.

---

FAITH STEP: *Ask Jesus to put on your heart the causes and people He cherishes; then ask Him to help you act on their behalf.*

—*Erin Keeley Marshall*

# FRIDAY, FEBRUARY 28

*Then the King will say, "I'm telling the solemn truth:*
*Whenever you did one of these things to someone overlooked*
*or ignored, that was me—you did it to me." Matthew 25:40 (MSG)*

I WANT TO WALK WHERE Jesus walked. The Mount of Olives. Gethsemane. Jerusalem. The Sea of Galilee.

I have my passport. And a longing to feel those identical paths under my feet. It's not the same to read about the garden tomb or view pictures of the John 4 well or hear audio of the birdsong in Bethany.

But I was reminded today that I *do* walk where He walked.

Every time I enter into other people's pain with them, I walk the path He walked. Every time I stoop to help a child or kneel to cry out to God or talk to someone shunned by society or listen to a breaking heart, I'm walking the same roads He did.

When I lay down what I want to do in favor of what God wants me to do, I'm walking in His footsteps. When I ignore my own discomfort in order to reach out to someone in need, I'm walking where He walked.

I can almost feel the coarse gravel underfoot, hear the rustle of olive trees, smell the bread and fish baking, see the hurting people in His path. They're now in mine.

The incarcerated, the hungry, the lame, and blind and deaf. "This is the path I walked too," He says as I sit beside a dying friend or pray with a family member. "You are in the virtual Holy Land, taking the same routes I did."

Might that be truer today than yesterday, truer tomorrow than today.

FAITH STEP: *Print out a list of memorable locations in the Holy Land and observe what Jesus accomplished at each of those historic sites. Take note of how your life is mirroring the route He took, the people He touched, the kind of difference He made.*

*—Cynthia Ruchti*

# SATURDAY, MARCH 1

*"So don't worry about tomorrow, for tomorrow will bring its own worries. Today's trouble is enough for today." Matthew 6:34 (NLT)*

WHAT WORRIES YOU? THERE ARE current worries that it seems I'm continually turning over to Jesus. Worries about missed work deadlines. Worries that I won't know how to handle the emotional needs of my newly adopted children. Worries that I'm never going to get that huge pile of laundry done!

And you know what? Worry sucks you dry. I'm pretty sure it kills brain cells and it fills up my heart with more gunk than a drain sewer.

"A day of worry is more exhausting than a day of work," writes John Lubbock. Isn't that the truth? And the funny thing is that it's unnecessary. Looking back, how many of your worries came to be? And if they did come to pass, wasn't Jesus there? Didn't He take care of you in every situation?

Thinking about the "work" of worry made me think of something my seventh-grade science teacher used to say, "Work smarter, not harder." And what should we be working smart about? Jesus tells us in John 9:4 (NLT), "We must quickly carry out the tasks assigned us by the one who sent us. The night is coming, and then no one can work."

When we are busy worrying, then we are using up all our thoughts, time, and energy on things that might never happen, instead of focusing on doing the work Jesus has asked us to do. We're robbing Jesus of the only thing He desires—all of us.

FAITH STEP: *Make a Not To Worry List. Anytime you find yourself focusing on a worry, write it down instead. Then write a prayer to Jesus after it, lifting it up to Him.*

*—Tricia Goyer*

# SUNDAY, MARCH 2

*Jesus answered, "I assure you, unless someone is born anew, it's not possible to see God's kingdom." John 3:3 (CEB)*

AFTER A PARTICULARLY GRIPPING SERMON one Sunday morning, our senior pastor invited anyone who felt a need to talk to someone or to pray or just to sit and consider God's Word to linger after the congregation dispersed. Many did.

A young friend of mine who'd been wrestling with some heavy issues, keeping Jesus at a distance rather than inviting Him into her situation, exited, then paused in the commons area. She glanced back through the double doors.

I asked if she was okay. As tears began to pool in her eyes, she said, "I... I think I need to...to go back into the...the..." She pointed toward the sanctuary but seemed unable to find the right word to describe it.

I put my arm around her. "Some of us call it the Birthing Room. It's where we labor over the things that have been causing us pain and allow Jesus to deliver new life in us."

She nodded. "It's time."

"Do you need someone beside you to help you remember how to breathe?"

She took my hand, squeezed it, and we walked back through the double doors together.

Jesus might appreciate the analogy. One of His favorite subjects was new life, giving birth to new creations, urging a glorious potential out of us, replacing illness with health, delivering us from the grip of sin and death.

Not just in sanctuaries, but anywhere Jesus is, life is being born. Because of the new things that come to life because of Him, His very presence is a Birthing Room.

FAITH STEP: *Babies are born in places other than birthing centers all the time. Reflect on the location where you were the last time Jesus birthed something new in you.*

—*Cynthia Ruchti*

# MONDAY, MARCH 3

*If only there were someone to arbitrate between us, to lay his hand upon us both,
someone to remove God's rod from me, so that his terror would frighten me no more.*
*Job 9:33–34 (NIV)*

I PAGED THROUGH A CONTRACT from a publisher for my new novel, and scratched my head. I don't speak legalese and couldn't make sense of most of the terms. But I knew I didn't need to stress out. I have an agent, and he flags issues we need to discuss. He also communicates with publishers on my behalf. I hate negotiations or conflict of any sort, so I'm always grateful that my agent is my representative and handles things for me.

Job also needed an arbiter. He felt as if God was unfairly punishing him, and he longed for someone to represent him. Arguing before God is even more intimidating than negotiating with a publisher. Job knew that on our own, we can't stand before a holy God. We need someone to arbitrate. Someone to stand in our place for us.

Jesus took that role. He represents us, speaks for us, and reconciles us with the Father. Later in the book, Job gives a prophetic proclamation that has inspired beautiful hymns. "I know that my Redeemer lives, and that in the end he will stand upon the earth" (Job 19:25, NIV). When trials close in on me and my heart is full of questions or confusion, I want to follow Job's example. I want to remember that I need an arbiter, and then rejoice that my Redeemer has come.

FAITH STEP: *Pull out some tax forms or legal documents and think of the difficulty found in getting these human requirements met. Think about the much more profound requirement to ransom a human soul. Thank Jesus for standing in your place, for reconciling you to God, and for being your ongoing Arbiter and Redeemer.*

*—Sharon Hinck*

# TUESDAY, MARCH 4

*A song. A psalm of the Sons of Korah. Great is the Lord, and most worthy of praise, in the city of our God, his holy mountain. Psalm 48:1 (NIV)*

IN THE PSALMS, KING DAVID spent a lot of time expressing his doubts and fears. I tend to like that about him. Then he would encourage himself by praising his Creator for all He had done, reminding himself of who was really in charge. I like that about him too.

So this morning, I am compiling my own psalm, a hymn of praise to the Savior who is really in charge. *You are steadfast. You are faithful. You are greater than what I can fathom. You are mighty. You are victorious. Your will always comes to pass. You are right and righteous in all of Your ways. You are bountiful and generous. You are all-knowing. You are kind and merciful. You are just. You are pure. You are holy. You are unchangeable. You are truthful. You do not let down those who follow You. You do not walk away from the ones whom You love. You are creative. You like surprises. You don't like to be boxed in. You are powerful beyond my wildest imaginations. You are wise. You are thoughtful. You enjoy the details. You know what is going to happen next. You are not concerned about overcoming obstacles. You can live out Your life through me if I can figure out how to get out of the way. You are rich. You are loving. You are compassionate even when we mess up. You know the past and the future, and the present is not too much for You to handle. You make dead things alive and sick things well. You redeem the unredeemable. You are in charge. You have told me that I am Yours. You take care of Your kids.*

Today, like King David, I am anchoring myself in the truth of who He is.

**FAITH STEP:** *Pen your own psalm of praise. Tell Jesus who He is in your life and what He has done for you.*

—*Susanna Foth Aughtmon*

# WEDNESDAY, MARCH 5

*If we confess our sins, he is faithful and just to forgive us our sins and to cleanse us from all unrighteousness.* 1 John 1:9 (ESV)

I WAS EXCITED TO RECEIVE the e-mail from the *Mornings with Jesus* editor telling the writers which specific holiday they'd been assigned to write about. I lost some of my enthusiasm when I saw my name paired with Ash Wednesday. What did I know about this observance? I've never attended a church that marked Ash Wednesday with any special service. The editor suggested that I stick with it and do some research.

I was surprised to learn how many denominations mark Ash Wednesday as the beginning of Lent, the season of preparation for Easter. A common practice is to mark the foreheads of worshippers with the sign of the cross, typically using ashes gathered when palm branches from the previous year's Palm Sunday are burned. This relates to the biblical tradition of throwing ashes over one's head to signify repentance before God. Ash Wednesday services may include some other symbolic act of confession and repentance, fasting, or appropriate readings from Psalms.

Confession of sins is one component of the model prayer that Jesus demonstrated when His disciples asked Him how they should pray. Even though I know confession and repentance should be included in my daily quiet time, too often they get pushed out of the way by my hurry to get to my needs and requests. If I neglect Ash Wednesday in my hurry to get to Easter Sunday, I run the danger of trivializing why Jesus died in the first place.

Setting aside a day to focus on this important facet of my relationship with my Savior only makes sense. So this year on Ash Wednesday, I probably won't have ashes on my forehead. But I will have confession and repentance in my heart.

**FAITH STEP:** *Spend some time examining your heart and your life for any sins that need confessing. You might want to write specific sins down on small pieces of paper, then shred them after praying for forgiveness.*

—*Dianne Neal Matthews*

# THURSDAY, MARCH 6

---

*Even though I walk through the valley of the shadow of death,
I will fear no evil, for you are with me; your rod and your staff,
they comfort me. Psalm 23:4 (NIV)*

---

MY HUSBAND AND I STOOD on a mountaintop waiting for the shadows to completely overtake us. My anticipation grew, for our Colorado hosts had tried to prepare us for this extraordinary moment.

Sure enough, as soon as darkness enveloped us, I saw it creeping up the horizon: first, a semicircle sliver of light forming near the bottom of a movie-like screen. Within minutes, it covered the entire picture from left to right. It was huge!

I had never viewed the moon rising through what seemed like a 1,000 percent or more zoom lens. It crowded out every other point in the sky, and I felt so... small, and yes, even giddy with delight. But we eventually had to descend the mountaintop. The moon rose higher, and the magic moment quickly passed.

When David was a shepherd, he must have seen many breathtaking moon risings as he guided his sheep up and down the mountains. The mountaintop brought beauty; the valley represented death. Predators lay ready to devour his sheep in the darkness. But the valley held only a shadow of death, and a shadow is merely a reflection of light. Life-giving green grass also lay in the valley for his sheep. And he had the Lord to protect and guide him. He couldn't stay on the mountaintop forever.

Jesus never wants us to fear the "shadows" of our lives. Each time I walk through a difficult valley, whether it's a personal loss or a difficult challenge, I try to remember that mountaintop moon rising. Although I'd like to stay on the mountaintop where everything looks perfectly beautiful, I know the true Light and Life of my soul waits for me in the valley with nourishing food, rest for my body, and protection for my journey.

---

**FAITH STEP:** *Memorize Psalm 23 this week. What mountaintop experiences has Jesus given you? How has He comforted you in the valleys?*

—*Rebecca Barlow Jordan*

# FRIDAY, MARCH 7

*But God shows his love for us in that while we were yet sinners*
*Christ died for us. Romans 5:8 (RSV)*

MY FIVE-YEAR-OLD DAUGHTER, ADELAIDE, LIKE me, is always trying to figure things out. I'm sure she heard something at church or during one of our family devotionals that prompted her to ask this, but I have no idea what it was.

"Mom, if we're nice to God, then He's nice to us, right?"

In her question I could see her trying to make sense of her faith. It was like she had figured something out, one of the secrets to the Christian life. Her eyes danced. She got it!

Except that she didn't.

"Well, Adelaide, it's not really that simple." I smiled, tucking a white-blonde strand of hair behind her ear.

Trying the best I could to explain a mystery I don't "get" myself, I said that God is nice to us even when we're not nice, but that sometimes bad things happen even when we're being as nice as we can be.

"Huh?"

Adelaide and I may ponder these questions our whole lives, but what we'll keep coming back to is that the core of the Christian life is love. Everything that happens to us, and everything we do, good or bad, flows through the filter of God's love for us, demonstrated by Jesus on the cross. *While we were yet sinners.*

We can and need to make choices for the right. That will save us a lot of heartache. But when things happen that we can't understand, we must cling to Jesus and trust that our Father knows best.

**FAITH STEP:** *Is your faith based on outward performance, whether yours or the Lord's? Ask Him to help you change that, taking you deeper into the mystery of your Savior's love.*

—*Gwen Ford Faulkenberry*

# SATURDAY, MARCH 8

*But our citizenship is in heaven. And we eagerly await a
Savior from there, the Lord Jesus Christ. Philippians 3:20 (NIV)*

IN SEVERAL VERSES THROUGH THE Bible, the church is described as Christ's bride. Like this verse, a bride eagerly awaits for her groom, and likewise, the groom eagerly awaits his bride.

This has never been more evident to me than this year, when our oldest son, Rene, married. His bride, Ariel, was a senior in college graduating with a degree in elementary education. Her degree required the last semester to be spent student teaching. At the time they planned their wedding, they believed she would be able to teach in the town where Rene worked as a youth minister. However, the university denied her request, and instead of spending their first three months of marriage together, she taught at a school three hours away, and they saw each other on weekends only. Each week, the newlyweds eagerly awaited the moment when they would be together again.

In Philippians 3 (NIV), Paul expresses how important it is to set our sights on heavenly things, when our "lowly bodies" will be transformed by Christ so that we will be "like His glorious body" (verses 20–21). Why wouldn't we eagerly await that transformation? No more sickness. No more sadness. No more pain. Seeing loved ones who have passed on. I know I can't wait to see my grandparents again or my dear friends who died way too young.

That, I believe, is the type of "eagerly awaiting" that is described in Philippians 3:20, a longing to see our Lord and Savior, the way Rene and Ariel longed to see each other each week and the way I long to see my loved ones again.

---

**FAITH STEP:** *Send a card to newlyweds this week with Philippians 3:20 written inside. Remind them that when they are apart, they should eagerly await the moment they see each other again. And throughout their lives together, they should eagerly await the moment they see their Lord.*

—*Renee Andrews*

# SUNDAY, MARCH 9

*How great is your goodness, which you have stored up for*
*those who fear you. Psalm 31:19 (NIV)*

MY HUSBAND AND I LIVED in Nepal for nearly three years. The nation ranked the world's fourth poorest at that time, and it showed.

Our villagers owned few material goods: cooking utensils and plates, grass sleeping mats, harvesting tools, and a couple changes of clothes. They cooked over an open fire in their homes, and they bathed in an irrigation ditch that trickled near our hut.

We minimized our possessions to live simply. Even then we owned a small metal table, two cane stools, a water filter, a tin-covered counter that held two camping stoves, and a portable kerosene heater.

One day a neighbor observed our belongings and said, "Everything that is, is here." His statement humbled me and caused me to be forever grateful for my material blessings.

Scripture says God's goodness is great toward those who fear Him. This goodness extends far beyond material possessions, but our belongings represent a good starting point for us to express gratitude. Even when we think we lack, we still have much for which to be thankful compared to the majority of the world's population.

**FAITH STEP:** *Look around your home. List at least five things for which to be thankful, and express gratitude to God for these material tokens of His goodness.*

—*Grace Fox*

# MONDAY, MARCH 10

*But the path of the righteous is like the light of dawn,*
*which shines brighter and brighter until full day. Proverbs 4:18 (ESV)*

MY FRIEND'S HUSBAND'S JOB HAD been eliminated in a company-wide downsizing. He'd applied for schooling that would train him in a career he wasn't excited about, but would pay the bills. His application was turned down.

"He's such a hard worker," she said. "How it's supposed to go is that you work hard, apply yourself, keep your nose clean, follow the rules, trust the Lord, and life gets better every year. Not worse." But when I had bled the same kind of disappointments months earlier, and asked the same kinds of questions, a familiar verse of Scripture caught me by the throat.

"The path of the righteous . . . shines brighter and brighter until [the] full day."

It seemed curious that the Lord hadn't chosen the word *better* for that promise. The gentle unfolding of its truth brought an uncommon peace to a common complaint.

We aren't guaranteed that our path will get easier and easier, better and better—in our eyes—but that as we lean into Jesus and plant our feet in the footprints He left, our path will grow brighter and brighter. Our faith will shine more and more as we negotiate the obstacles and faithfully trust Him whether we get a promotion or lose our job, whether the diagnosis is benign or malignant, whether we receive the answer to our agonized prayer now or later...much, much later.

What gets noted in Scripture—and by those observing—is that no matter what happens, our path may not get better, but as we reflect more and more of Him, it will grow more radiant until it practically glows!

**FAITH STEP:** *If you've recently had what the world would call a setback, are you mired in "This isn't how it was supposed to turn out"? Or are you handing out sunglasses because your faith path is blindingly bright?*

*—Cynthia Ruchti*

# TUESDAY, MARCH 11

*I will bless you...and you will be a blessing to others. Genesis 12:2 (NLT)*

I STILL REMEMBER A HYMN from my childhood called, "Make Me a Blessing." All of us love Jesus's blessings and want to know that our lives can touch others. But we don't always like what accompanies those blessings.

As I read about the lives of two faith-filled people recently—Abraham, and Mary, the mother of Jesus—I realized afresh that obedience and blessing go hand in hand. Abraham received a promise from God that he would become the father of many nations. He passed God's supreme test of obedience and faith when he was willing to do what God asked: to sacrifice his promised son, Isaac. God accepted Abraham's obedience and provided a lamb instead of taking Isaac's life.

Mary, as a virgin teenager, chose to receive God's impossible-sounding words that she would bear the Son of God (Luke 1:31). Did her obedience usher in blessing? Absolutely!

God used both of these servants as major players in His bigger plan for salvation. As believers, our lives have been blessed beyond measure as a result of these two faith-filled people.

It's easy for me to look at those "giants" in Scripture and see myself as insignificant, not someone God could use to bring blessing to others in such a monumental way. But our simple "yes" to Jesus, no matter how small it may seem to us, gives Him all the material He needs to make our lives "bless-worthy."

Like Abraham and Mary, we may not know or understand God's plan, but we can find joy and purpose knowing we are part of His greater purpose. He has no major or minor players. We're all a part of His team. He wants both to bless us, and to make us a blessing. How He does that is up to Him. Our part is simply to obey.

FAITH STEP: *Thank Jesus today for making you a team player. The next time He asks you to do something, tell Him "yes."*

—*Rebecca Barlow Jordan*

# WEDNESDAY, MARCH 12

*These are a shadow of the things that were to come; the reality, however, is found in Christ. Colossians 2:17 (NIV)*

WHEN MY CHILDREN WERE LITTLE, sometimes we tried using our hands to make "shadow puppets" on the wall. I never managed anything fancier than a bunny created from a balled-up fist hopping up and down with two fingers sticking up. One evening our little game became more amusing when the cat tried to jump up and grab a shadow. After that, the kids made sure their shadow puppets were low enough on the wall for her to chase after, darting away just when she pounced.

The New Testament explains that Jesus is the reality that many things in the Old Testament foreshadowed. The tabernacle, and later the temple, the Mosaic laws, the festivals, and all the rituals pointed to Him and His future role as our Savior. Many times God rebuked the priests and the people for placing more importance on sacrifices and special holy days than on sincere worship of Him. In the New Testament, Jesus accused the Jewish leaders of concentrating on following rituals and traditions without having a heart for God. Their wrongly placed focus caused them to miss the Messiah when He stood right in front of them.

Even though I know who Jesus is, I can also be guilty of chasing shadows. This happens whenever I get more caught up in rules or traditions than in my relationship with Him. Or when I go to church and pay more attention to the music, programs, or even the building itself than the One I went there to worship. How ridiculous it would be to try to have a relationship with a person's shadow instead of the actual person. Instead of obsessing over external shows of faith, I need to keep my focus on Christ, the real thing.

FAITH STEP: *Have you been focusing on external displays of faith more than on Jesus Himself? Spend some time in prayer simply praising Him for Who He is.*

—*Dianne Neal Matthews*

# THURSDAY, MARCH 13

*But our citizenship is in heaven. And we eagerly await a Savior from there, the Lord Jesus Christ, who, by the power that enables him to bring everything under his control, will transform our lowly bodies so that they will be like his glorious body. Philippians 3:20–21 (NIV)*

I WOKE UP AND STRETCHED, easing the stiffness out of my muscles and sitting up slowly. Then I remembered that it was a special day. I'd looked forward to this for weeks. My friend Patti was downstairs in the guest room. I quickly got ready for the day, eager to spend time with her.

Each day of her visit, that little bit of extra anticipation brightened my morning. I couldn't wait to pad out to the living room and see if she was up yet. We went for walks, giggled over cups of tea, and caught up on everything in our lives from the important to the silly. I thanked Jesus for the blessing of her visit, and the blessing of friendships.

When I noticed the joy I felt as I looked forward to spending time with her, I asked Jesus to deepen that same sort of eagerness toward Him. He is my best friend, and I don't have to wait months for Him to stay in my guest room. He's there to greet me each day.

I also asked Him to stir that eagerness in me for the future. I waited for my friend's arrival with excitement, and I can look forward to Jesus's return with that same joyful anticipation.

FAITH STEP: *What is the last thing you looked forward to with great eagerness? Ask Jesus to give you that same sort of eagerness to be with Him. Tomorrow morning when you first wake up, tell yourself that your Best Friend is waiting to spend time with you and greet the day with eagerness.*

—*Sharon Hinck*

# FRIDAY, MARCH 14

*Do not lose your temper—it only leads to harm. Psalm 37:8 (NLT)*

"Step away, Mom. Just *step away*."

Sage advice from my pip-squeak. When Calianne's words reached my conscience, I did indeed step back from the stuck blender or the dripping faucet or whatever kitchen catastrophe confounded my composure.

*Ahhhhhhh* . . . the glory of stepping back temporarily from the chaos. There's a lot to be said for grown-up time-outs. I was due for one, which my daughter granted me when she repeated the exhortation I've often given to her and her brother.

Sometimes the most holy, faith-filled, productive action we can take is to *step away* from what's testing our temper so Jesus can have room to *step in* to our trouble. No, He wasn't going to materialize and fix my blender or wipe the floor, but He is always ready to diffuse my anger. My patience and our home's atmosphere needed me to drop the towel and let the mess remain a mess for a bit. Spewing a mess of words could have been much more destructive than whatever was frustrating me in the first place.

Does it surprise you to know that Jesus got frustrated? You may recall Him flipping over tables in the Temple (Matthew 21:12–13). Not a picture of calmly stepping away. It isn't wrong to act on our anger to protect what's godly or pure; in fact, that's right and good. Jesus got angry at the right things, such as tax collectors defiling His Father's house.

Weigh the situations you're struggling with. Step away, even if it's just a moment or two alone, to gain perspective before your limits cause additional harm.

**Faith step:** *What flips your lid, fries your bacon, steams your boat, pops your bubble . . . just makes you crazy angry? Now, before you face it again, commit to step away to breathe a prayer for help from Jesus. He knows what's worth getting steamed about, and He can help you process productive ways to handle your anger.*

—*Erin Keeley Marshall*

# SATURDAY, MARCH 15

*And let us run with perseverance the race marked out for us. Hebrews 12:1 (NIV)*

LIFE IS LIKE A RELAY race. I discovered that while creating a complete backyard and (partial) front yard makeover last year. I described my dream gardens, the kind I could afford, and my husband sketched the plans. But how would we get it all done?

I was surprised at how much we could accomplish, and how much time it required. I spent hours researching plants, visiting nurseries, and reading books on perennial gardens. I measured plots, drew pictures, and dreamed about the finished product.

When the time came to begin, I handed the baton back to Larry, who completed most of the long, hard hours preparing the ground. But we also hired some help to redo pebbled paths, carve out garden plots, plant new sod, and even install a sprinkler system. Together we bought and planted flowers, and I found fun yard art to complement the picture. When we finished, we celebrated, amazed at the final product. Not once did I complain or wish that I had accomplished that makeover alone. I valued—and received gratefully all the extra help.

Throughout my life I've often struggled with whether my "ministry" through writing and as a minister's wife was enough. Could I have discipled more? Should I have exercised more hospitality? But wait. Just like it takes more than one person to create and maintain a beautiful garden, so it takes the entire body of Christ to "run the relay race" and grow believers into mature Christians. We each do our part, using our God-given gifts.

When we're gone, others must take up the baton and run the race set before them. Jesus, our Faithful One, will add His blessing when we run for Him. And in the end, we'll all share in the joy of that completed prize.

FAITH STEP: *What gifts has Jesus given you to share with the body of Christ? Thank Him for those gifts—and for those who are running the race with you.*

—*Rebecca Barlow Jordan*

# SUNDAY, MARCH 16

*He is before all things, and in him all things hold together. Colossians 1:17 (NIV)*

MY HUSBAND, J.R., CO-OWNS SEVERAL cheer and tumbling gyms in the Southeast. There are several hundred athletes at each gym ranging in age from toddlers to college students. We try our best to get to know all of the children at the gyms and tend to learn a lot about what is important in their world by their daily conversations with us or our coaching staff.

Recently Chloe, a tiny blonde five-year-old, entered our gym for her weekly tumbling class with even more animation than usual. She could hardly wait to tell everyone what had happened.

"Kaitlyn and I were in the car, and ants were on her feet, and she swiped at the ants and then the car went off the road and flipped and caught on fire. And I lost all of my brand-new fake fingernails."

I concentrated on the important part. Obviously Chloe was okay, but what about her sixteen-year-old sister? "Chloe, how is Kaitlyn?" I asked.

"She was in the hospital but she's better. But didn't you hear? I lost *all* of my fake fingernails."

Obviously, at five years old, Chloe hadn't developed her priorities enough to know that her sister's well-being was more important than her press-on nails.

Often, I'm like that five-year-old. I start my day thinking about deadlines, laundry, dirty dishes, groceries, and cleaning. But Christ taught us how to prioritize. He taught that you should love the Lord your God with all your heart, soul, and mind, and love your neighbor like yourself.

When we start our day in God's Word and in prayer, everything—even the most difficult things—fall into place. May we learn to prioritize like Christ, focus on our God, and watch the worries of this world pass away.

FAITH STEP: *Do not let the laundry, deadlines, cleaning—or even brand-new fake fingernails—take your focus off of your Lord today. Remember His priorities and make them your own.*

—*Renee Andrews*

# MONDAY, MARCH 17

*Let us then approach the throne of grace with confidence,
so that we may receive mercy and find grace to help us in our time of need.*
Hebrews 4:16 (NIV)

I RECENTLY HOSTED A WEEKEND getaway for businesswomen. An event planner suggested finding sponsors to help cover expenses. Doing so meant approaching corporate decision-makers to request their partnership.

The mere thought made my heart pound. What if these people felt my endeavor was pointless or my request inappropriate? What if they considered my presence an annoying interruption in their busy schedule?

Perhaps you experience the same misgivings when you need to approach someone with a request:

- your employer—to ask for a raise
- your ex—to ask for cooperation with child custody agreements
- your neighbor—to ask him to quiet his barking dog
- your spouse—to ask for forgiveness

Sometimes we fear approaching people with our needs lest we offend or be considered a bother. That's never the case with God.

He invites us to approach Him through faith in Jesus Christ. He welcomes our presence and our requests. He never considers us an annoyance. "In him [Jesus Christ] and through faith in him we may approach God with freedom and confidence" (Ephesians 3:12, NIV).

What are your needs today? Take them to God. Do so with gratitude and boldness knowing He promises to listen and respond.

FAITH STEP: *Read Esther's story (Esther 4:8–11). Approaching King Xerxes carried the threat of death for this young woman. Compare this with Hebrews 4:16 and Ephesians 3:12. Thank God for the freedom we have to approach Him.*

—*Grace Fox*

# TUESDAY, MARCH 18

*"But the Counselor, the Holy Spirit, whom the Father will send in my name,*
*he will teach you all things, and bring to your remembrance all that I have said to you."*
John 14:26 (RSV)

THESE PAST SIX MONTHS, WE have not had any curtains on our kitchen windows. It has made the kitchen bright and full of light. But now as we have entered the semifrigid season of winter, it has made it so cold that it encourages one to don a parka while eating cereal.

I found some white curtains the other day and thought, *I should get these for the kitchen and see if they make a difference.* The difference of the last few mornings has been amazing. There is a sense of cocooning warmth around the table in the morning and my son, Will, is no longer wearing his blanket to breakfast. Scott walked through the kitchen and said, "Curtains are blankets for houses."

It got me thinking about the "curtains" of my own life. What keeps me warm and protected against the winters of real living? In all of His love and mercy, Jesus has surrounded us with His Holy Spirit. Jesus didn't want to leave us on our own to face the trials and difficulties of life. He knew we would need Him like never before. He sent the Counselor to guide us, nurture us, convict us, and help us.

Not only are we not alone, but His presence fills us with joy and hope. When we are facing the arctic winds of life, the constancy of the Holy Spirit is a warm blanket for the soul, letting us know that we are protected. Loved. Cherished. Understood. Cared for. Heard. Held.

While I am thrilled that my kitchen is feeling warmer, I am more thrilled to know that I am not alone on this journey of life.

FAITH STEP: *Wrap yourself in a blanket on the couch. Feel its warmth and comfort, knowing that you are not alone on this journey of following Jesus. Take a moment to thank Him for His constant presence.*

—*Susanna Foth Aughtmon*

# WEDNESDAY, MARCH 19

*I am sure of this, that He who started a good work in you will carry it on to completion until the day of Christ Jesus. Philippians 1:6 (HCS)*

THE HARDER I WORKED TO clean my house, the more overwhelmed I felt. Evidences of unfinished projects greeted me everywhere I turned. Half-written articles and half-read magazines cluttered the desk. Unhemmed pants lay on the sewing machine. The ribbon in my Bible marked a passage I had determined to memorize three months earlier.

In the kitchen a huge pile of recipe clippings waited to be filed. The closet was stuffed with several years' worth of craft materials for grand projects I'd planned but never gotten started. Suddenly I wondered: *How often do I get exhausted not so much from the work I'm doing, but from the pressures of unfinished and half-finished tasks?*

When Jesus lived on the earth, He never procrastinated. He always spent His time doing exactly what needed to be done—no more and no less. Just before His crucifixion, Jesus was able to say that He had completed the work His Father had given Him to do (John 17:4). Now Jesus is working on an assignment that involves us. My life, and yours, is a grand project He has planned down to the last detail. His goal is to help us become transformed into His image, and to use us to bring honor and glory to His name.

Thank goodness Jesus never procrastinates like I do! Because of His faithfulness I can be sure that He will bring His purposes for my life to completion. Nothing in heaven or on earth can sidetrack Him from His plans, not even my own willful disobedience. I never have to worry about Jesus giving up on me. And one day, when I see Him face-to-face, the project of my life will be completed—right on time.

FAITH STEP: *The next time you feel like a failure as a Christian, thank Jesus that your life is a work-in-progress.*

—*Dianne Neal Matthews*

# THURSDAY, MARCH 20

*"Seek first the kingdom of God and His righteousness, and all these things shall be added to you." Matthew 6:33 (NKJV)*

THE OTHER DAY MY SISTER was grieving a final "first" that occurred in her home. Her youngest lost his first tooth, and it was a bittersweet celebration for her.

Our family has experienced its share of firsts in recent months, as well. Our oldest started kindergarten and got his first visit from the tooth fairy. My daughter began to write her first letters by herself, and she learned to draw flowers and people and other newly recognizable characters. We hosted our first holiday in our new home.

Some firsts are bittersweet, as in my sister's case. Some firsts can be downright hard; we all remember being wounded by a friend or losing something we love.

But believers in Jesus can celebrate regardless, because we have a host of beyond-wonderful firsts to look forward to. First glimpse of His face. First step into heaven. First feeling of complete joy. First flooding of unchallenged peace, of no more doubting we're loved, of freedom from weaknesses we haven't been able to conquer.

Consider the first hug with fellow believers in heaven, loved ones you long to see again. The first moments of restored health, the lifting of every burden. Every pain gone. The first moments knowing that suffering is a thing of the past.

The first time hearing, "Well done, good and faithful servant."

We're constantly saying good-bye to elements of this world, a reality that can be tough to live with. Unbearable, really, if not for Jesus's promise of eternal firsts.

What first are you craving most? If you know Jesus as your Savior, why not celebrate that first early? Feel some of that future-first joy now. In fact, before getting on with your day, do that first!

FAITH STEP: *Jot down three negative experiences you grieve on earth. Then, next to each one, write how Jesus wants to trade that negative with a healing "first" one day.*

—Erin Keeley Marshall

# FRIDAY, MARCH 21

*We are therefore Christ's ambassadors, as though God were
making his appeal through us. We implore you on Christ's behalf:
Be reconciled to God. 2 Corinthians 5:20 (NIV)*

I RECENTLY ATTENDED A TALK given by a Pakistani-American woman. She had
been invited to speak about her experience as a Muslim in America to a group
of literature students at the college where I teach.

The woman was young, hip, and very articulate. Like most of the students,
I listened to her story with interest. I thought she presented it in an intelligent
way, not trying to convert anyone to Islam but fulfilling the request to inform
her listeners about her particular experience.

One student, who I knew already to be vocal in classes about her faith, was obviously uncomfortable with the subject matter. During question-and-answer time
she tried to engage the speaker in an argument about such things as jihads, the
validity of the Koran, and finally, the notion that the speaker was in danger of hell.

At this point, the speaker looked to me for help, and I had to intervene. I reminded the group that the speaker was there by invitation, and that the purpose
was education, not conversion to any religion. When I said we would proceed
with respect for our differences, the student got up and stormed out of the room.

Afterward, I offered the speaker a snack in my office. She said something
to me that I will never forget.

"I have great respect for people who are passionate about what they believe.
What I wish I could tell that student, however, is that if I were ever to consider
converting to Christianity, her behavior would serve as a hindrance, not a help."

Sometimes in our zeal to stand up for what we believe, we forget what
matters most. But Paul wrote that we are to be representatives of Jesus in the
world, letting God speak through us.

**FAITH STEP:** *If you get the opportunity to share your faith today, be sure you do so in the
spirit of reconciliation, lest you hinder the cause of Christ.*

*—Gwen Ford Faulkenberry*

# SATURDAY, MARCH 22

*Jesus wept. John 11:35 (NIV)*

Messenger. Pony Express. Telegraph. Radio. Telephone. Television. E-mail. All have bowed to the superior "get the word out" power of social media.

I'm tucked into my cozy writing chair, with my mood-setting little French lamp on my desk and a cup of tea brewed extra strong at my side. Between projects, I check the newsfeed on my timeline and find dozens—soon to be hundreds—of posts about another school shooting. The fact that I had to use the word *another* is enough to sicken both heart and stomach.

Parents and grandparents are hugging their children tight. "You're still here. You're still here." Others are plummeting into the tarry, stinging blackness of young grief.

And I'm stuck on a two-word verse. "Jesus wept."

Where would we be if we didn't know Jesus was capable of weeping? Knowing the end from the beginning, knowing the ultimate outcome, cradling even now those little ones and their parents in His arms, He doesn't pass it off as the tragedy *du jour. What's all the fuss about?* No.

He grieves. He weeps with us. He feels the daggers of pain, bears the horrors we find unbearable.

Such a simple truth: Jesus weeps. Not just wept, past tense. He weeps.

Some days, it seems like one of the longest and strongest Scriptures, not the shortest.

**Faith step:** *Have you considered using a folded facial tissue as a bookmark in your Bible? Maybe it will serve as a reminder that when your heart breaks, you can count on the comfort of a Savior who cries real tears.*

—*Cynthia Ruchti*

# SUNDAY, MARCH 23

*As he was going into a village, ten men who had leprosy met him.*
*They stood at a distance and called out in a loud voice, "Jesus, Master, have pity on us!" When*
*he saw them, he said, "Go, show yourselves to the priests." And as they went, they were cleansed.*
*One of them, when he saw he was healed, came back, praising God in a loud voice. He threw*
*himself at Jesus's feet and thanked him—and he was a Samaritan. Jesus asked, "Were not all ten*
*cleansed? Where are the other nine?" Luke 17:12–17 (NIV)*

THE FIRST TIME I HEARD this story, I was shocked that only one man showed gratitude. Even as a little girl, I'd been coached on the importance of saying, "Thank you."

In later years when I reread the story, I continued to feel quick to condemn and perhaps a bit smug. Jesus healed these men of a horrible, degenerative, and very isolating disease. Certainly if Jesus did something that dramatic in my life, I'd race right back to Him and pour out worship and thanks. Wouldn't I?

One day a new truth struck me. My soul had been disfigured by sin, my entire being caught in a living death, isolated from God and from others by the effects of my sinful nature. And Jesus brought me healing. Certainly as I wake each day, I race right back to Him and pour out worship and thanks. Don't I?

To be honest, I often race to Him to pour out needs and requests. And He welcomes me, and wants to hear the hurts and longings of my heart. But I wonder if He sometimes grieves that I so quickly forget the biggest miracle He's already given me—even bigger than healing from leprosy: a new life in Him.

FAITH STEP: *In honor of the ten leprous men, for the next ten days, when you wake each morning, thank Jesus for healing your soul through His sacrifice on the cross.*

—*Sharon Hinck*

# MONDAY, MARCH 24

---

*Again he said, "What shall we say the kingdom of God is like, or what parable shall we use to describe it? It is like a mustard seed, which is the smallest seed you plant in the ground. Yet when planted, it grows and becomes the largest of all garden plants, with such big branches that the birds of the air can perch in its shade." Mark 4:30–32 (NIV)*

---

MY BACKYARD IS LOOKING A little sparse these days. The rosebushes are squat and trimmed back and the hydrangea bushes look like a clump of twigs. The Japanese maples have yet to bloom. Even the lemon tree looks forlorn.

But I know that the beauty is coming. Spring is just around the corner. Soon the rosebush will be sprouting leaves and the maple will fill out with its vibrant greenery. It happens every year.

It is so easy to think that things are what they seem. That things will stay the same. But Jesus sees things differently. Taking the tiniest seed possible, the mustard seed, He says, "The smallest seed will become the largest plant."

This is how things work when it comes to Jesus. He turns everything on its ear. The blind shall see. The lame shall walk. The least significant will become the most significant. The first will be last, and the last will be first. This should give us great hope. As His truth takes root in our hearts, we have no idea of how large His kingdom can grow within us. How His love will change us. How His mercy will shape our lives and give shelter to those around us. He will grow us and form us into more than we can ever hope or imagine.

He takes small, unruly lives and makes them large and lovely. Just take it from the mustard seed.

---

**FAITH STEP:** *Plant a seedling in a cup by your window. Check out its progress each morning. As you watch the seedling, remind yourself that Jesus is growing His kingdom in you.*

—*Susanna Foth Aughtmon*

# TUESDAY, MARCH 25

*In light of this hope that we have, we act with great confidence and speak with great courage.* 2 Corinthians 3:12 (VOICE)

I SAT IN THE ROOM filled with teenaged girls. I took a deep breath as I opened my mouth to share my story of being a young mom and of finding Jesus. I also wanted to share the importance of turning over our lives to Jesus.

I'm always nervous when I give this talk because my words conflict with everything young women hear in the culture. Hollywood is filled with un-married couples having babies, women choosing to have a baby without a husband, and everyone—in real life and on the screen—becoming sexually active at the drop of a hat. *Will they even give me the time of day?* I wondered.

What made this talk even more difficult was the fact that I was giving it in the Czech Republic through the use of a translator. This is a country with less than 1 percent Christians. A country where young women are put on birth control at a young age and are expected to be sexually active. It took courage to stand up before them and share a different way—but doesn't telling the truth always take courage?

And you know what? The truth made sense to these young women. Many of them thanked me for my talk. They told me that hadn't heard such things before, but they wanted to make different choices in their lives. And, yes, there were those who hardened their hearts to my message, but at least they heard. And at least I could go to bed that night knowing that I had opened up and shared my whole heart.

That's really all we're responsible for . . . telling the truth, pointing to Jesus Christ, and offering hope. The rest is in His hands.

**FAITH STEP:** *Pray for courage and ask Jesus to help you share your story with someone who needs to hear truth today.*

—*Tricia Goyer*

# WEDNESDAY, MARCH 26

---

*And we know that all things work together for good to those who love God, to those who are the called according to His purpose. Romans 8:28 (NKJV)*

---

IN MY DEVOTIONAL MOMENTS WITH Jesus, I often analyze true Bible stories like I do novels, wondering about the characters' motivations and why the writer made a certain plot twist. That happened recently with the life of Joseph. This protagonist and favored son of Jacob didn't exactly use the best judgment when bragging about his crazy dreams to his brothers. Still, I always thought he got the rough end of the deal.

It was one thing to be thrown in a pit and sold to slaves. But that eventually put Joseph smack in the middle of God's plan to help rule Egypt, especially when his faithful behavior and integrity earned him favor with Potiphar, one of Pharaoh's officials.

But why did God further complicate the plot and allow Joseph to be falsely accused of rape and thrown into a dungeon for two years? Why did God delay to act?

I discovered the answer is the same reason God waits to act in our own lives at times. He has a bigger—and better—ending, one that will bring ultimate glory to Him.

For two years Joseph kept serving God faithfully in prison, earning his godly reputation, including interpreting a few dreams for some thankless recipients. And at the end of those two years, God gave Joseph his freedom. This time, Joseph the dreamer became Joseph the interpreter for Pharaoh. As a result he earned the title of everyone's hero—including his own family (Genesis 37–47).

At times our lives may play out more like a novel. But we see no "hero" in sight. The wait is nail-biting. But if we'll look in the pages of Scripture, we'll find a real page-turner, and the answers our "hero," Jesus, promised all along through Paul: "All things will work together for your good. Just wait on Me."

---

**FAITH STEP:** *Take time to review the events of Joseph's life in Genesis 37, 39–47. Do you remember a time when God's delays worked out for your (much better) good?*

*—Rebecca Barlow Jordan*

# THURSDAY, MARCH 27

*But you, my Lord, are a God of compassion and mercy; you are very patient and full of faithful love. Psalm 86:15 (CEB)*

A POPULAR SPORTS BROADCAST CONTAINS a segment called, "C'mon, man!" The commentators show a video clip of a play or series of plays that leaves them and the audience dumbfounded, scratching their heads, saying, "C'mon, man!"

Life is like that sometimes. You're late for an appointment. That's the day you get a flat. And it's raining. And your cell phone isn't charged.

"C'mon!"

That's how I felt on a day that taxed my patience. One frustration after another. Some of them could have been categorized as major. Spent and fully aware that the frustrations weren't over, just postponed until morning, I collapsed into my chair.

A mouse ran out from underneath it.

*Seriously?*

Too tired to scream, way too tired to jump up and run out of the room, I stared at the beady-eyed rodent. "Ser…i…ous…ly? Tonight of all nights?"

Jesus never reached His last straw. He still hasn't, after all these years, all these disappointments by the humans He helped create. Even from the cross, when He seemed to reach His limit of emotional pain—"My God, My God, why have You forsaken Me?"—He remained faithful and told His Father, "Into Your hands I commit My spirit."

No matter how much I frustrate Him, He keeps loving, even if He does stop from time to time to ask me, "Seriously?"

FAITH STEP: *Can you "hear" the voice of Jesus on the verge of asking, "Seriously?" about your "old familiar sin"? What decision can you make right now that will keep Him from having to ask?*

—*Cynthia Ruchti*

# FRIDAY, MARCH 28

*Being found in appearance as a man, He humbled Himself by becoming obedient to the point of death, even death on a cross. Philippians 2:8 (NAS)*

WHEN THE STORY OF LANCE Armstrong's epic fall broke, one of my friends made this comment: "That man needs Jesus." The story of Armstrong's cycling life, as told to Oprah Winfrey, had been nothing but a big lie. He had gone to unthinkable extremes to use performance-enhancing drugs in order to be the best cyclist in history, winning seven Tour de France titles. These, along with everything else he'd ever won, were all stripped from him when he was caught.

His confession was stunning to watch. People speculated about whether Armstrong seemed contrite enough, but to me, he just looked lost. His eyes were dead. Utterly and completely dead.

Amy Carmichael once wrote, in a little book called *If*, that "if I covet any place on earth but the dust at the foot of the cross, then I know nothing of Calvary love."

Like many of us (who have considerably less athletic ability), Lance Armstrong coveted fame and fortune. He wanted to be somebody in the sports world, and enjoy all the perks of superstardom. For this he traded everything—character, reputation, relationships with family and friends, his health, and finally, his dignity. His pride led him down the path of destruction, as pride always does.

But there is another road we can choose. It is the road of humility, following in Jesus's footsteps on the way to the cross. Ironically, this is the path to victory, to real and abundant life. No matter what we may covet, Jesus is the only One Who truly satisfies.

FAITH STEP: *Are you looking to something or someone other than Jesus for your purpose in life? Look no further. Die to self, be obedient, and find out what it means to really live in Him.*

*—Gwen Ford Faulkenberry*

# SATURDAY, MARCH 29

*Fear not, for I have redeemed you; I have called you by name,
you are mine. Isaiah 43:1 (ESV)*

As I WAITED FOR MY husband to come out of the woods from bow-hunting, an odd spurt of screaming hot oil set the kitchen cupboards on fire, melted the stove, and reminded me of the value of a fire extinguisher.

Charred cupboards and an unrecognizable backsplash greeted the eight fully garbed volunteer firemen from our community who crammed into my tiny kitchen to reassure me the fire was completely out, with no hot spots in the walls or the electrical system.

The team leader called me by name. Even with soot and ashes hovering in the air, I could draw a deeper breath because of the personal connection. The firemen knew me and cared all the more.

My husband didn't come home from the woods that night. While I said good-bye to the only major appliance we hadn't had to replace in the last year—my stove—he was falling fifteen feet from his tree stand. The impact broke his femur and back. An hour after calling 911 about the kitchen, I was on the phone again, asking the team to rescue my husband from the woods.

When they returned that second time, the crew began their rescue with hugs.

They knew us. Their normal high level of caring about the victims they served ramped even higher.

Jesus knows my name. He doesn't just care about me on a global level. It goes beyond that. He knows me individually. My cries for help land on the ears and heart of Someone Who already invested in me, Who calls me His own.

FAITH STEP: *As you read the Bible today, insert your name in the promises and directives—"Cynthia, be kind to one another, tenderhearted, forgiving..." And stay aware of the difference it makes to consider the words of Jesus a message of comfort, hope, encouragement, and challenge to you personally rather than to people in general. He's called you by name.*

*—Cynthia Ruchti*

# SUNDAY, MARCH 30

*The Lord is near to the brokenhearted and saves the crushed in spirit.*
*Psalm 34:18 (ESV)*

MY STEPDAD, RON, WAS THE only father figure I knew for many years. He married my mother when I was four, and they divorced when I was eighteen. Growing up, my stepdad was distant. He provided, but he didn't connect. He wasn't an angry person, but he rarely extended love, either. I can't remember hugs, or curling to his side, or sitting on his lap.

When Ron divorced my mom, it would have been easy to allow our relationship slip away, but his new wife made sure we stayed connected. She was a good person. She would call and update us on their lives, but sadly she passed away from cancer. Ron was distant before, but with her death he withdrew. Even today he lives alone, hundreds of miles away from any family member. I don't hear from him unless I call, and even when I talk to him the conversation doesn't last more than fifteen minutes.

There are some people who are easy to connect with, but others are harder to build a relationship with. Part of the disconnect is Ron's quiet nature, but there is more there too. He is a Vietnam veteran—a medic during the war—and he saw horrible things that no one ever should. He also grew up with alcoholic parents—life hasn't been easy for him.

I'm thankful that God is close to the brokenhearted and crushed in spirit. I contact Ron often, and I also remind him that God is only one prayer away. Perhaps you have a family member who has isolated himself or herself from others. While it may be easy to give up on that person . . . don't. Continue to offer prayers and love. And when you can't do it, ask Jesus to do it through you.

---

FAITH STEP: *Do you have a family member or friend who has isolated himself or herself? Give that person a call today and express your care—even if it's only a five-minute phone call.*

—*Tricia Goyer*

# MONDAY, MARCH 31

*When Simon Peter saw this, he fell at Jesus's knees and said, "Go away from me, Lord; I am a sinful man!" For he and all his companions were astonished at the catch of fish they had taken. Luke 5:8–9 (NIV)*

ONCE AGAIN, THE RESPONSIBILITIES OF a busy day had squeezed out my time alone with God. Sure, I'd talked with Him on the fly throughout my activities. But even though I'd set a resolution to spend more time in quiet prayer and Bible reading, I'd let the opportunity slide past.

I've always believed that we make time for what is truly important to us, and nothing was more important to me than my relationship with Jesus. So why was I having such a hard time? Was there a deeper reason behind my excuse of being too busy?

When I took my questions to Jesus and looked honestly at my heart, I realized that I have the same impulses as Peter did. While I long to draw close to my Savior, part of me also wants to run and hide—or stay distracted. Although Jesus offers love and mercy, part of me gets stuck noticing my old sinful nature, and slides into habits of avoiding Jesus because He is so holy. Yet falling at His feet is exactly what I need to do when guilt and shame coax me to avoid Him.

The irony of this story is that Peter's reaction didn't come after Jesus delivered a scathing sermon against hypocrisy, or drove out scary demons, or explained the painful calling of the cross. Jesus had just given loving provision. Let's confess our sins to Jesus, acknowledge His holiness, power, and loving provision. Then, instead of pushing Him away, let's thank Him for His presence and ask for faith to draw closer to Him.

FAITH STEP: *Ask Jesus to deepen your hunger for friendship with Him.*

—*Sharon Hinck*

# TUESDAY, APRIL 1

*"For I did not come to judge the world, but to save the world."*
John 12:47 *(NIV)*

NORMALLY WE THINK JUDGING OTHERS equals verbal accusations, maligning them with everything from character assassination to nitpicking criticism of irksome habits. Once in a while we offer "constructive criticism" to the ones we target, attempting to "speak the truth in love." But most of the time our whispers find attentive ears elsewhere, out of earshot from our intended victims.

Our judgmentalism may never pass our lips, but unspoken words can still hurt. Body language cuts just as deep as verbal words. Clenched fists, ugly frowns, "silent treatment"—ignoring someone—are only a few ways I remember both judging and receiving judgment in the past. I'm not proud of those moments.

I read about Jesus's reactions to people in the gospels one day and realized afresh that He didn't "judge" people. He definitely spoke the truth, and those words angered some. But Jesus's body language always revealed love. In the pages of Scripture I visualized one arm wrapped around a child in His lap, and the other beckoning and blessing others surrounding Him. I saw Him walk the extra miles to include a hated and ignored Samaritan woman in His kingdom. I watched Him touch lepers, blind eyes, and bent limbs.

I admired Him as the Pure One Who knelt before His disciples, washing dirty feet, and Who broke bread, even with the one who would betray Him. And I saw His hands reach outward to invite the multitudes and upward as He gave thanks to His Father repeatedly.

But most of all, I felt the sting of His own willing death as He extended bloody hands nailed to a rugged cross. And in that unspoken body language, I saw the heart of God and both felt—and heard—the words: "I love you this much!"

FAITH STEP: *In what ways have you experienced or exercised judgmentalism through body language? Be intentional about encouraging others with positive verbal and body language this week.*

—*Rebecca Barlow Jordan*

# WEDNESDAY, APRIL 2

*Then Jesus placed his hands on the man's eyes again, and his eyes were opened.*
*His sight was completely restored, and he could see everything clearly.*
Mark 8:25 (NLT)

As MY FRIEND LISA DROVE me home from the clinic, I marveled at structural details on the buildings we passed. I read out phone numbers from billboards. Once home, I stood looking out my kitchen window at the subdivision across the open field, noticing new details about the homes and yards. When my husband walked in the door that evening, I missed what he said because I was fascinated by the design of the stitching on his belt. I had not realized what I'd been missing until I had the cataracts removed from my eyes.

The Bible records several instances of Jesus giving sight to blind people. Some of them had been born blind; others had lost their sight. Jesus also worked to heal spiritual blindness. On more than one occasion, He accused the Jewish leaders who refused to believe in Him of being "blind guides" (Matthew 23:24, NIV). After His death and resurrection, Jesus opened the spiritual eyes of His followers to understand what the Scriptures taught about the Messiah and how He had fulfilled those very passages.

As I spend time in the Scriptures, I need to remember that Jesus wants to improve my spiritual eyesight. He wants to open my eyes so I can see and comprehend things that I never have before—truths that will help me know Him better and understanding of how to apply spiritual principles to my life. Commentaries and other Bible study tools are valuable resources, but I don't want to forget to invite Jesus to open my eyes every time I open the Bible. With His help, I will see things in the Scriptures I didn't even know I had been missing.

FAITH STEP: *Have you been grappling with a difficult verse or passage of Scripture? Ask Jesus to open your eyes so you can grow in understanding and see how to apply it to your life.*

*—Dianne Neal Matthews*

# THURSDAY, APRIL 3

*He heals the brokenhearted and binds up their wounds.*
*Psalm 147:3 (NIV)*

MY FRIEND SHELLY RECENTLY PASSED away from ovarian cancer.

The last morning I was with Shelly I just hugged her and wept. She whispered, "I'm going to see you again . . . I'm going to see you again." And I said, "I know . . . I'm just going to miss you so much."

Because sometimes Heaven seems far away. I am stuck in the perpetual "Why?" of the situation like a three-year-old. Why didn't Jesus choose to heal when He is so able to do so? My mom says, "We don't like it when we think Jesus is being stingy with the miracles."

No . . . we don't. I'm pouting. Disappointed. Confused. Upset. I've seen the look of it on every one of my children's faces when they don't get their way and I have told them, "Nope . . . not this time."

I wish I was one of those people who takes life's hardship with a keen sense of God's sovereign plan. I'm more like a toddler caught midtantrum over here. But I have found that even when I am midpout, Jesus is still reaching for me, arms open, saying, "I know you don't get it. You probably never will. But let Me love you anyway."

And all of a sudden it's like I am three again, crawling up into my dad's lap, wrapping my chubby arms around his neck, sobbing into his shirt. I think when Jesus heals the brokenhearted, He does it by holding us so tightly that we can feel His heart beating for us. Accepting us . . . questions and all. Keeping us safe in His care. Showing us mercy. Holding us in His arms. Whispering in our ears, "I've got you."

And pouting or not, that is where I want to be.

FAITH STEP: *Sometimes we get caught up in the hurts and disappointments of this life. Write down a disappointment you are struggling with now. Offer it to Jesus in prayer, knowing that only He can heal the hurt in your heart.*

—*Susanna Foth Aughtmon*

# FRIDAY, APRIL 4

*What counts is whether we have been transformed into a new creation.*
*Galatians 6:15 (NLT)*

IN CONVERSATION WITH A FRIEND the other day, I was asked whether I am plagued by a sense of my shortcomings. My friend stated that he is; it keeps him from wanting to speak in front of crowds.

Later that day I got a text from my daddy. Keep in mind I am forty years old, the mother of four, and a college professor. I received this between classes: *Just thinking of you. I love you, and I want you to know that you have made your dad look good your whole life.*

It would probably be good to show that text to my friend, because I think it explains a lot.

Unlike many people, I grew up with a sense that I was highly valued. There were consequences when I did something wrong, but they were presented as learning opportunities rather than causes for shame. The one overriding message I received from my parents was this: *You are loved, and we believe the good in you wins out, no matter what.*

There were no delusions that I was perfect. Instead, emphasis was placed on cultivating a relationship with Jesus, who lived in me from a very young age, and was the source of everything good.

With this foundation it has been fairly natural to build my adult faith on the concept that in Christ I am a new creation, and when I am weak He is strong. It's not really about my shortcomings. It's about who Jesus is in me.

FAITH STEP: *Are you plagued by a sense of your failures? Remember this promise today: Greater is He who lives in you, than he that is in the world.*

—*Gwen Ford Faulkenberry*

# SATURDAY, APRIL 5

*"Consider how the wild flowers grow. They do not labor or spin. Yet I tell you, not even Solomon in all his splendor was dressed like one of these."*
Luke 12:27 (NIV)

NORTHERN ALABAMA OFFERS AN ABUNDANCE of scenic visions: the Lookout Mountains, the Tennessee River and Charolais cattle farms. We had plenty of picturesque scenes during our morning commute, but I'll never forget the first time we passed cotton fields in full bloom, white puffs so vivid we marveled at their beauty. With both of us growing up in the South and, at that time, neither having traveled much, we'd never seen an abundance of snow, but we assumed that if we did, it would resemble those white fields of cotton.

Twenty-five years have passed since we first saw the cotton fields. Living in Alabama, we see them often now. We've also traveled to places covered with snow. Unfortunately, over the years, as the familiarity increased, the awe-power decreased.

Have you ever noticed how easy it is to do the same thing with our spirituality? As familiarity with worship increases, we catch ourselves merely going through the motions. Singing a song without concentrating on its meaning. Bowing our heads without focusing on the words of the prayer.

But God gave us those beautiful white fields, and He gave us the most precious, awe-inspiring gift of all, His Son. Let Him know how much you appreciate the beauty of His creation, and let Him know how much you appreciate the sacrifice of His Son.

FAITH STEP: *Walk or drive past fields in bloom today, or use the Internet to search for "gorgeous landscapes." Marvel at the beauty God made, and look at the world today as though seeing it for the first time. Then transfer this view to your daily devotion, and worship your Lord today as though worshipping Him for the first time.*

—*Renee Andrews*

# SUNDAY, APRIL 6

---

*The priests could not continue their service because of the cloud, for the glorious presence of the Lord filled the Temple.* 1 Kings 8:11 (NLT)

---

HAS THERE EVER BEEN A time in your life when you were so amazed at God's presence that you simply had to pause? Pause to take Him in, pause to rejoice, pause to reflect on how amazing God truly is? This happened to me just last week. I was folding a load of laundry, and I almost sank to my knees at the sight of dozens of tiny socks that needed to be paired up. No, it wasn't the overwhelming task that stilled the movement of my hands (although that can be overwhelming at times), but the revelation of answered prayer.

You see, my husband and I have felt God's call to adopt for the last seven years. After many years of paperwork and disappointment, God blessed us with a baby girl. And then recently we had two more little ones added to our home. Words of thanksgiving flowed through my lips as I folded those little socks, remembering the many, many times I was on my knees in my bedroom, crying out to God and asking Him why this adoption thing was so hard and why it took so long. The truth was, because God knew the children He had for us . . . at the right time. For a while the work was waiting . . . and now the work is just work! But what a glorious work it is.

When I think of the priest who worked at God's temple, I can imagine the awe they felt when God's glorious presence came down. How spectacular! I can see those priests on their knees before God. Work can wait at times like this!

Work can wait in our lives too. "God's true presence requires that we stop working in our strength and rely on His," writes author Rachel Wojnarowski. This is true whether we are seeking to expand our family, seeking to find a loving husband, or seeking to further our career. Work can wait when God's presence meets you . . . and your work will never be the same after that.

---

**FAITH STEP:** *Put your work aside for a while and just enjoy God's presence.*

*—Tricia Goyer*

# MONDAY, APRIL 7

*Therefore, since we are surrounded by such a great cloud of witnesses,*
*let us throw off everything that hinders and the sin that so easily entangles.*
*And let us run with perseverance the race marked out for us. Hebrews 12:1 (NIV)*

OLYMPIC ATHLETES TRAIN FOR YEARS with a strict diet and exercise regime. Discipline is critical if they hope to win, so they throw off negative habits or attitudes that might hinder their success. These include eating unhealthy foods, staying up too late at night, becoming overly self-confident, and engaging in negative self-talk.

We may not be professional athletes, but we're in a race nonetheless. Ours is of a spiritual nature. We begin when we place our saving faith in Jesus Christ, and we press on until we cross the finish line and meet Him face-to-face. In the interim, we keep our eyes on the One Who is invisible, as Moses did (see Hebrews 11:27). We obey His Word because we believe it's truth and we want to demonstrate our love for Him by doing what He says. We also do as athletes do—we throw off anything that hinders us from running our race to win.

This includes hindrances such as the fear of inadequacy or of an unknown future, comparison, procrastination, prayerlessness, believing the enemy's lies that cause us to doubt God, and listening to others' negative voices.

This also includes sins that entangle—unforgiveness, unresolved anger, selfishness, lust, idolatry, and pride. These and others weigh us down and prevent us from running well, so shedding them is a must.

Scripture says a huge crowd of witnesses to the life of faith surrounds us. They cheer us on as we run. Let's run strong. Let's run for the prize and finish well.

FAITH STEP: *What hindrances are making your faith race difficult? Tell a godly friend, and ask that person to pray with you for the ability to throw them off. Invite him or her to hold you accountable if necessary.*

—*Grace Fox*

# TUESDAY, APRIL 8

*Then Peter came to Jesus and asked, "Lord, how many times shall I forgive my brother or sister who sins against me? Up to seven times?" Jesus answered, "I tell you, not seven times, but seventy-seven times." Matthew 18:21–22 (NIV)*

A COWORKER HAD MADE SOME choices that made my job ten times harder. Again.

In the past year, I'd had ample opportunities to practice forgiveness because of her actions. Some issues could be resolved, but many times I was left with problems she wouldn't take responsibility for, problems I had to untangle. Each time I prayed and asked for the grace to forgive and find a way to have a healthy work situation.

A new e-mail from her dumped yet another unnecessary problem into my lap. I pushed away from my desk, letting my righteous indignation take over my thoughts. I'd tried to understand, worked to negotiate. But now I'd had it. I pictured myself as a poor pack mule, loaded down with hassles and unneeded problems placed on me by the irresponsible coworker. Rubbing my throbbing temples, I glanced upward. "Lord, this is the last straw."

*Have you been collecting those straws?*

The gentle voice of Jesus interrupted my rant. Of course I hadn't. I'd forgiven. Seven times seventy, just like He said.

Except, if I'd truly forgiven, I wouldn't feel weighted by this huge collection of straws. There would be only this latest offense to forgive…a much easier task.

A rueful smile tugged my lips. "You're right. I've been keeping a tally. I mentally rehearse all the evidence of how rough I have it because of her. Forgive me. And help me forgive."

---

**FAITH STEP:** *Grab a backpack or shoulder bag. Thinking of someone who irritates you, review each grudge, and with each, place a soup can or sauce jar in the bag. Feel the heavy weight of those "last straws." Thank Jesus that you don't have to carry that weight anymore, and as you put away the cans, forgive each grudge and let it go.*

—*Sharon Hinck*

# WEDNESDAY, APRIL 9

*You gave your good Spirit to instruct them. You did not withhold your manna. Nehemiah 9:20 (NIV)*

"THE DAY IS HALF GONE, and I've only begun!"

That and other negative statements had recently crept into my mornings. This day a string of unplanned but necessary actions stole away the writing time I had mentally "assigned" myself. The day was indeed half gone.

Maybe it's the Bible study my husband and I are doing together each morning at home on "Believing God" that convicted me a few minutes after I had verbalized my displeasure. At any rate, Jesus reminded me that there's more than one way to view a situation.

I knew better. Repeatedly I had seen God work in that mysterious way of His, multiplying my time like oil in the widow's jar, and providing "manna" for a chapter in less time than I could blink an eye. But sometimes I forget that Jesus is our *Jehovah-jireh*, the provider of every need, every day. I forget that He is the Maker of time itself.

I backed up mentally and began the day again: "Wow! This morning I woke up after a good night's sleep. I enjoyed Bible study with my husband, entered Jesus's prayerful throne room, fixed a delicious breakfast, cleaned the kitchen, washed some clothes, pampered my face to look nice for our date tonight, sent some texts and e-mails to make others feel special...and it's only eleven o'clock. So much done!"

Same morning. Different outlook. Later I scooped up the manna Jesus readily provided—and completed my desired daily quota in record time.

I just love the way Jesus works.

---

FAITH STEP: *Are you surprised at how Jesus works in your life sometimes? What "manna" has He provided for you lately?*

*—Rebecca Barlow Jordan*

# THURSDAY, APRIL 10

*And you will seek Me and find Me, when you search for Me with all your heart.*
Jeremiah 29:13 (NKJV)

"DID YOU LOOK IN THE laundry room?"

"Of course," I told my husband. "That's the logical place. It's where we've always kept it. I looked there. Twice."

The back and neck massager was too significant to ignore with an "Oh well. It'll turn up." So we plowed into an intense search. Every logical and illogical place—by daylight, lamplight, and flashlight—succumbed to the search.

Wonder of wonders, I eventually found it. In the laundry room, where we'd both looked multiple times. I pulled out a bin on a storage shelf, lifted a top layer, and there it was.

The isn't-that-just-like-humanity part of the story is that the next day I walked out into the garage to get something out of the freezer and had a flash of a thought. "I wonder if someone could have brought it out here by mistake?"

A second later, I caught myself. The search was over. The item was no longer lost. But we'd become so accustomed to the search that it was habit to wonder where the thing was hiding.

Does Jesus wave His arms, jumping up and down to get our attention, because we sometimes act as if we're as lost as we were before we found Him?

"Jesus, where are You?" we call out in distressing times.

"I'm right here," He might answer. "You've already found Me. You can quit looking. Keep seeking Me in My Word. But you can quit acting as if you haven't found Me. I'm right here."

**FAITH STEP:** *The faith to believe Jesus is the Son of God and our only Hope is the same faith it takes to remember He's still there—found—when shadows hide His face. Does that reminder encourage you like it does me?*

*—Cynthia Ruchti*

# FRIDAY, APRIL 11

---

*You can make many plans, but the Lord's purpose will prevail.*
*Proverbs 19:21 (NLT)*

---

MY FIRST THREE MONTHS OF 2013 were to include attending two missions conferences, hosting a businesswomen's retreat, and traveling to Russia and Romania. I also had four book contracts to fulfill.

My plans fell apart when my left Achilles tendon ruptured. I landed in a knee-high cast for three months with no weight-bearing. I managed with crutches for nine days, and then my knee on the opposite leg gave out. Crutches no longer an option, my lack of mobility became a major issue. I realized doing those events was beyond my capability and, sadly, canceled them.

Canceling brought disappointment, but I suspect God's purposes prevailed. I spent the next eleven weeks in a wheelchair, studying His Word and writing and editing at my kitchen table while dozens of people prayed me through the process. I learned the reality of God's strength perfected in my weakness.

Scripture says we can make plans, but ultimately God's purpose prevails. Sometimes we wouldn't choose that purpose, or the methods used to accomplish it. We can fight it, or we can accept it and learn to trust God in the midst of it.

I chose to trust, and I experienced peace. Granted, I shed a few tears when utter exhaustion swept over me during my recovery, but in the depths of my heart, I knew God was in control and was up to something good.

We make many plans, but we do well to keep them in an open hand. Let's invite the Lord to work out His purposes for our lives, and let's trust Him even when we don't understand His ways.

---

FAITH STEP: *Recall an experience when your plans fell apart. How did you see God at work? What did you learn from it?*

*—Grace Fox*

# SATURDAY, APRIL 12

---

*For I am the Lord your God, who stirs up the sea, causing its waves to roar.*
*My name is the Lord Almighty. And I have put my words in your mouth and*
*hidden you safely within my hand. I set all the stars in space and established the earth.*
*I am the one who says to Israel, "You are mine!" Isaiah 51:15–16 (NLT)*

---

FOLLOWING JESUS IS A MIXED bag for most of us. We triumph…we fall…we get back up and Jesus helps us dust off our knees…and we continue on the journey of following, listening, questioning, and worshipping, asking Him to shape our lives into something that glorifies Him.

It seems that in this season in my life, Jesus is once again gently prying my fingers off of my own life. He is asking me to live in a place of uncertainty and anchor myself in who He is rather than try and rearrange my circumstances. He is asking me to wait on His direction instead of barging ahead on a frantic path of anxiety. It's hard. It seems that I am incredibly human after all. I don't bend to His will or words so easily.

But when I read His words in Isaiah I think, *Why would I choose to step out of His hand when He has laid the foundations of the earth and breathed life into all of humanity? How can I not turn my face toward the One Who has set the sun in the heavens and named the stars?*

So this morning, I'm taking a deep, noncontrolling breath and saying to Jesus, "You are right. I am Yours. Do Your thing. I will trust You." Even when I don't have a clue about what is coming around the next corner. Because according to the One Who established the earth…He's got this too.

---

FAITH STEP: *Get up early and watch the sun rise. Notice the beauty in the creation that surrounds you. Remind yourself that Jesus, Who formed the earth with His words, is shaping your life too.*

—*Susanna Foth Aughtmon*

# SUNDAY, APRIL 13

*And the crowds that went before him and that followed him were shouting,*
*"Hosanna to the Son of David! Blessed is he who comes in the name of the Lord!*
*Hosanna in the highest!" Matthew 21:9 (ESV)*

WHEN I READ THE TRIUMPHAL Entry story, I wondered where the angels were. We're not told. Can we assume they were somewhere in the heavenly audience that day?

Angels played key roles in the significant moments of the life of Jesus. To Mary, an angel announced the results of the celestial pregnancy test. An angel visited Joseph to tell him everything was going to be all right. Angels filled the sky the night Jesus was born. An angel warned Joseph and Mary to flee to Egypt.

We know the rest of the Palm Sunday story—that within days of the hosannas, the crowd turned ugly, demanding His crucifixion. We know that after the crucifixion and death of Jesus, angels stood guard over His tomb and announced to the women who came to give Him a proper funeral that it wasn't necessary. Jesus had conquered death. The tomb was empty.

I wonder if the Palm Sunday hosannas rang hollow in the ears of the heavenly host who'd witnessed His incarnation, His birth, His ministry. I wonder if they clasped hands or huddled or even rested their hands on the hilt of their swords during the Palm Sunday chaos. How much had God let them know ahead of time? Did they know the celebration would be short-lived, but that God Himself through His Son was about to put new meaning to the term *long-lived*?

On that day when He makes all things clear, I wonder if Jesus will let me know that detail.

FAITH STEP: *Does your "Hosanna" turn quickly to "Jesus, what are You doing?" when crises hit? I'm aiming for sustained hosannas in my life. How about you?*

*—Cynthia Ruchti*

# MONDAY, APRIL 14

*I pray that God, the source of hope, will fill you completely with joy and peace because you trust in him. Then you will overflow with confident hope through the power of the Holy Spirit.*
Romans 15:13 (NLT)

THERE IS NOTHING THAT THROWS my three young kids into an excited tizzy more than hearing the garage door opening. That sound means that Dad is home! They run excitedly to the door, and when it opens all three try to talk at once. They tell him about their day. They share what they liked best, what they ate, what they played with, and even what they didn't like . . . like nap time. Their excitement brings a smile to my husband's face. It's proof of the relationship. It also makes me consider how I approach my heavenly Father.

"Much of prayer expresses the fullness of the soul rather than its emptiness," writes James Stalker. "It is the overflow of the cup. Prayer at its best is, if one may be allowed the expression, conversation with God, the confidential talk of a child who tells everything to his father."

Do you see God in that way . . . as a Father Who cares? As Someone Who wants you to run to Him and hear all about your day? Often we feel we can only talk to God about the important stuff. We believe that He doesn't have time for all the normal stuff in our day. Yet when we go to God about the normal stuff, too, it's proof of our relationship. It shows Him we want to connect. And the more we go to Him the more we *want* to go to Him—the words will overflow and prayer will be a natural part of our lives.

This is what 1 Thessalonians 5:16–17 is talking about: "Be joyful always; pray continually." It's not just about sharing our needs, but needing to share everything with God or we'll burst!

**FAITH STEP:** *Try to spend the next few hours talking to God about all the normal stuff you're doing . . . and see what a difference it makes in connecting with Him!*

—*Tricia Goyer*

# TUESDAY, APRIL 15

*"Don't let your hearts be troubled. Trust in God, and trust also in me."*
John 14:1 (NLT)

IT'S HARD TO IMAGINE HOW confused and troubled the disciples must have felt. They had witnessed the crowds adoring Jesus as He rode into Jerusalem on a donkey. They had heard people hailing Him as King of Israel. But now, as the twelve disciples celebrated the Passover meal with Jesus, the mood had abruptly switched. Jesus had predicted that one of them would betray Him. He said that Peter would deny knowing Him and they would all desert Him. Jesus had even said that He would be going away—that He would soon die. His words made no sense to them.

There are times when I feel confused and troubled. Maybe it's a phone call or a message relaying bad news. Or some strange turn of events that makes no sense at all. Or even the cumulative effect of repeated disappointments and failures. Just as a child who is hurt or scared runs to a parent to be held and hear soothing words spoken in their ear, I need to know where to turn. During that Passover meal, Jesus spoke comforting words to calm His disciples' hearts: "Don't let your hearts be troubled…trust in Me." Those words are also spoken for me.

Jesus knows exactly what troubles my heart and He knows the words I need to hear. But I have to trust Him enough to go to Him with my need and then listen to His voice. He may speak to me through a stirring in my spirit or by a strong sense of His abiding presence. Or He may lead me to a passage of Scripture that addresses my situation and brings encouragement and comfort to my hurting heart. Either way, I can depend on Jesus to speak soothing words when I need them.

FAITH STEP: *Do you need to hear comforting words from Jesus today? Ask Him to speak to your troubled heart, either through His Spirit within you or through the written Word.*

—*Dianne Neal Matthews*

# WEDNESDAY, APRIL 16

*Then I looked and heard the voice of many angels, numbering thousands upon thousands, and ten thousand times ten thousand. They encircled the throne and the living creatures and the elders. In a loud voice they were saying: "Worthy is the Lamb, who was slain, to receive power and wealth and wisdom and strength and honor and glory and praise!" Revelation 5:11–12 (NIV)*

"THEY'RE AMAZING PEOPLE AND THEY deserve our help," the television carpenter declared on camera. His team planned to build a new home for a family with dire struggles. I loved seeing the support of a community and the joy of a family receiving an overwhelming gift. But whenever I watched the program, I was struck by the frequent comments about the recipient's worthiness. I thanked Jesus that His gift of life and blessing comes to us in spite of our unworthiness. It also got me thinking about how humans determine worth.

A politician with charisma and strong communication skills may be judged worthy to receive the power of an elected position. An entrepreneur who worked tirelessly and built up a business is considered worthy to receive wealth. A professor with a list of degrees who has committed his whole life to learning may be counted as wise. An athlete who trained her whole life for the Olympics has earned her strength. An actor, singer, or dancer with the greatest talent and training may be considered worthy to earn the highest awards of honor in his field.

But these human achievements are only pale shadows of what we see in this glimpse of Heaven in Revelation. Only the Lamb of God—Jesus—is completely worthy to receive all the power, wealth, wisdom, strength, honor, glory, and praise. Only His declaration of love makes us worthy to enter His presence.

FAITH STEP: *Are you focused on chasing power, wealth, wisdom, strength, or honor? Or do you struggle with feeling unworthy? Does it ever distract you from allowing Jesus to be your all in all? Today, spend time praising the Lamb for Who He is: the One Who is worthy, and Whose sacrifice brings us undeserved grace.*

—*Sharon Hinck*

# THURSDAY, APRIL 17

*Jesus knew that the Father had put all things under his power, and that he had come from God and was returning to God; so he got up from the meal, took off his outer clothing, and wrapped a towel around his waist. After that, he poured water into a basin and began to wash his disciples' feet, drying them with the towel that was wrapped around him. He came to Simon Peter, who said to him, "Lord, are you going to wash my feet?" John 13:3–6 (NIV)*

I ATTENDED MY FIRST MAUNDY Thursday service a few years out of college. It was going to be a foot washing service along with a time of prayer and worship. There is something intimate and vulnerable about having someone touch your toes. I wasn't sure I was quite ready for it. My friends, Shelly and Laurie, said, "Just come on...you will be fine."

During the service we reflected on what lay before Jesus the night He was betrayed. Jesus knew He was in his last moments on earth. He knew what was coming. He knew that torture, abandonment, and a brutal death lay before Him. Yet He chose to spend His last moments serving His friends, humbling Himself, and washing their feet. He focused on showing them what was important, loving God and loving each other.

That night my friends and I washed each other's feet. As we poured water over the tops of each other's toes, we also prayed for each other. And we cried. Because it is overwhelming and humbling to be served by a friend. It is an act of extravagant love. Jesus showed us how to love each other.

On this Maundy Thursday, it is beautiful to know that when we love each other, we are loving Him too.

FAITH STEP: *Think of a way to serve one of the people you love, whether it is bringing them a meal or watching their kids so they can take a break. Know that when you love them, you are emulating Jesus and loving Him too.*

—Susanna Foth Aughtmon

# FRIDAY, APRIL 18

---

*When Jesus had cried out again in a loud voice, he gave up his spirit.*
*At that moment the curtain of the temple was torn in two from top to bottom.*
*The earth shook, the rocks split and the tombs broke open. The bodies of many*
*holy people who had died were raised to life. Matthew 27:50–52 (NIV)*

---

HOW COME THIS DETAIL DOESN'T get more notice? Many people came back to life on the day Jesus died. That's a big deal! In all the Easter weeks I've spent in church, never once do I remember a single mention of the life that began at the moment of Jesus's death.

Each year when Good Friday arrives, the sky seems to hang lower, the atmosphere subdued by the weight of the universe and eternity and loss. We can't wait for Easter, when we can give a standing ovation for Jesus's victory. The hope of Easter brightens the darkness of Good Friday.

I've always thought Jesus's Father God waited until Easter to clarify His victory, but He did not! He began bringing His people back to life immediately. Eternal rebirth for humanity began immediately after Jesus paid the price for us.

Jesus won, a truth that unequivocally means *life*. Eternal life in all its healing, saving glory began on Good Friday.

Whatever the day looks like from your perspective, whatever season of happiness or sorrow you are in today, celebrate His gift of your life as you thank Jesus for dying to buy you back from death.

---

**FAITH STEP:** *Spend a few minutes imagining the scene in Heaven's throne room after Jesus died as faithful followers were reborn. Thank Him for life.*

—*Erin Keeley Marshall*

# SATURDAY, APRIL 19

*After the Sabbath, at dawn on the first day of the week, Mary Magdalene and the other Mary went to look at the tomb. Matthew 28:1 (NIV)*

THERE ARE EVENTS IN LIFE that take precedence over all others, things that move you to drop everything and hurry to where you are needed. The death of a loved one will cause you to leave something that seemed drastically important and go to be with family and friends and to mourn the one who has passed on.

For the days between the death and the funeral, families mourn together and often wish they'd have said something differently, done something differently. They reflect on the life of the one they've lost and try to cope with moving on without them.

When I think about Jesus's death on the cross and those days between the death and resurrection, I can only imagine the pain saturating His disciples. Not only did they lose a loved one, but they'd seen Him endure unmerciful suffering. They didn't yet realize the truth of His promise that He would rebuild the temple in three days, and they mourned their Savior and Friend.

How glorious on that first Easter Sunday when the angel announced the blessed news, "He is not here; He has risen."

**FAITH STEP:** *Wake early tomorrow on Easter morning and witness the sunrise. Think of that first Easter when the Son rose!*

—*Renee Andrews*

# SUNDAY, APRIL 20

---

*Carrying the cross by himself, Jesus went to the place called Skull Hill (in Hebrew, Golgotha). There they crucified him. John 19:17–18 (NLT)*

---

MY CHILDHOOD BEST FRIEND LOST her battle with cancer at age fifty-three. She'd undergone a successful bone marrow transplant, but another cancer invaded her body following that procedure.

We'd gone separate ways after high school. We married, moved overseas, and eventually lost track of each other. We were reunited only two weeks before she moved to Heaven.

I sat at her bedside, watching her sleep and wondering, *Why, God? Why have You allowed her to suffer like this? Why are You taking her from her family? This makes no sense.*

Two years later, I still have no answer.

I suspect Jesus's followers asked "Why?" as they watched Roman soldiers crucify Him. He was the Messiah, after all. He was God incarnate—able to feed the masses, heal the sick, and raise the dead. Why would He allow them to falsely accuse and kill Him? It made no sense.

The answer came three days later when Jesus rose from the dead as prophecy foretold, conquering death once and for all and providing forgiveness of sin for all who trust Him for salvation.

Life's painful experiences often confound us and leave us asking "Why?" Sometimes God reveals His purpose, and it's more amazing than we could dare to imagine. Sometimes, however, He conceals it and asks us to trust Him.

One day we'll meet Jesus face-to-face. Maybe He'll answer our questions then, or maybe His magnificence will silence them. Either way, we'll worship the risen Christ as the One Whose purposes are always great and always good.

---

FAITH STEP: *Someday we'll worship Christ face-to-face. Make today a joyous dress rehearsal for Heaven's performance by praising Him for His sacrificial love and His power to conquer death.*

*—Grace Fox*

# MONDAY, APRIL 21

*Therefore, brothers, since we have confidence to enter the Most Holy Place by the blood of Jesus,*
*by a new and living way opened for us through the curtain, that is, his body,*
*and since we have a great priest over the house of God, let us draw near to God*
*with a sincere heart in full assurance of faith, having our hearts sprinkled to cleanse us*
*from a guilty conscience and having our bodies washed with pure water.*
*Let us hold unswervingly to the hope we profess, for he who promised is faithful.*
*Hebrews 10:19–23 (NIV)*

MY DAUGHTER HAS BEEN TAKING aerial art classes, and last night my husband and I went to see the school's end-of-the-year recital. Before the performance, we watched as the instructors examined the equipment. They checked the riggings of the trapeze and tested the fabric and ropes.

Soon, performers climbed above us, wrapping and unwrapping into beautiful poses. They hovered overhead in ways that defied the laws of physics, as they spun, rolled, and flew.

None of that heart-stopping beauty would be possible unless the students had total confidence in the cables, ropes, carabineers, and scaffolding. When they did ensemble work, they also needed faith in their partners. I was impressed by all the trust exhibited by the students. Trust that their teachers had trained them well. Trust that their bodies had the physical strength to maintain their positions clinging to moving fabric or narrow pipes. Trust that partners wouldn't drop them. Trust that the resin would help their grip. Trust that the audience would support and appreciate their efforts.

I want to have that sort of confidence and trust in Jesus. Each day, I want to remember that He has given me everything I need to climb, to fly, to accomplish feats that look impossible. He invites us to "hold unswervingly to the hope we profess" because He is faithful.

FAITH STEP: *Thank Jesus today that, because of His life, death, and resurrection, we can draw near to God with confidence, and face today's challenges with faith and hope.*

—*Sharon Hinck*

# TUESDAY, APRIL 22

*For I am not ashamed of this Good News about Christ.*
*It is the power of God at work, saving everyone*
*who believes—the Jew first and also the Gentile. Romans 1:16 (NLT)*

As I STROLLED IN MY parents' yard that early April afternoon, I pulled my heavy sweater tighter to ward off the chilling breeze. It was unusual to have such a cold spring day in west Tennessee. I looked at the gray, leafless trees in the woods across the road. They seemed to doubt that spring had really arrived.

My mother's flower bed, however, told a different story—one that contrasted sharply with the weather and the trees' appearance. The bright yellow daffodils and vivid pink and purple hyacinths rose up from the ground as though they were boldly standing up for some unpopular cause. The more I gazed at those flowers, the more I felt as though they offered a picture of faith, the kind of faith that Jesus wants me to have.

On some days my world seems cold and gray. Circumstances crop up that don't make sense to me. During those times I have to make a choice. Will I look at my situation and give in to doubts? Or will I keep my eyes on Jesus and trust that He has a plan for whatever is happening and He will see me through it?

Then there are times when I'm tempted to blend in with my environment rather than stand out as a follower of Jesus. Do I really want to bow my head and pray as people watch in a crowded restaurant? When someone makes a statement mocking Jesus or the Gospel, do I dare risk speaking up and possibly being labeled a fanatic? It might be easier to keep a low profile, but how can I be ashamed of the One Who gave His life for me?

FAITH STEP: *As you go about your day, ask Jesus to help you watch for opportunities to take a bold stand for your faith rather than blending in with your environment.*

—*Dianne Neal Matthews*

# WEDNESDAY, APRIL 23

*"Remove the heavy yoke of oppression. . . . Feed the hungry, and help those in trouble. Then your light will shine out from the darkness, and the darkness around you will be as bright as noon. The Lord will guide you continually, giving you water when you are dry and restoring your strength. You will be like a well-watered garden, like an ever-flowing spring. . . . Then you will be known as a rebuilder of walls and a restorer of homes." Isaiah 58:9–12 (NLT)*

FOR SEVERAL YEARS MY HUSBAND, Steve, and I have wanted to live more off of our property. He built a garden and hauled in organic soil. The kids chose which fruits and veggies to grow, and last weekend Steve plotted where to plant several fruit and nut trees.

The plants will need my TLC to thrive and, in turn, to help us thrive. The amount of care I offer them will determine to a large degree how much my family benefits, but it's going to require me to spend my efforts on them.

I love what Isaiah 58 says about our level of others-centeredness and our own well-being. We thrive when we give. When we live to heal and nurture others, Jesus's light shines through us and we gain strength ourselves. Glowing from the inside out sounds like a pretty abundant lifestyle. *The Message* version of this passage says the Lord will "give you a full life in the emptiest of places."

The Lord gave Isaiah this message when His people, the Israelites, were in exile. These were dark times for them. Knowing the context offers hope to us today. Everywhere we look we find reasons to feel uncertain about the future. Cancer and disease, natural disasters, faltering economies, human trafficking, families in crisis, global bullies . . . you've heard the list. Still, the Lord told them to give.

Our first steps in preparing for the future are to look upward to Jesus for help and outward to see how we can help. We're excited to see how Jesus multiplies the produce as we give from our garden.

FAITH STEP: *Find some way to help today. You could take a meal to a sick friend; offer to mow the lawn, clean, or run an errand; or donate to a shelter.*

*—Erin Keeley Marshall*

# THURSDAY, APRIL 24

---

*Therefore do not throw away your confidence, which has a great reward.*
*Hebrews 10:35 (ESV)*

---

AT A RETREAT, I HEARD a clear challenge to dream bigger than normal, to dream Jesus-sized dreams, things only He could do, things He delights in doing.

The retreat instructor offered us time to pray and write down those courageous, adventuresome dreams. I wrote in pencil, not only because writing in pen seemed arrogant, but because no dream is worth it if God isn't in it. I needed more time to listen to Jesus stirring in my heart through His Holy Spirit.

Two days after returning home from the retreat, life got messy. It started with a grease fire in the kitchen. The smoke, soot, and extinguisher dust scattered to every corner of the house. The cleanup took three weeks. The crew put a rush on it because my husband was hospitalized that same night, had surgery the next day, and spent more than a week in Room 530, Bed 1. He spent the following many months in a back brace and used crutches the brief times he could be out of bed or off the couch.

"My dreams went up in smoke," I whimpered. I didn't even know where those pages were anymore.

Jesus—the epitome of Truth—seemed to whisper something profound to my spirit. "No, they didn't. They're in the garage."

I'd hastily thrown office items into bins and hauled them to the garage when the fire remediation crew cleaned and painted the office.

My dreams didn't go up in smoke. They were temporarily relocated. To the garage.

---

**FAITH STEP:** *Misplace a dream? Is it truly gone or temporarily relocated? Spend some time today asking Jesus to revive the dream He planted in your heart.*

*—Cynthia Ruchti*

# FRIDAY, APRIL 25

*We are hard pressed on every side, but not crushed; perplexed, but not in despair; persecuted, but not abandoned; struck down, but not destroyed. We always carry around in our body the death of Jesus, so that the life of Jesus may also be revealed in our body.*
2 *Corinthians 4:8–10 (NIV)*

MY MEDICAL CLINIC UPDATED THEIR records to a new computer system so that patients could easily access their files and see lab and test results. I was delighted with the convenience and signed up. But when I pulled up my file, my heart sank.

A stark summary of various problems glared at me from my computer screen. It wasn't new information, but the terse phrases and summaries hit me again with the reality of how damaged my body was from an ongoing illness.

I called my friend Amy, who also had some tough diagnoses and health issues to grapple with. I shared how discouraged I felt from confronting facts I'd rather ignore.

"Look at it this way," she said, her voice full of firm encouragement. "You're a walking miracle. It's a miracle that you can function at all."

In a flash, my perspective shifted. Instead of focusing on the ever-increasing physical problems, I realized that the very presence of those problems made each day an even more amazing gift.

Whatever our level of health, we are all walking miracles. Each breath, each beat of our hearts, each thought is a reminder that the life of Jesus is revealed in our bodies.

FAITH STEP: *Look in a mirror and remember that you are a walking miracle. Jesus lives in you. However strong or weak, healthy or sick you are, ask Him to be revealed through you.*

—*Sharon Hinck*

# SATURDAY, APRIL 26

*Trust in the Lord and do good; dwell in the land and cultivate faithfulness. Psalm 37:3 (NAS)*

LAST YEAR OUR PASTOR LED us through a "What's Next?" campaign. Unlike a building emphasis to raise funds for a new church auditorium, this was like a mission strategy for reaching people for Jesus both locally and globally. Our pastor ended with a thirty-day challenge for each member to pray daily and ask God personally, "What's next for me?"

I wasn't sure whether Jesus would answer me with, "Here are some definite actions to take"; "Just go with the flow"; or "Prepare and wait." But I took the challenge.

In the next month I wrote; I listened; I read; and I prayed. There were times of low motivation when I felt physically spent for no reason, moments when "sameness" challenged my productivity, and other days when exhilaration filled me with expectation and creativity.

When I finished the thirty-day challenge, Jesus impressed something on my heart that had been growing already in this season of my life. I'm so grateful for each day, and Jesus's "Well done" is what I long for daily—just to love and serve Him any way I can. But sometimes my crazy ideas and activities still push me ahead of Him.

I decided "What's next?" for me would consist of a simple philosophy: "Show up, and be faithful." I would plant a "garden" and cultivate faithfulness. And I would let Jesus grow that garden any way He wanted.

How's it working? Jesus has showered me with tons of surprises, pruned me with ample reminders, and blessed me with much grace! Productivity matters less; Jesus matters more. I've decided I'll make "What's next?" a lifelong challenge.

FAITH STEP: *How can you "cultivate" faithfulness this year? Consider your own thirty-day challenge, and ask Jesus to show you, "What's next?"*

*—Rebecca Barlow Jordan*

# SUNDAY, APRIL 27

*"Don't store up treasures here on earth, where moths eat them and rust destroys them, and where thieves break in and steal. Store your treasures in heaven, where moths and rust cannot destroy, and thieves do not break in and steal. Wherever your treasure is, there the desires of your heart will also be." Matthew 6:19–21 (NLT)*

DURING A FLIGHT HOME, I had to change planes in Atlanta. I boarded the second plane and waited for the last leg home. And waited.

It didn't take long sitting on the filled flight to realize that we were experiencing a delay. And then the flight attendant called my name and asked me to come to the front. I wondered what I'd packed that wasn't allowed, but the flight attendant quietly said, "There was an accident with your luggage." I said, "Okay, what happened?" She winced. "It fell off the cart and was run over." I winced. "Run over by the cart? Is it okay?" And then she explained, "It fell off the cart, but it was run over by another plane."

Christ repeatedly commanded us not to be attached to material things. In Luke 12:15, He said to guard against every kind of greed because life is not measured by how much you own. In Matthew 6:24, He tells us we cannot love God and money.

I'll admit I was more than a little sad to lose all of the books that were packed so carefully in the suitcase that was literally smoking on the runway. But those books won't save my soul, and truthfully, I can no longer even remember the titles. They aren't important in the entire scheme of things. They were nice to have, but I can live without them. Christ, however, I can't live without.

FAITH STEP: *Find one item in your closet that you really like but can live without. Donate it to Goodwill or a women's shelter today.*

—Renee Andrews

# MONDAY, APRIL 28

*"There is nothing concealed that will not be disclosed,*
*or hidden that will not be made known." Luke 12:2 (NIV)*

BACK IN MY TWENTIES I was facing a difficult decision and didn't know if I was approaching it with all the wisdom I needed. I wanted to do the right thing for my future, but did I know all I needed to know to make such a life-changing decision? I wished I was as clear on the answer as I was about my feelings of inadequacy. I felt myself drawn in one direction but hesitating for one reason or another. I needed more security than my fallible human reasoning offered.

When I turned to a trusted friend for advice, she said something that has stuck with me to this day. She prayed with me and asked God to "let nothing remain hidden that needs to come out." How free I felt with those simple words!

Our futures are in the Lord's hands. Yes, it's our part to give our all, but the final result is up to Jesus, Who is abundantly capable to guide us on the best path. He wants us to rely on Him. Like a Shepherd leading His sheep, Jesus promises to guide us; He even says we'll hear His voice (see John 10:27). This news ought to be revitalizing and confidence building. He will reveal all that needs to be revealed in time for us to take the steps He knows are best. Put the responsibility back on Him where it belongs; your job is to listen for Him and trust Him to be Himself, your Leader.

FAITH STEP: *If you're confused by circumstances, ask Jesus to open your mind and heart to the facts you need to know to follow Him.*

—*Erin Keeley Marshall*

# TUESDAY, APRIL 29

*As they sailed, he fell asleep. A squall came down on the lake, so that the boat was being swamped, and they were in great danger. The disciples went and woke him, saying, "Master, Master, we're going to drown!" He got up and rebuked the wind and the raging waters; the storm subsided, and all was calm. "Where is your faith?" he asked his disciples. In fear and amazement they asked one another, "Who is this? He commands even the winds and the water, and they obey him." Luke 8:23–25 (NIV)*

EVERY TIME I GET ON an airplane during a rainstorm, my stomach lurches. I don't like being high up in the air near lightning. I know in my mind that a giant metal tube in proximity to high-voltage electricity is not a good combo. My palms sweat, and I pray a lot. I have a time of silent praise when we touch down.

I'm sure there was a lot of praise going on when the disciples reached the shore after their near-death experience. I think they were a lot like me. They were scared. They were thinking that a little boat in a giant storm was not a good combo. From what they could tell, Jesus's napping was not helping. When He finally stopped the storm, they were even more freaked out. Who was this guy Who calmed hurricanes with a word?

The truth is, we really don't understand how Jesus works. Wrapping our minds around His power is beyond us. Our frame of reference is too small to comprehend His greatness.

But one thing we can know is that during the stormy times in our life, even when we don't get Him, He is with us. Jesus is taming waves and speaking peace, and He is in control. And that is good to know...even when we don't understand it.

FAITH STEP: *Think about a rough situation in your life right now. Ask Jesus to be with you, to calm your fears and give you peace even when you don't understand all He is doing.*

—Susanna Foth Aughtmon

# WEDNESDAY, APRIL 30

*"They look beautiful on the outside. But inside they are full of dead bones and all kinds of filth. In the same way you look righteous to people. But inside you are full of pretense and rebellion."*
Matthew 23:27–28 (CEB)

I CAN REMEMBER THE BIRD. I can't remember the setting, other than that it was a beautiful garden. Was it Buchart Gardens in Victoria, British Columbia? Or was it Cypress Gardens in Florida? Maybe it was the San Diego Zoo.

As my companions and I walked the sculpted paths that took us from one awe-inspiring scene of beauty to another, kept in a perpetual state of "Wow! Look at that!", we first saw and then heard a brightly colored, long-tailed, crested bird that looked like a piece of artwork perched on a delicate branch.

Until it opened its mouth.

What came out was no birdsong. It sounded like an aviary version of a smoker's cough. Rough. Coarse. Like the difference between a concert violinist and fingernails raked down a ridged guitar string.

Such beauty in form. Such ugliness in voice. It grated on our nerves.

How disturbing it must seem to Jesus when people created in His image open their mouths and what comes out is the verbal equivalent of a smoker's cough—rough language, angry words, cruel sounds, harsh blatting...

"What's wrong with this picture?" Jesus could well ask. "Your 'song' doesn't match the faith image you show on the outside."

Matthew 23:27–28 expresses how He said it to those who lived a fake faith when He walked this earth.

Jesus doesn't leave any doubt about how He feels about the mismatch between the image we present and the reality of our "song."

FAITH STEP: *Ask yourself throughout the day if the words and attitudes coming out of your mouth match your faith and the love with which you were created. Does your song match your plumage?*

*—Cynthia Ruchti*

# THURSDAY, MAY 1

*Do not be anxious about anything, but in everything by prayer and petition, with thanksgiving, present your requests to God. And the peace of God, which transcends all understanding, will guard your hearts and your minds in Christ Jesus. Philippians 4:6—7 (NIV)*

I WALKED INTO MY OFFICE and settled into my desk chair, my mind racing. I was on a writing deadline for a project I had been thrilled to accept. But when I looked at the number of days left until the deadline, the amount of work to do, and the amount I was able to accomplish each day, my mouth went dry. The numbers didn't add up. There was no way for me to get the work done on time. And of course, the more time I spent with my mind spinning in circles with worry, the further I slipped behind.

"Lord, I know You sent me this work. I know I should trust You. But I'm feeling panic."

I love to feel peaceful, but my kind of peacefulness happens when work is done, all the pieces are in place, the house is tidy, no one in my life is upset about anything, and the soundtrack of my life is a Bach prelude. Yet most of the time loose ends abound, chores pile up, people I care about are hurting, and my heart's background music is closer to Chopin's "Minute Waltz," or Rimsky-Korsakov's "Flight of the Bumblebee."

The verse in Philippians gave me a clue about what I needed as I faced my desk that morning. I didn't need *my* kind of peace. I needed the peace of God that is found in Christ Jesus. His is the peace that infuses us even in the midst of stress. His is the love that reassures us we aren't alone in the chaos. His is the strength that holds back pressures that threaten to crush us.

FAITH STEP: *Ask Jesus to guard your heart and mind with His peace today.*

—*Sharon Hinck*

# FRIDAY, MAY 2

*And if by grace, then it cannot be based on works; if it were, grace would no longer be grace.* Romans 11:6 (NIV)

GROWING UP, MY SISTER AND I shared a room. One night I woke to her screaming, "He's got me! He's got me!" I just knew someone was in our bedroom and had my sister so I joined in, "He's got Gina! Someone's got Gina!"

My parents burst into the room practically falling over each other, ready to save us. Daddy turned on the light and saw Gina's hand covering her face. Her arm was asleep, so she didn't realize the hand suffocating her was...her own.

We laugh about it now, but the instance reminds me of my first years as a Christian, when I never believed I would be good enough for Heaven. I didn't pray enough, didn't study enough, didn't give enough. Quite honestly, I was miserable, because like my sister that night, I couldn't see past the hand on my face. Grace was something I didn't understand and definitely didn't study. I had a fear mentality that controlled my every thought and every action. Finally, after years of study and a better understanding, I realize by God's grace I no longer have to worry about being "good enough." I will never be "good enough," but through Christ, in God's eyes, we are all good enough. Christ wants to set me free, in the same way Daddy lifted Gina's hand and showed her she was okay, that she was indeed free.

FAITH STEP: *Place your hand on your face covering nose and mouth. Feel your struggle to breathe. Now move it away...and remember Christ's grace sets you free.*

—*Renee Andrews*

# SATURDAY, MAY 3

*"The thief comes only to steal and kill and destroy; I have come that they may have life, and have it to the full." John 10:10 (NIV)*

I AM CURRENTLY WORKING ON a book with Leonard Ravenhill's daughter-in-law, Nancy, that features vignettes from her remarkable life as well as quotes by the great Bible teacher. One of my favorite quotes of his reads, "Jesus came that we might have life, not that we'd have more theology and more knowledge."

That is such a good word for me. I tend to place a lot of value on academics, studying, knowledge. I am drawn to people who specialize in theology and can teach me things I don't know about the original languages of the Bible, church history, and other matters. I read lots of books.

Not long ago I was on a kick of reading books about Jesus. I liked *The Jesus I Never Knew* by Philip Yancey, parts of *Beautiful Outlaw* by John Eldredge, and the Bible study *Jesus the One and Only* by Beth Moore. After I finished those books, I felt more knowledgeable about Jesus. But, as Ravenhill suggests, unless all of that reading brings me closer to Jesus, it's not worth much. His purpose for me is life.

FAITH STEP: *As you spend this morning with Jesus, ask Him to lead you…not merely into more knowledge about Him, but a deeper experience of Him and the beautiful Life He is.*

—*Gwen Ford Faulkenberry*

# SUNDAY, MAY 4

*All the treasures of wisdom and knowledge are hidden in Him.*
*Colossians 2:3 (HCS)*

YEARS AGO OUR FAMILY HAD a kitten who loved to sit in the bathroom window and look out at the backyard. Unfortunately, the window didn't have a sill. Jasmine quickly learned to hop up on the toilet, jump up and grab the lower part of the window frame, then pull herself the rest of the way up and lie against the screen. One day she made the mistake of not looking first to see if the window was raised.

After Jasmine grabbed the window frame, she saw that she had no place to go. The scrawny little kitten hung on with all her might, meowing pitifully. Hearing her cries, I rushed into the bathroom. After one glance at her little face, I quickly raised the window and gave her rear end a boost up.

I started laughing at how Jasmine had looked, but stopped abruptly. *How often do I look that way?* I wondered. So often I rush into my own little schemes, ignoring the privilege of going to the Source of all wisdom to ask for guidance first. Then I cry out to Him in the middle of the mess I've made, when I'm barely hanging on by my own strength. In spite of my foolishness, my Savior's loving hands are always there, ready to lift me up.

During Jesus's ministry on earth, He often amazed the people and the Jewish leaders with His teaching. They knew He hadn't been formally trained as a rabbi, yet His deep knowledge and understanding of the Scriptures were evident. As a believer, I can draw upon that wisdom through prayer and Bible study. Just as my cat learned to check and make sure the window was raised before jumping up, my goal is to always ask Jesus for wisdom before I act.

FAITH STEP: *Do you have a decision to make or a new project to begin? Before jumping right in, why not first go to the Source of all wisdom and knowledge to ask for guidance?*

—*Dianne Neal Matthews*

# MONDAY, MAY 5

*Set a guard over my mouth, Lord; keep watch over the door of my lips.*
*Psalm 141:3 (NIV)*

ONE DAY AS I WAS visiting my daughter's family, I corrected my grandchild at the dinner table in front of her parents. I immediately realized what I had done and soon apologized for my hasty words. First, it was not my job to discipline my grandkids in the presence of their parents. But mostly, I had set in motion *my* rules, not theirs. In fact, those *rules* really had no substance. They focused more on my *preferences* and did not necessarily involve acts of disobedience.

As I was reading about the Pharisees one day, I observed their behavior pattern and understood more about what grieved Jesus. So much of the time these religious leaders rebuked others, including Jesus, for not agreeing with their religious "laws." They ignored the spirit of the law, insisting on crossing every *t* and dotting every *i* (Matthew 23:23). They even invented their own rules, which often amounted to preferences, not biblical laws.

No wonder Jesus rebuked them for their short-sightedness and grace-less understanding. He came to bring life, not death. He never condoned disobedience but often spoke words of conviction. Jesus *was* the Authority. For them to feign superiority in His presence was both foolish and wrong. Jesus came to fulfill the law through mercy and love.

We can all take matters into our own hands if we're not careful. That day I asked Jesus to set His authoritative guard at the door of my lips—and to fill my heart with His mercy and love.

FAITH STEP: *Have you ever spoken too hastily or exercised misplaced authority? Ask Jesus today to set a guard at the door of your lips.*

*—Rebecca Barlow Jordan*

# TUESDAY, MAY 6

*Where can I go from your Spirit? Where can I flee from your presence?*
Psalm 139:7 (NIV)

CELL PHONES ENABLE US TO stay in touch with friends and family almost everywhere we go. This proved handy on the way home from a family vacation recently.

Driving in three vehicles meant the possibility of being separated on the freeway, so we made plans ahead of time to meet in a specific city for dinner. Our son arrived in the city first, so he chose a restaurant and phoned me and my husband with directions. We, in turn, called our daughter in the third car.

My eighty-year-old mom observed the goings-on from the backseat and laughed. "I've never seen anything like it," she said. "I'm amazed at how these new-fangled phones keep everyone in touch so easily."

I agreed. It's wonderful to know that nearly everywhere we go, whether in North America or overseas, we can enjoy each other's presence, albeit via technology.

Know what's far more wonderful than that? We, as believers, can enjoy Christ's presence even without technology. No matter where we go, He is there. No phones are needed to talk with Him.

"If I go up to the heavens, you are there; if I make my bed in the depths, you are there. If I rise on the wings of the dawn, if I settle on the far side of the sea, even there your hand will guide me, your right hand will hold me fast," says Psalm 139:8–10 (NIV).

The Lord's presence surrounds us, so we have constant access to Him. Even when we're beyond cell coverage.

FAITH STEP: *This very moment, thank Jesus for His never-ending presence in your life. Talk to Him throughout your day—when you're driving, walking, doing chores, waiting in line. Engage Him even in the mundane. And keep in touch with Him throughout your day, wherever it may take you.*

—*Grace Fox*

# WEDNESDAY, MAY 7

*And he said to her, "Daughter, your faith has made you well; go in peace, and be healed of your disease." Mark 5:34 (ESV)*

IT HAD BEEN A MORNING of one interruption after another strung together like pop-beads.

I'd get started on my Bible study lesson—for instance—and the phone would ring with a friend who needed encouragement.

Back to the Bible study, and a few minutes later I'd be called away by a prayer need.

Pen in hand and study guide open again. But not for long. Delivery man at the door. "Thank you. God bless you."

Jesus's ministry was a continuous stream of interruptions. How many times do we read that Jesus was "on the road to…" or "on His way to…" when something significant happened? He was a guest at a wedding—a *guest*—when the party ran out of wine. The only way to solve the problem was for Jesus to jump-start the miracle part of His ministry.

I'm especially moved by the story of the woman who tugged on the hem of His garment. Crawling along the ground in pain, weakness, and utter despondency over her problem, the woman interrupted His former plan to heal a man's young daughter. Jesus stopped, met the bleeding woman's need for healing, called the once-crawling one "Daughter," even though her problem had left her feeling abandoned, useless, and repulsive. Then, once her need was met, He proceeded to what He originally intended to do.

Well acquainted with interruptions, He created some of the most moving scenes in Scripture while on the way to something else.

FAITH STEP: *Jesus didn't let interruptions spoil His mood for living fully engaged in the business of carrying out His Father's instructions. What can you and I do today to adopt a similar attitude? See how many times you can genuinely thank the Lord for interruptions today.*

—*Cynthia Ruchti*

# THURSDAY, MAY 8

*Do not conform any longer to the pattern of this world, but be transformed by the renewing of your mind. Then you will be able to test and approve what God's will is—his good, pleasing and perfect will. Romans 12:2 (NIV)*

THIS PAST WEEK I HAVE been struggling. In one corner of my mind lurk all the longings that I have for my life. In the other lingers the bright truth that I need to yield myself to Jesus's will no matter what the outcome.

It's easy to say, "You just need to give it over to the Lord. He is in control." But it is an entirely different story to rip one's heart free from the dreams that have consumed your thinking and offer them back to the One Who gave them to you. Sometimes our dreams can grow so large we can't see anything else.

My friend Stephanie told me, "I had to give back to Jesus the thing I wanted most—to go be a missionary in a Muslim nation." Now that is a rockstar dream. Why would Jesus want her to give that up? I don't know. But I do know that when I am holding on to a dream so tightly, I can start becoming obsessive and weird about it. (Think Gollum from *Lord of the Rings*… "Precious…my precious"…)

When I am only clinging to my desires, I am no longer clinging to Jesus. So this morning, I am saying, "Jesus, these hopes and dreams that You planted in me…the desires that have shaped and driven me…I am taking them (i.e., ripping my tightly clutching fingers from them) and handing them back to You." Tears are brushed aside, followed by a long, exhaled breath.

I know it is all for the best. His hands are the only ones big enough to hold them.

FAITH STEP: *Find a quiet place to think about the things that you long for most. Saying them out loud, offer each dream back to the One Who gave it you, telling Him you want His will for you most of all.*

—*Susanna Foth Aughtmon*

# FRIDAY, MAY 9

*And God will generously provide all you need. Then you will*
*always have everything you need and plenty left over to share with others.*
*2 Corinthians 9:8 (NLT)*

TODAY MY TODDLER WAS SCRIBBLING in a small notebook. I'm not sure where she found it. (It's always a mystery where she discovers things....) As I looked at it, I found it's a journal from four years ago, filled with prayer needs. One of the short entries lists projects that overwhelmed me at the time—conference calls I needed to take, edits I needed to finish, and books I needed to write. Yet even after the long list I wrote the following, "Lord, be glorified by all I do—not just through the writing. Be glorified by the love and care I have for my family too!"

There are a few things I found interesting. First, years later, all the projects were complete. The conference call led to a great project, and the books were written, edited, and have been enjoyed by readers for many years now. Those things were completed, and God continued to get the glory.

Also, what I didn't know was that soon those stressors would pale in comparison to what was to come. In less than five months from the date in the journal, we were chosen by a birth mom to adopt her baby girl, and in the same time frame we also made the decision to move two thousand miles for my husband's job. Yet, even then, God provided for all my needs.

I'm thankful my toddler found this old journal. It's helped me to remember all God had done. And as two more children have recently joined my home, it reminds me that I'll someday be looking back over this challenging time with a smile, saying, "God worked it all out."

FAITH STEP: *Do you have an old prayer journal? Read through past entries and thank God for all the answered prayers.*

—*Tricia Goyer*

# SATURDAY, MAY 10

*"I am the Lord your God who takes hold of your right hand and says to you, Do not fear; I will help you." Isaiah 41:13 (NIV)*

WHEN WAS THE LAST TIME you felt the sweetness of a little hand in your own, a child's complete trust and dependence on you all wrapped up in five small fingers cocooned in yours?

Yesterday my daughter and I arrived home to discover our garage door had been wide open while we were gone. We live in a safe neighborhood, so I really wasn't worried, but you never can be too careful.

"Mama, do you think someone got in our house?" Uncertainty showed on her face.

"Probably not," I assured her, "but we'll check all the rooms to be sure."

Throughout our search, Calianne insisted on holding tight to my hand, grabbing on quickly if we became unlinked. Her unabashed trust in me gave my heart a thrill, and I was reminded again of the lengths I'd go to unhesitatingly protect my children. It'd be instinct.

Today's verse became more real to me through that experience with my little girl. Jesus holds *my* hand as securely as I held my child's. No, even more so. He never lets go, and He has power to ensure my security amidst anything.

And based on the feeling it gave me to ensure my daughter's well-being, I can trust that Jesus absolutely loves to feel me trust Him. It had never occurred to me that Jesus doesn't just want me to trust Him for my own good— He adores being trusted by me!

Why not put a smile on your Savior's face today by trusting your hand in His?

FAITH STEP: *Tell someone this week that Jesus adores being trusted by him or her. Then tell yourself the same truth and trust it to be true.*

—*Erin Keeley Marshall*

# SUNDAY, MAY 11

*But as for you, continue in what you have learned and have become convinced of, because you know those from whom you learned it, and how from infancy you have known the Holy Scriptures, which are able to make you wise for salvation through faith in Christ Jesus.*
2 Timothy 3:14–15 (NIV)

MY MOM'S BIRTHDAY WAS APPROACHING and I wanted to do something special for her. Mom insisted she didn't want a party and didn't want any fuss at all. I reminded her that we all wanted to celebrate her, and asked again if there was anything she would enjoy. She admitted she loved getting cards in the mail, and had heard of a friend who had a "card shower."

My husband, daughter, and I dove in to the project with gusto. My husband put up a notice at work. My daughter posted online to her friends. We passed out slips of paper at church with her address, and I sent info to an e-mail loop of writers. A few days before her birthday, cards, postcards, and even gifts of books from people she'd never met began to arrive. She was thrilled. Each day was an adventure when she'd bring in the large stack of mail, and pour through return addresses from all over the country.

Her joy at receiving, opening, reading, and savoring her mail made me think of the full mailbox that Jesus has provided for us through His Word. Every day, I can open the pages of my Bible and find His greeting of love expressed in various ways: letters, songs, poetry, historical accounts, parables, and more.

Had Mom let all those colorful cards and well wishes sit unopened, she would have missed out on a fun blessing. Yet some days, I ignore the wealth of encouragement and love that Jesus has sent to me.

FAITH STEP: *Open your mail from Jesus—your Bible—and rejoice at His personal greeting to you today. Then mail a card to a friend to lift their spirits.*

—Sharon Hinck

# MONDAY, MAY 12

*But Jesus gave her no reply, not even a word. Then his disciples urged him to send her away. "Tell her to go away," they said. "She is bothering us with all her begging."*
Matthew 15:23 (NLT)

IS THERE ANYTHING MORE FRUSTRATING than feeling like someone is ignoring us when we need their help? Whether waiting in a crowded emergency room or standing in a long line while customer service reps chat with each other, we want to scream out for attention. But who would expect Jesus to ignore someone, especially a mother pleading for healing of her demon-possessed daughter?

The passage in Matthew 15 can be difficult to understand, as it looks like Jesus is ignoring the cries of the Canaanite woman. His seeming callousness is the opposite of His usual way of responding to those who sought Him out for healing. Commentaries can help us understand the nuances and the context of the dialogue between Jesus and the woman—comments that at first glance sound vague or even insulting.

Still, it's not easy to explain why Jesus acted reluctant to heal the woman's daughter. Perhaps He wanted to help the mother's faith and understanding develop. Maybe He wanted to make sure that everyone watching would see that He accepted all people who came to Him in faith, including Gentiles. The most important point is that this distraught mother refused to give up, and Jesus granted her request.

Sometimes I start to feel like Jesus is ignoring me. I have prayer requests that have been on my heart for years. After a while, it's tempting to just give up. But when I remember Jesus's loving and merciful nature, I can trust that He has a reason for not yet answering. It might be a timing issue or a test of my faith, but there's no reason to give up.

**FAITH STEP:** *Do you feel that Jesus is ignoring one of your prayer requests? Ask Him to use this struggle to help your faith grow. Tell Him you trust His goodness even though you don't yet see His answer.*

—*Dianne Neal Matthews*

# TUESDAY, MAY 13

*For he himself is our peace. Ephesians 2:14 (ESV)*

IN MY SOMETIMES MISGUIDED ATTEMPTS to operate in constant efficiency mode, I balk when a television show or movie comes on that I've already seen. A rerun. Except in rare cases, I usually think, *Why spend two hours on this? Let's watch something* new.

But by default, I saw a classic—*The Hunt for Red October*—for the second or third time the other day when stuck in a chair with my feet elevated. This time through I noticed nuances and layers I couldn't appreciate as much unless I'd already seen the movie and viewed it through the lens of knowing how it all turned out.

One line gripped me by the heart muscle. The Russian submarine captain confessed, "It's a war with no battles, no monuments, only casualties."

I wonder if Jesus feels that way about those who resist what they know He's asking them to do. Does He think, *You might as well surrender, child. It's a war with no honorable battles, no monuments worth visiting, only casualties?*

The strain of guilt is one of those casualties of living in defiance to what God wants of us. Misery's another. Sabotaging God's plans is yet another.

An old hymn of the faith rings out, "Nothing between my soul and the Savior." No casualties need litter the landscape between where we stand and where He stands. Peace.

Today I'm more determined than ever to keep the peace between us. He has it mastered. I'm still working on it.

FAITH STEP: *Although we tend only to reflect on a particular character quality of Jesus near Christmas, even in the Old Testament He was proclaimed our Prince of Peace. I have a small pillow with the word* peace *embroidered on it. Do you? Let's rest our heads against it and let Him speak peace over our situations and relationships this day.*

—*Cynthia Ruchti*

# WEDNESDAY, MAY 14

*This is the day which the Lord has made; let us rejoice and be glad in it.*
*Psalm 118:24 (RSV)*

IT SEEMS LIKE WE HAVE a choice each day: to embrace the life we have been given or to dwell on the life that we thought we would have and are not currently living.

It is a choice of the will to choose to face the sun and accept what the day is offering, love the goodness that can be found in it, or to bend under the burden of unmet expectations and dive into the darkness of anxiety.

There is Jesus, who stands at the foot of the path, hand extended, waiting for us to place our palm in His and step into the day that He has given us. As I put my hand in the hand of the One Who created me, Who molded my days and shaped my nights with a single word, I am learning to set my mind on Him. On who He is. On what He has already done in my life. On His presence. On His good, strong love. On the amazing blessings He has unleashed upon me. On His unchanging mercy. On His faithfulness even in the face of my wavering heart.

In Psalm 91 (RSV) it says: "He who dwells in the shelter of the Most High will abide [rest] in the shadow of the Almighty." Our rest, our hope, and our joy come when we are tucked inside His shadow. You have to stick pretty close to someone to be in their shadow.

So this morning, I am aware of where I am and who He is. He is the Almighty, the Most High, and I am covered by the benevolence of His shadow and the hugeness of His grace. I think I made the right choice.

FAITH STEP: *Go sit outside in the shadow of a large tree. Remind yourself that no matter what you are facing in your day, you can be content and joyful knowing you are resting in the shadow of the Almighty.*

—*Susanna Foth Aughtmon*

# THURSDAY, MAY 15

*Each time he said, "My grace is all you need. My power works best in weakness."*
*So now I am glad to boast about my weaknesses, so that the power of*
*Christ can work through me.* 2 Corinthians 12:9 (NLT)

ABOUT TWENTY YEARS AGO I experienced multiple medical tests and heard conflicting diagnoses before one doctor spoke the foreign word, "fibromyalgia." He actually read to me from a medical textbook. At that time neither the doctor nor I knew much about that syndrome. I felt like a test case, to say the least.

Through the years I've managed the condition well with exercise, rest, a healthy diet, and stress reduction: learning what I could and couldn't do. I also take half a tiny pill to keep my muscles from partying all night. I've never wanted to make any physical condition the main topic of my conversation. So I've always told others my fibromyalgia is "mild." And I believe that, especially when I observe others who have experienced many more painful symptoms than my own.

Jesus, my Jehovah-Rapha, has answered my frequent prayers and healed 80 percent of those challenging symptoms. But I still experience moments when too little sleep, sore muscles, or fatigue conflict with my desires and productivity. I am not a "Type A" person, but I often try to push myself too far. God's Word and the words of Oswald Chambers in his book *My Utmost for His Highest* help me keep the right perspective: "We are not here to prove God answers prayer; we are here to be living monuments of God's grace."

Jesus teaches me constantly that grace is not an excuse for grumbling but a reason for gratitude. Instead of focusing on what I don't have or can't do, I choose to be grateful for what I do have and for what I can do—or rather, what Jesus can do through me. I'm always open to 100 percent healing. But in the meantime, I'm extremely grateful to be a living monument of His grace.

FAITH STEP: *How has Jesus made you a living monument of His grace?*

—*Rebecca Barlow Jordan*

# FRIDAY, MAY 16

*"Come to me, all you who are weary and burdened, and I will give you rest. Take my yoke upon you and learn from me." Matthew 11:28 (NIV)*

I SAT IN MY BIBLE study group and looked around at the women of all ages, backgrounds, and races. We were sharing prayer requests and the list was long. And as we sat there I could hear this Scripture echoing.

"Come to Me, all you..."

Jesus wooed. He woos all of us. He woos each of us.

"...you who are weary and heavy burdened."

Jesus walked this earth, and He understands both weariness and burdens. He knows that not a day passes when we don't experience either or both.

"Take My yoke upon you..."

Jesus knows we can only be yoked with one guiding force. He wants to be that guiding force. Unlike the world, He will not place more burdens upon us than we can bear.

"and learn from Me..."

Jesus may not lay out the whole plan, but He teaches us as we're on our way. His Word is a companion to us on our walk. His lessons meet us at the right place at the right time.

When we gather, share our requests, and bring them before Jesus, we are exactly where we need to be . . . coming before Jesus. The weariness grows, and the burdens increase, when we try to carry them ourselves. Share them with each other. Share them with Him.

FAITH STEP: *Do you have a trustworthy friend with whom you can share your burden? Find time to talk with your friend in person—or on the phone—to encourage and pray for each other.*

—*Tricia Goyer*

# SATURDAY, MAY 17

*"To what can I compare this generation? They are like children sitting in the marketplaces and calling out to others: 'We played the flute for you, and you did not dance; we sang a dirge, and you did not mourn.'" Matthew 11:16–17 (NIV)*

I TRIED PHONING MY SON, but he didn't answer. I crossed my arms and frowned at my husband. "Do you realize it's been three whole weeks since we've had even a glimpse of our granddaughter?"

Ted gave me a sympathetic smile and a hug. "I know you miss her, but we'll manage another trip in a few months."

A month earlier, we'd had the privilege of meeting our sweet grandchild in person. It's hard to describe the level of joy I felt holding her for the first time.

Yet along with the joy came the sadness of living across the country. I kept reminding myself to be grateful for modern communication tools like Skype. But we soon found that it was a struggle for the busy young parents to find time to connect—at least enough to satisfy me.

I wonder how often I've slipped into this pattern. Jesus sends an amazing blessing. I thank Him, overwhelmed with gratitude. Then shortly after, I find something to grouse about. A new freelance job arrives just when we need the income, but soon I'm muttering about the problems that arise with the project. I get a quiet day to myself that I've longed for, but soon feel restless and lonely. I'm blessed with a beautiful grandchild, but fuss that she doesn't live next door.

When I read this verse in Matthew, I heard Jesus gently chide that no matter how He blesses us, we find a way to complain. I asked His forgiveness, thanked Him again for His generosity to me, and resolved to nip my complaints in the bud.

FAITH STEP: *Have you noticed complaints slipping past your lips too frequently? Ask Jesus to help you notice His blessings, then write a thank-you note to Him.*

—*Sharon Hinck*

# SUNDAY, MAY 18

*As He who called you is holy, you also be holy in all your conduct...*
*knowing that you were not redeemed with corruptible things...*
*but with the precious blood of Christ. 1 Peter 1:15, 18–19 (NKJV)*

WHEN MY DAUGHTER STELLA WAS a few months old, my sister-in-law Rene and I went out with some friends to dinner and a movie. The movie was to be a real "chick flick," something ladies everywhere were raving over.

Because Stella was nursing, she went along with us. My sister-in-law and I took turns eating while the other one stood with her, swaying her gently as she required. The ladies all fussed over her, declaring her supreme cuteness, and she and I both enjoyed their company.

By the time we sat down in the theater, Stella was ready to nurse and go to sleep. It was perfect timing. Rene and I relaxed, glad that Stella was obliging us by snuggling peacefully under a blanket in my arms.

However, within the first few minutes of the movie, we were looking at each other aghast. We hoped it would get better, even as image after inappropriate image flashed before our eyes.

Rene and I are Christians. But we don't consider ourselves prudes. The last thing we want to do is to offend a sister by acting holier-than-thou, because we know for a fact we're not. So for several scenes, we squirmed in our seats, wondering what Jesus would do.

When Stella pulled back the blanket and flashed me a gummy smile, reality hit me like a brick to the head. This was nothing I'd want my daughters to sit and watch. Therefore, I needed to get out of there. Rene felt the same way, so we excused ourselves and headed for the door.

FAITH STEP: *It's easy, sometimes, to see life through shades of gray. But the calling to be holy is very clear. Ask Jesus to sharpen your focus today.*

—*Gwen Ford Faulkenberry*

# MONDAY, MAY 19

*Every day they continued to meet together in the temple courts.*
*They broke bread in their homes and ate together with glad and sincere hearts,*
*praising God and enjoying the favor of all the people.*
*And the Lord added to their number daily those who were being saved.*
*Acts 2:46–47 (NIV)*

WHEN J.R. AND I MARRIED, there were no cell phones, no texting or e-mailing. Communication occurred via a landline, handwritten letter, or—*drumroll please*—speaking in person.

However, I think back to those first years of marriage. We had a "young marrieds" group at church that gathered in a home each month to eat, play games, and have Bible study. Several of those couples are still close friends because of the bond we developed during those fellowships.

As technology has boomed with cell phones, the Internet, and video games, gatherings like the ones we had back then started dissipating and our chances to grow real friendships became lost in today's technological world. Our family went several years where we were so busy that we didn't believe we had time for additional fellowship beyond scheduled church services. But this past year we started having a "life group" meeting weekly in our home. The small group discusses the Bible, but we also discuss what is happening in our lives and how we can support each other and pray for each other as we journey through life's struggles together.

Those early Christians ate together and praised God together. Christ wants us to edify each other, lift each other up, and grow closer (see 1 Corinthians 14:3). Truly caring for one another involves more than being social network friends. It involves fellowship…and love.

**FAITH STEP:** *Invite a family to your home for lunch after Sunday worship. Open your home; open your heart.*

*—Renee Andrews*

# TUESDAY, MAY 20

*Do not let any unwholesome talk come out of your mouths,*
*but only what is helpful for building others up according to their needs,*
*that it may benefit those who listen. Ephesians 4:29 (NIV)*

TODAY'S VERSE HAS ME THINKING about grace. Just how broad is grace, and how much wrong does it cover? What does it look like in everyday life, in those demanding relationship?

None of us deserves grace—unmerited favor—from Jesus, but he gives it to us freely. Does giving grace to others mean we overlook every wrong, that we accept all mistreatment from them?

Breathe a sigh of relief with me over the answer, a resounding *no*.

Truthful grace is perhaps grace in its most heroic form. Which sounds more uplifting to you in the midst of conflict? Stuffing down our feelings to avoid truly dealing with a situation or, on the flip side, ranting and raving? Neither passive nor aggressive is good. True, rare grace thoughtfully carves a path through issues toward a healthy, healed conclusion. Grace is patient not hotheaded, gutsy not passive. Grace says, "I will be patient yet firm with you regardless of your response."

We know this because of Jesus's example. He offered his life for all of us, including those who treated Him badly and killed Him, and for everyone throughout time who has loved, hated, or acted carelessly toward Him. Yet He did not hesitate to speak truth in a spirit of building up those who needed to change a sinful course (Luke 19:1–10; John 4:1–42). His example of grace is deliberate and purposeful, not passive-aggressive.

FAITH STEP: *Does someone in your life need your gutsy grace in the form of gentle honesty? Ask Jesus to provide the timing and wording if He wants you to offer the gift of truthful grace to that person. Finally, ask Him to show you if he wants you to remain silent with someone whose heart is hardened to the truth (Matthew 26:63).*

—*Erin Keeley Marshall*

# WEDNESDAY, MAY 21

*Don't worry about anything; instead, pray about everything. Tell God what you need, and thank him for all he has done. Philippians 4:6 (NLT)*

OUR FAMILY HAD RECENTLY MOVED to a year-round Christian camp where my husband became program director. He received no income. Instead, we depended on friends' financial donations to meet our obligations. Talk about nerve-racking.

We had to pay for kids' clothes, orthodontics, medicine, groceries, gas, insurance, and more—like all other families we knew—but with no guaranteed income. We asked God to supply for our needs, but worry became my constant companion.

The camp secretary tallied donations on the tenth of every month. We lived in an apartment above the office, so that day saw me run the stairs every hour until she placed our paycheck in our mailbox.

Worry tied me in knots even though I was familiar with Scriptures such as Matthew 6:25, 27, 32–33 (NLT)—"So I tell you, don't worry about everyday life—whether you have enough food, drink, and clothes...Can all your worries add a single moment to your life? Of course not...Your heavenly Father already knows all your needs and he will give you all you need from day to day if you live for him and make the Kingdom of God your primary concern."

One day, exhausted from stress, I made a conscious decision to focus on God's truth rather than on my fears. I also established a daily habit of thanking God in advance for supplying our needs. I practiced this for months. Doing so helped untie the worry knot and set me free.

Are you a worrier? Focus on God's truth rather than on your fears, and thank Him in advance for answering your prayers. Then you'll experience freedom too.

FAITH STEP: *Write down the things that worry you. Now write out Philippians 4:19 across that list.*

—*Grace Fox*

# THURSDAY, MAY 22

*For I consider that the sufferings of this present time are not worth comparing with the glory that is to be revealed to us.* Romans 8:18 (ESV)

WHEN MY HUSBAND BROKE HIS femur and back, eight days in the hospital weren't enough to send him home mended. He came home broken, bedridden, and in need of constant care.

Every movement brought pain. The rod the surgeons inserted in his thighbone was secured by a screw at the top and two screws just above the knee. His back fracture made a confining back brace a constant necessity.

Getting him into the car for doctor appointments resembled the trouble Prince Charming had trying to cram a stepsister's oversized foot into a delicate glass slipper. At nearly six foot three, my husband was used to ducking and twisting to get into a vehicle. But with his leg unbending and his back forbidden to bend, it was a circus act that left us both gasping for breath.

After settling him and climbing behind the wheel one day, I turned the key in the ignition, which started the radio. My husband braced his hand on the ceiling of the car's interior, near the skylight.

"Honey? Are you okay?"

He pointed to the radio. The music rang out with the reminder that we can become suddenly unaware of our afflictions when they're eclipsed by the glory and wonder and love of Jesus.

Bill wasn't bracing himself against pain. He was raising his hand in praise.

Jesus seared that picture into my memory. It sustained us through many more months of recovery. How differently He calculates suffering. According to His Word, there's no comparison to what waits for us at its end.

FAITH STEP: *Do you have a mental picture of a sterling moment—a grace moment that reminded you how different things are because of Jesus? Try expressing that moment with art or song or capture it in words. Find some creative way to give it voice.*

*—Cynthia Ruchti*

# FRIDAY, MAY 23

---

*I had fainted, unless I had believed to see the goodness of the Lord in the land of the living. Psalm 27:13 (KJV)*

---

WHO HASN'T BEEN CHALLENGED WHEN trying to keep the "R & R" part of family vacations intact? I remember one year when our well-worn Chevrolet we affectionately dubbed "Ol' Yellar" took us on a wrong turn, then broke down by the side of the road, delaying our trip overnight. Did I say "one year"? How about *multiple* years?

Vacationing isn't always easy! Through the years I learned to lean on the psalms in God's Word for peace, and yes, sometimes for sanity! It often helped me to paraphrase my own psalm-prayers to Jesus, grateful that He understood my limitations:

> *O give thanks to God, for He is good—even when the car is stalled,*
> *before we ever leave the neighborhood.*
> *Cause us to hear Your voice, O Lord, above the fighting of noisy children.*
> *Make haste to help us,*
> *for our enemies of mosquitoes, ants, and flies have overtaken us.*
> *Your Spirit and love refresh us with cool breezes in the midst of our air-*
> *conditioning loss and GPS disasters.*
> *Your mercies are enduring; Your love is everlasting.*
> *Help us, Jesus, to endure this day and last until the end of this trip.*
> *We would have fainted, unless we had believed to see Your goodness*
> *in the land of this vacationing nightmare.*
> *We shall again praise You, O Lord… if we can just make it home in one piece.*

---

FAITH STEP: *How has traveling—with or without children—tested your patience? Write your own psalm declaring your faith in Jesus in the midst of challenges. For inspiration, read Psalm 107:1, Psalm 143:5, Psalm 38:22, and Psalm 42:5–6.*

—*Rebecca Barlow Jordan*

# SATURDAY, MAY 24

---

*It is for freedom that Christ has set us free. Stand firm, then, and do not let yourselves be burdened again by a yoke of slavery. Galatians 5:1 (NIV)*

---

MY KIDS AND I LIKE watching Looney Tunes. They love any episode featuring banter between Daffy Duck and Bugs Bunny, but my favorite is an old one in which Porky Pig travels across the globe to find a rare dodo bird. To do so, he must first go through Wackyland, a wonderful place for someone who loves puns.

In Wackyland, Porky comes across things like a "Rubber Band," which is a marching band made up of rubber bands playing musical instruments. There are all sorts of creative things like this in Wackyland, but the one that stands out most in my mind is a prisoner who carries around his bars like a window frame. It never occurs to him to set it down and be free; he just walks through life looking out at the world from behind bars.

Now that's wacky! But it occurs to me as I write this that many Christians do the same thing. Jesus came to set us free, but we still carry around bars like we're slaves to sin. Whether it's guilt, condemnation, fear of failure, or whatever…we need to cast off those bars and walk through life in the freedom of His grace!

---

**FAITH STEP:** *Is there an area of your life in which you still carry the yoke of slavery? Stand firm in the freedom Jesus offers you today.*

*—Gwen Ford Faulkenberry*

# SUNDAY, MAY 25

*Do not conform any longer to the pattern of this world, but be transformed by the renewing of your mind. Then you will be able to test and approve what God's will is—his good, pleasing and perfect will. Romans 12:2 (NIV)*

THIS PAST YEAR YANKED THE joy out of me. But I like joy and laughter and hope better than crankiness and irritability. What would it take for me to wake up and feel a sense of expectation of what the day holds instead of dread at the thought of what is required of me? What would it take to turn my heart inside out, empty it of the sadness, and fill it with hope?

I know that some of my sadness comes from losing a dear friend recently. But I also know that some of it comes from choosing to focus on the hard things in life instead of choosing to see the beauty that each day holds.

So I have decided I am going to change. Because I am the only one who can do that. This is my old to-do list: 1. Do the laundry. 2. Pick up the house. 3. Finish the bills. 4. Clean out the shed. No wonder I am sad.

This is my new list. 1. Listen to a good song. 2. Write a love note to my boys. 3. Dance for ten minutes. 4. Go for a walk. 5. Have coffee with a friend. 6. Sit in the sun and read Psalm 139.

I may still have to fold laundry, but between dancing and reading about how I was formed with love and a purpose seems to make it better. I am on a mission to be joyful. I am asking Jesus to reshape how I think—to transform me by the renewing of my mind. I am on a path toward seeing life differently and embracing that loveliness that is already surrounding me. Feel free to join me!

FAITH STEP: *Write a new joy-full to-do list for yourself. Ask Jesus to help transform the way you think.*

—*Susanna Foth Aughtmon*

# MONDAY, MAY 26

---

*My child, pay attention to what I say. Listen carefully to my words. Don't lose sight of them.*
*Let them penetrate deep into your heart, for they bring life to those who find them,*
*and healing to their whole body. Proverbs 4:20–22 (NLT)*

---

MY MOTHER-IN-LAW ALWAYS SAID MY husband was a strong-willed child. I didn't understand what that meant until our daughter, Leslie, turned out just like him. If I gave her the blue cup, she wanted the orange one. If I chose pants for her to wear, she wanted a dress. If I picked out her very favorite book to read, then she'd want something else. Everything was a fight. Everything.

Through the years my husband and I worked on different techniques that would teach her to obey while still allowing her to be the independent, creative child that she was. It was a lot of work, and even when she did obey, I noticed her obedience was more with her body than her heart.

*Dear Lord, won't You help me with this girl? Show me what I need to do to help her . . .*

My daughter's change happened one week during junior high. She'd gone away to summer camp and came back bubbling with joy after she accepted Christ. I'd find her awake in the morning reading her Bible and journaling. Over the years I'd read the Bible to her—and I helped her to memorize Scripture—but now there was no need to force and push.

Life and healing will come to our children when we pray . . . but don't be surprised when it comes from the inside out. Your hard work over the years, in teaching and leadership, and your prayers make it possible for your children to open their hearts to Jesus's extraordinary grace—the final ingredient to all your hard work. An ingredient that Jesus alone can produce.

---

**FAITH STEP:** *Are you weary from trying to force someone else to be good and act right? This week instead of focusing on a person's actions, focus instead on prayer. Trust Jesus to work in people's hearts.*

—*Tricia Goyer*

# TUESDAY, MAY 27

*Jesus said, "Father, forgive them, for they do not know what they are doing."*
Luke 23:34 (NIV)

A REVIEWER WROTE A SARCASTIC and condemning analysis of one of my novels. While I appreciate balanced critique and try to learn from it, anonymous people on the Internet can sometimes post cruel, angry, or mean-spirited reviews.

I was already at a low point, discouraged and exhausted from the hard work of finishing the book and working with the publisher to promote it. The words of the review seared into my heart like a hot poker, charring my spirit. No matter how many times I coached myself to develop a thick skin, the truth was, my sensitive nature was part of what enabled me to be a writer in the first place.

Jesus calls us to pray for our enemies, but I usually skimmed over those verses. There were people I didn't enjoy as much as others, or people who had wronged me—as I'd probably wronged them, as well. But "enemy" had always seemed like a more vicious and intentional word. However, that day as I read the review, I did feel attacked by an enemy.

I struggled in my prayer time to forgive the attack, but kept bumping up against one barrier. The reviewer had no idea what a vulnerable place I was at when he dashed off his unkind comments. He would never know how deeply I'd been hurt. He'd never feel sorry for the pain he had caused. Forgiveness would be a lot easier if the person I was forgiving felt remorse.

Then I remembered Jesus's words from the cross. He offered forgiveness for people oblivious to the damage they were causing. They didn't know what they were doing.

Forgiving hurts from oblivious people continues to be difficult for me, but Jesus's words from the cross challenge me to follow His example.

FAITH STEP: *Has someone hurt or wronged you recently? Write it on a slip of paper. Ask Jesus for the grace to forgive, then tear up the paper and throw it away.*

—*Sharon Hinck*

# WEDNESDAY, MAY 28

*Pray continually. 1 Thessalonians 5:17* (CEB)

IT ADDED SEVERAL MINUTES TO my mile-long walk to school, but was worth it to take a slight jog on the side street in my hometown and time it so my high school sweetheart and I could walk the remaining way together. Yes, in snow. And yes, uphill. (But no, not barefoot. That was way before my time.)

We've been married more than forty years now. And we still treasure stolen moments together. Sneaking a kiss in the church narthex when no one's looking. Holding hands under the table at a family dinner. Showing up at his workplace during his break when I have errands to run in town to let him know I was thinking about him.

So we see each other a lot.

But those stolen moments are so sweet. They rekindle our love and affection for one another.

Jesus is always with us. We're never separated. Lingering in His presence with long stretches of time together in Bible reading or prayer builds the foundation of our relationship.

But He must love the stolen moments too. When I'm moved by a single word in a Scripture verse, or rendered breathless by some miracle of His creation and know Whom to thank, or wake with a praise song on my mind, or sneak a brief glance at Him in a devotion book, or thank Him for helping me figure out the problem with the checkbook balance…

**FAITH STEP:** *If you've been laboring under a load of regret for how long it's been since you lingered in His presence, try two action steps. First, linger in His presence. Find a way. Second, savor those sweet but brief stolen moments when you tell Him how much you love Him.*

*—Cynthia Ruchti*

# THURSDAY, MAY 29

*In all things God works for the good of those who love him,*
*who have been called according to his purpose. Romans 8:28 (NIV)*

"WE'RE RETURNING TO NORTH AMERICA," said Gene. My brain, groggy from anesthetic due to my Caesarean delivery, struggled to understand. "Our baby is very sick and needs medical care unavailable here."

*Here* was Nepal, our home for three years prior. Our daughter was born with hydrocephalus (too much water on the brain).

Our plans for lifetime missionary service blown to smithereens, we'd land in the USA with no job, no car, no home, and no medical insurance. Could God redeem this for good? Yes. And He did.

Our faith matured in ways we'd never imagined as we watched God provide employment, a housesitting opportunity, and government funds to pay our daughter's first year of medical bills.

Our situation became an opportunity to minister to others. The first two years of our daughter's life were filled with hospitalizations, surgeries, and a bout with meningitis. We met and encouraged numerous other parents with sick children during that time.

God truly does work all things for the good of those who love Him and who have been called according to His purpose. Sounds obvious sometimes, I know. But it's true.

Whatever tragedies we face, God can turn them to triumph. Believe it.

**FAITH STEP:** *Don't allow fear or anger to overwhelm you when tragedy strikes. Instead, ask God to use the situation to reveal Himself in new ways to you and others involved.*

*—Grace Fox*

# FRIDAY, MAY 30

*How great is the love the Father has lavished on us,*
*that we should be called children of God! And that is what we are!*
*The reason the world does not know us is that it did not know him. 1 John 3:1*

THIS MORNING OUR YOUNGEST, ADDISON, came and crawled up in bed in between Scott and me. Hunkering down in the warm slip of space between us, he positioned his chilly feet perfectly on the backs of my calves, and his breathing began to settle into a sleepy rhythm. Once my legs rewarmed themselves, I fell back asleep too. The cool of the room and the heaviness of covers can do that to you.

I awoke to feel a small finger tracing the lines of my face. Over each eye. The slope of my nose. The dip above my lip. And finally, a flat palm laid against the warmth of my cheek. Addie finished tracing my face and rolled over for his dad to snuggle him. It was a moment of affection that warmed me from the inside out. It is a beautiful thing to be known and loved.

I try to think about how Jesus loves us so much, and I still can't wrap my mind around it. He has known us intimately since we were crafted in our mothers' bellies and even in our failures and imperfections. He has lavished His love and forgiveness on us at every turn. Jesus chases us down with His incomprehensible grace and mercy and fills us with His Holy Spirit as we follow Him on this journey of life.

There is no way to repay such an extravagant gift. All we can really do in response is love Him back. It is good to know that that is what He wants most of all.

FAITH STEP: *Write a love note to Jesus. Remind Him of all the things you love about Him and how He has changed your life with His incomprehensible love.*

—Susanna Foth Aughtmon

# SATURDAY, MAY 31

*They will hold to the outward form of our religion, but reject its real power.*
*2 Timothy 3:5 (GNT)*

IN THE BACK OF OUR minds, we know the images we see in magazines are retouched. The model's skin is not that flawless; her teeth not that bright naturally; her knees are knobby, not smooth.

Technology makes a retouched photo harder to identify. But the frequent use of retouching makes us default to the assumption that a perfect image owes its perfection to computer-generated fixes.

It may work in marketing, but it doesn't work with faith. A Photoshopped faith may look pretty and sound pretty—"I'm just trusting Jesus in this. He's so faithful." But if we scratch at the surface, will we find faith only skin-deep? Painted on?

Among the few times Jesus grew truly livid were when He found people living fake faith—Photoshopped faith. Tradition plastered over where relationship should be. Token compassion slapped on top of day-to-day self-absorption. Mama's heart of faith pasted on our body rather than our own faith shining through.

Genuine. Authentic. They were the only kinds of faith that blessed Jesus. And they're the only kinds that bless us and others too.

Do our scars show? They're real. Is the faith the world around us sees genuine, or has it been retouched for the public?

FAITH STEP: *The only way we'll be comfortable letting the world see our real, unretouched faith is if it is genuine. Touched by Him, not retouched to cover what it's really like. What's one change you can make today to improve the look of your faith without makeup? (Hint: Immersing ourselves in God's Word makes faith glow.)*

—*Cynthia Ruchti*

# SUNDAY, JUNE 1

*What, then, shall we say in response to these things?*
*If God is for us who can be against us? Romans 8:31 (NIV)*

THERE IS A LOT OF clutter in my life.

It is what happens when you have a husband, three children, a hamster, and a cat. I find myself trying to clear a pathway from the front door to the couch on a regular basis. Mostly, because I want to lie down on the couch and take a nap. All the piles of dishes, the stacks of bills, and the trails of toys just make me tired. Because the clutter is a constant reminder that my work will never be done.

My husband, Scott, doesn't get it. "Just let it go." He doesn't let the detritus of life affect him. That is why he is so happy. I, on the other hand, alternate between frantic cleaning and a semicomatose depression. Scott just raises an eyebrow as I moan, "It's never done. You are all against me. It's hopeless."

Clearly, I am the picture of a loving wife and mother almost every day. But life is a work in progress. The clutter of life mirrors the clutter of the heart with all its excess baggage, the hurts that need to be mended, and the habits that need to be broken. The truth is that we will remain a work in progress until the day we see Jesus. It does us no good to let ourselves be overwhelmed by the process. We can still be energized and joyful if we choose to focus on the One Who is on our side instead of what we are up against.

That would be Jesus. His boundless mercy and grace. His overflowing love and His ever-present forgiveness. And really, it doesn't get more hopeful than that.

FAITH STEP: *Let go of the clutter in your mind that has you worried and stressed out. Offer it to Jesus with this prayer: "Jesus, I know that You are here for me. Help me to focus on You and Your love for me today."*

—*Susanna Foth Aughtmon*

# MONDAY, JUNE 2

*For God is working in you, giving you the desire and the power to do what pleases him.*
*Philippians 2:13 (NLT)*

MY TODDLER—WHOM WE NICKNAMED BUDDY—HAS a bubbly personality, but one thing he doesn't like is getting strapped into his car seat. "Down. Down please, Mommy!" he cries. He doesn't like to be restricted. He doesn't like sitting still in his car seat.

It takes energy to strap him into the seat, and I try to calm him with my words. "I know you don't like this now . . . but just wait and see where we're going!" There are times I have to fight to strap him in to go to the park or the zoo. I'm hoping the stage will pass, and Buddy will learn to trust me—trust that I have his best interest in mind, even if it feels confining for a time.

I've found the same true in my own life. There are times when I feel God confining me and shutting doors I wish were open. I pray. I plead. I cry, "Please, God." But with no avail. Usually I'm too busy complaining to hear His reassuring voice. *I have something good in mind for you, Daughter. Trust Me.*

It's not that God isn't answering my prayers . . . it's just that He has something better in mind for me. Something wonderful I can't even imagine. I can either struggle with Him, question His motives, and plead for my own desires, or I can pray, trust His motives, and listen to His heart.

"Prayer is not an argument with God to persuade him to move things our way," writes Leonard Ravenhill, "but an exercise by which we are enabled by his Spirit to move ourselves his way."

Do you want to be able to trust God's way? Pray for wisdom. Pray for the desire and power to follow His will and not fight for your own. You'll never know what God has waiting for you right down the road.

**FAITH STEP:** *Next time you see a mom wrangling with a toddler, pray for that mom. Also pray that you'll better submit to God's will in your life.*

—*Tricia Goyer*

# TUESDAY, JUNE 3

*Fix our eyes on Jesus, faith's pioneer and perfecter. Hebrews 12:2 (CEB)*

MY BRAIN HAS A MUFFIN top.

It's not visible to the naked eye, but I'm sure high-tech medical equipment could reveal my brain is spilling over with too much information: facts, ideas, concepts, future books, trivia, minutiae, and useless thoughts.

And moments with Jesus.

The less crowded my brain, the more those moments with Him stand out. Did I just write that? Did I just admit it to myself?

Should I take a more minimalist approach to what's stored in my brain so the Jesus moments have room to shine? That was rhetorical.

What does the Bible say is the secret to successfully maneuvering the labyrinth called life? "Fixing our eyes on Jesus, the Author and Finisher of our faith."

Like a woman—not that I would know—who can't see her feet for the excess around her middle, it's hard to fix my eyes on Jesus with excess in the way. So, I'll discard this thought, and that one, and that whole fileful over there, so I can maintain better eye contact with Jesus. I'll purge my overloaded brain circuits of the broken bits of information that don't connect to anything else or that block my view like fog which prevents me from seeing more than the street below, even though I paid for an *oceanfront* room.

It's the Jesus moments that keep me going, that infuse meaning into what I'm muddling through.

Time to do some brain purging.

FAITH STEP: *Dumping information isn't as easy as pushing a Delete button on a computer. What works for you? Time alone in a retreat setting? A hike through the woods or along a beach? A virtual "ceremony" surrendering unnecessary thoughts to Him? Try one of those brain and stress purges today.*

—*Cynthia Ruchti*

# WEDNESDAY, JUNE 4

*"Indeed, the very hairs of your head are all numbered. Don't be afraid; you are worth more than many sparrows." Luke 12:7 (NIV)*

AFTER THE BIRTH OF OUR first son many years ago, two of our good friends stopped by the hospital for a visit. We chatted for several minutes, and then Wayne quietly slipped out the door. He soon came back, bringing me a PayDay candy bar and a can of Dr. Pepper from the vending machines. Until that moment I would have never guessed that Wayne knew my favorite brands of candy and pop.

It's comforting to know that we are understood, that someone cares enough to take the time to learn our likes and dislikes, our needs and desires, our personal history and our dreams for the future. Yet even those who love us the most often miss important aspects of our life or our character. Sometimes it's because of a lack of perception on their part; other times we work hard to hide certain details from the people around us.

There's absolutely nothing we can ever hide from God, no matter how hard we try. Jesus explained that not only does God know every time a sparrow dies, He also knows the exact number of hairs on our head at any given moment. He is aware of our deepest thoughts, feelings, and longings. He sees everything about us—the good, the bad, and the ugly.

It might seem unnerving to be so thoroughly exposed unless we remember that the One Who knows us most intimately loves us more than we can imagine. Once we accept the forgiveness of sin that Jesus made possible, we can rest in the knowledge that Someone understands us fully, completely. And there is nothing He will see that will ever make Him love us any less.

FAITH STEP: *Is there anything that makes you feel ashamed when you come to Jesus in prayer? Talk to Him about it, thanking Him for loving you in spite of your flaws, failures, and shortcomings.*

—*Dianne Neal Matthews*

# THURSDAY, JUNE 5

*"I am with you..." declares the Lord. Jeremiah 1:8 (NIV)*

A PROMISE GOD MADE TO Jeremiah helped me through our first pastorate, while my husband and I were still in college.

We struggled through wasp stings, as the heat would rise in our little sanctuary, and the winged creatures would descend. One time Larry was preaching and a wasp landed right on the pages of his open Bible. He quickly emphasized a point in his sermon by slamming the Bible shut, killing the intruder. One day I was playing the piano, and a wasp flew onto my arm. I paused for a moment and kept playing, but I felt the sting.

We ate dinner in barns and even caught our own fish for Sunday lunch one time. Our ninety-year-old church member challenged us repeatedly, like the time she jangled her coin purse during Larry's sermon when we failed to take an offering, and our tug-of-war with her over her "Bud" (beer bottle) vase of artificial flowers that kept appearing and reappearing on the church piano. One day she even backed her car in reverse all the way to the local post office, crashing into the building. And those are just a few of her escapades.

But throughout that three-year pastorate, I remembered God's promise when His hesitant prophet was wondering why in the world God had chosen him. "'Ah, Sovereign Lord,' I said, 'I do not know how to speak; I am only a child.'"

To which God replied, "Do not say, 'I am only a child.' You must go to everyone I send you to and say whatever I command you. Do not be afraid... for I am with you" (Jeremiah 1:6–8, NIV).

And just like with Jeremiah, God has been—with us. And we've never looked back.

FAITH STEP: *Have you ever felt like a child when Jesus asked you to do something? What Bible promise has helped you the most?*

—*Rebecca Barlow Jordan*

# FRIDAY, JUNE 6

*I planted the seed in your hearts, and Apollos watered it, but it was God who made it grow.*
1 Corinthians 3:6 (NLT)

FOR THE LAST THIRTEEN YEARS I've worked with teenage girls. It's a great ministry, and a hard one too. I want to help them, but I don't want to help too much and make them dependent on me. I want to know about their lives and be involved, but there are too many girls, too many problems, hard family issues, and conflicts that trail along after them. I want to make sure that the ways I serve them will help them, but I get impatient when I don't see immediate results. I know their "change" isn't up to me, but it's hard when more seeds are planted than crops are harvested. And—if I'm being completely honest—I wouldn't mind a little approval for a job well done.

This makes me think about the women who reached out to me during my teen years. The women who helped me weren't concerned by approval, because 99 percent of the time they didn't get it from me. They might have been frustrated when I didn't change as quickly as they'd hoped. They might have been impatient, waiting to see if any of the seeds of love, of God's Word, and of wisdom would take root in my heart.

I haven't connected with most of these women in twenty years. I wish I could find them and tell them that they did make a difference. It also reminds me to be patient, be faithful, and be diligent . . . even when I can't see results. The women who mentored me had no idea I'd be writing and speaking, telling their story all these years later. They most likely don't even see it as their story. It was God's story, and they just got to be a part . . . just like God has granted me the opportunity to be a part of the story of the young women I serve.

FAITH STEP: *Think of someone who impacted you during your teen years. Write a letter to that person, thanking him or her. If you have that person's address, then mail it!*

—*Tricia Goyer*

# SATURDAY, JUNE 7

*Fight the good fight of faith.* 1 Timothy 6:12 (NAS)

I HAD A STUDENT NAMED Ivy in two of my classes at the college. Her clothes were baggy on her small frame, and she kept her head ducked most of the time, never saying a word. I thought she probably hated English, and hated me.

When I assigned the first essay, it doubled as a way to get to know one another. Students were to bring five objects in a bag to serve as visual aids.

Ivy looked down as she walked to the front of the class. Red splotches covered her neck. She had on a tank top that day and I noticed that her arms were surprisingly muscular as she set down her bag, a large black duffel.

"I may not look like it, but I'm a fighter."

She pulled out a boxing glove and proceeded to tell the class how she had lost her best friend in a car wreck a few years before, nearly gone over the edge with depression, and started boxing as a way to release her feelings.

The other students sat still and speechless in their seats.

Ivy and I became friends. I found out that she came from a dysfunctional background and felt unloved all of her life. I decided to sort of adopt her, which meant, among other things, that I prayed for her, preached to her, and hounded her about coming to class and making good grades. She texted me the night she got saved.

At the end of the year, Ivy was on the Dean's List. She brought a present by my office with a letter. "Thanks for fighting for your students."

The present was a boxing glove with Philippians 4:13 on it. It stays on my bookcase to remind me to fight the good fight every day.

FAITH STEP: *Commit Philippians 4:13 to memory. You can do all things through Jesus!*

—*Gwen Ford Faulkenberry*

# SUNDAY, JUNE 8

---

*Let us then approach God's throne of grace with confidence, so that we may receive mercy and find grace to help us in our time of need. Hebrews 4:16 (NIV)*

---

LAST YEAR WE LET OUR employees borrow our van for a trip to Orlando. They had an abundance of luggage, and it wouldn't fit in the back, so our newest employee shoved the door with his hip . . . and dented the van.

Rather than tell us, if the employees saw us approaching, they turned the van in the other direction to keep us from seeing the dent. Eventually, they realized we would see the damage, and so T.J., the new employee, confessed. He was so nervous, and without reason. My husband told him it was fine. The van had nearly 300,000 miles, and a dent wasn't going to make a difference. Plus, no one was hurt, and that was the important part.

T.J. received grace, in the same manner that we receive grace from God, with Christ as our high priest pleading our case. Do we deserve it? No. Did T.J. deserve it? Not really. But we receive it, and so did T.J.

Lamentations 3:58 (NLT) says, "Lord, you are my lawyer! Plead my case! For you have redeemed my life." Christ *is* our lawyer, always ready to plead our case. And like T.J. felt toward his boss, we can feel extremely grateful for the grace freely given by our Lord and Savior.

---

**FAITH STEP:** *Is someone in your life needing grace from you today? Treat them as Christ treats you.*

—*Renee Andrews*

# MONDAY, JUNE 9

*"And why do you worry about clothes? See how the flowers of the field grow. They do not labor or spin. Yet I tell you that not even Solomon in all his splendor was dressed like one of these. If that is how God clothes the grass of the field, which is here today and tomorrow is thrown into the fire, will he not much more clothe you—you of little faith?" Matthew 6:28–30 (NIV)*

MY HUSBAND AND I WERE driving down isolated back roads, looking for a trailhead to a hike deep in the north woods. He slowed the car as I studied the directions in our hiking guide. When I looked up, I saw a large pond along the left side of the road.

Thousands of wild irises poked out of the marshy water, an amazing border of color. No one had cultivated them. This wasn't a garden designed by human hands. In fact, there had probably been centuries where no one but God had witnessed the beauty of this wetland. Even now, very few people traveled this road. The iris pond shared its beauty for the glory of God alone.

I often feel insignificant or invisible. I spend most days home alone, and often wonder if I'm of any use to His kingdom. Yet God creates hidden, tucked-away places of beauty. Maybe my life can be one of those little hidden places that bring Him glory.

My husband and I were stunned by the beauty of the irises, and thought of all the other hidden treasures around the planet never witnessed by human eyes. God takes pleasure in His creation. And as Jesus shared, we are of even more value to Him than the flowers. Even when we feel we aren't seen by anyone else, He takes pleasure in the beauty of our lives.

**FAITH STEP:** *Do you worry about whether your life has value? Buy a flower and set it on a windowsill. Each time you look at it, let it remind you how precious and beautiful you are to Jesus.*

—Sharon Hinck

# TUESDAY, JUNE 10

*"Surely I am with you always, to the very end of the age." Matthew 28:20 (NIV)*

WHEREVER YOU'RE READING THIS, STOP a moment and enjoy the quiet. The phone may be ringing, the office buzzing with coworkers, your house full of loud children. But stop where you are and listen behind all that.

Can you hear it? Maybe you can, maybe you can't. I often have a tough time hearing it through the busyness of life, but I believe it's there.

It's the hush of Jesus's Spirit. It may seem impossible, but we really can hear it no matter how loudly life shouts.

Jesus's Spirit has always hovered in a hush. Genesis 1:2 (NLT) says, "The earth was formless and empty, and darkness covered the deep waters. And the Spirit of God was hovering over the surface of the waters."

How different a crazy day affects us when we stop in the chaos to acknowledge that the Savior of the world and of our present moment hovers all around us, never leaving us alone, always covering us with His presence. What a picture that provides of His promise to be with us always, even to the end of the age.

Okay, so then what happens at the end of the age? More good news. Jesus's holy presence will still beckon His own to Him when this earth passes away: "When everything is ready, I will come and get you, so that you will always be with me where I am" (John 14:3, NLT).

If you belong to Jesus, you always have His holy hush covering you. Listen for it; you can be sure of it despite the din around you.

**FAITH STEP:** *What daily circumstances threaten to drown out the beckoning hush of Jesus's Spirit in your life? Talk to Him about it, and ask Him to sensitize your own spirit to hear His.*

—*Erin Keeley Marshall*

# WEDNESDAY, JUNE 11

---

*The mind of sinful man is death, but the mind controlled by the Spirit is life and peace,*
*[because] the sinful mind is hostile to God. Romans 8:6–7 (NIV)*

---

How would you describe the state of your mind? I'll be honest—I struggle with mine.

It easily recalls conversations with difficult people. "Remember what that woman said three years ago? Well, she probably meant such-and-such. You should have told her a thing or two!"

It also tries to convince me that I'm not good enough. It reminds me of past failures and says they determine my identity. And it sometimes insists I know better than God how to fulfill His purposes.

When my mind pulls these stunts, I respond with a prayer: "God, fill and control me with Your Holy Spirit. Drench every part of me, especially my mind. I ask this in the power of Jesus's name. Amen." I also recall Scripture verses or sing a praise song to turn my thoughts toward the Lord.

What happens? The struggle subsides, and peace prevails. That shouldn't surprise me because Scripture says that the Spirit-controlled mind is life and peace.

I've been honest with you. Now it's your turn to be honest. What's the state of your mind? What negative or inappropriate thoughts have run through it recently? Have you allowed them to linger, or have you fought the battle with the means God has provided?

Let's invite the Holy Spirit to control our minds, and we'll experience life and peace.

---

**FAITH STEP:** *Each time a negative or impure thought comes to mind, turn it immediately to prayer: "Father, thank You that Your Holy Spirit lives in me. By His power I have victory over this thought. Replace it now with truth. In Jesus's name, amen." Then recite a Scripture verse or sing a praise song to put your mind where it ought to be—focused on the Lord.*

*—Grace Fox*

# THURSDAY, JUNE 12

---

*Who will separate us from Christ's love?* Romans 8:35 (CEB)

---

"IT WOULDN'T HAVE BEEN SO bad if the kitchen weren't on fire."

The string of rapid-fire—pardon the pun—family disasters had reached comedy routine status for sheer numbers alone. Like a bad movie or a poorly written novel, the crises came so fast and furious, one on top of another, that the plot lost its believability factor. Even we who were experiencing it didn't think it sounded credible anymore.

When crises hit, especially a rash of them, overlapping one another in their race to make us miserable, we can confidently depend on grace gifts hidden among the ashes. The kindness of a friend. Generosity showing up at the door. An opportunity to tell someone how you can keep calm in the middle of a storm like that.

Romans 8:35–39 in *The Message* version reads, "Do you think anyone is going to be able to drive a wedge between us and Christ's love for us? There is no way! Not trouble, not hard times, not hatred, not hunger, not homelessness, not bullying threats, not backstabbing, not even the worst sins listed in Scripture . . . None of this fazes us because Jesus loves us . . . Nothing living or dead, angelic or demonic, today or tomorrow, high or low, thinkable or unthinkable—absolutely nothing can get between us and God's love because of the way that Jesus our Master has embraced us."

Troubles too numerous to make a believable plot for a novel? Still can't separate us from the love of Jesus!

---

FAITH STEP: *Where's the crisis not covered by the promise that nothing can drive a wedge between us and how much God loves us through His Son, Jesus? Write out that passage in your journal or on sticky notes you post all over the house. Let its truth penetrate deep and anchor your soul.*

—*Cynthia Ruchti*

# FRIDAY, JUNE 13

*Whoever is wise, let him give heed to these things; let men consider the steadfast love of the Lord. Psalm 107:43 (RSV)*

THIS PAST SUMMER WE WENT to Cayucos, a little beach town on the coast of California. The mornings are cool with fog and the afternoons stretch out before you, warm and lovely.

All we had to do was walk two blocks down the street and we were eye-to-eye with the majesty of the Pacific Ocean. The gulls swooped and soared. The dull roar of the waves crashed on the sandy shore sending the boys scurrying away from the water with shouts of laughter. It was beautiful. The gray-green water disappeared into a strip of the horizon. It continued as far as the eye could see. Its immensity was awe-inspiring.

This is what Jesus's great love for us is like. It is so vast that we cannot see it or understand it in its entirety. This is the type of love that surpasses knowledge and blows our minds. Just when we think we know the measure of His love for us, nope, it's more. It is deeper than we can fathom. Wider than we can grasp. Longer than we can imagine. Higher than we can climb.

And this is the love we get to root ourselves in. A grandiose, rich, never-ending breadth of love that Jesus has for us, the ones He loves. It doesn't get any better than that!

FAITH STEP: *Imagine you are on the beach, hearing the pounding of the waves on the shore. Now remind yourself that Jesus's love for you is wider, deeper, higher, and longer than any ocean you can picture.*

—*Susanna Foth Aughtmon*

# SATURDAY, JUNE 14

*For you know very well that the day of the Lord will come like a thief in the night.*
1 Thessalonians 5:2 (NIV)

WHEN I WENT INTO LABOR with our oldest son, I was shocked. He was due the second week of July, but in mid-June, he was ready to make an appearance. I felt certain that the pains were false labor. I was at work and continued trying to work until the pains became harder and harder . . . and every two minutes. Those were my warning signs that my baby was ready to enter the world. A trip to the doctor, and he confirmed that these were not false labor pains. My baby was coming, and I needed to get to the hospital ASAP. Less than six hours later, we had a beautiful baby boy.

Nine AM, 1:42 PM, 1:45 PM, 7:30 PM, 9:40 PM, and 11:00 PM. On April 14, 1912, the *Titanic* received six warnings concerning icebergs, the last one coming merely forty minutes before collision.

There are times in life when we receive warnings. I heeded the warnings that my baby was coming and went to the hospital. The *Titanic's* captain didn't, and the ship went down.

The Bible gives us numerous warnings about the coming of Christ (Acts 24:25; 26:27–28; 2 Corinthians 5:11; Acts 22:16). No one knows the day and time of Christ's coming, but we do know one thing: He is coming. To go through life ignoring this truth will send you on a destination that is sure to meet destruction, like that fated ship in 1912. However, to heed the truth, live your life for Christ, and set your final goal on eternity with Him, will result in a glorious miracle, much like the miracle I received on June 13, 1989, when God gave us that beautiful baby boy.

FAITH STEP: *Concentrate on the beauty of this verse: "But you, brothers and sisters, are not in darkness so that this day should surprise you like a thief. You are all children of the light and children of the day. We do not belong to the night or to the darkness"* (1 *Thessalonians 5:4–5, NIV*).

—*Renee Andrews*

# SUNDAY, JUNE 15

*Being confident of this, that he who began a good work in you will carry it on to completion until the day of Christ Jesus. Philippians 1:6 (NIV)*

MY COUSIN, BETH, AND I were talking the other day about relationships. Marriage. Friendship. Family bonds. We were laughing at how different we are from the people we love. Mostly, we were talking about how relationships require a lot from those involved. Seriously.

Beth said, "If someone were to tell me that marriage should be easy, I would tell them, you have no idea what marriage really is. It is work!"

Work. That sounds horrible. Why should a good relationship be something we have to work at? Shouldn't it flow easily out of our great abundance of love for the person? But I have found that anything that really matters requires work, dedication, and perseverance. With all of those things comes value and appreciation. What we invest in is precious to us.

Our relationship with Jesus is no different. He has invested infinitely in us. The amount of effort He unleashed in order to heal the breach between Himself and mankind is unfathomable. He left heaven to come to a broken earth and a wounded people, took the weight of our sinfulness upon Himself, endured unbelievable suffering, and stormed the gates of hell to triumph over death. That sounds an awful lot like work to me. And in return? He asks for our shattered lives…so that He can begin a good work in us. It seems that work is born out of love after all.

As for me? I am ready to roll up my sleeves and get to work.

**FAITH STEP:** *Take some time to sit in Jesus's presence. Ask Him what work He wants to do in your life at this time. Thank Him for His love and the work that He has already begun to do in your life.*

—*Susanna Foth Aughtmon*

# MONDAY, JUNE 16

*Let us fix our eyes on Jesus, the author and perfecter of our faith, who for the joy set before him endured the cross, scorning its shame, and sat down at the right hand of the throne of God.*
*Hebrews 12:2 (NIV)*

WHEN MY GRANDSON WAS SEVEN months old, I enjoyed a weeklong visit with my daughter and her family. The days were busy but in the evenings we enjoyed relaxed conversation, especially after my granddaughter went to bed and Roman was nursing. After he finished, Holly held him in her lap facing her as we talked. Roman always gazed up at her face, seeming to hang on every word even though he didn't know what she was saying. He smiled at her even when she wasn't looking at him, and chuckled whenever she laughed.

Each evening I watched Roman's face as he gazed at his mom's face. I felt mesmerized by the love reflected there, and by the sense of security he seemed to gain from looking into her eyes. When she looked at him and spoke, his face flushed with joy and his whole body wiggled. That nonverbal exchange between little Roman and his mom made me start thinking about what I miss out on when I don't keep my eyes on Jesus.

Some days my mind is focused solely on the pressures of my to-do list: household chores, bills to pay, writing deadlines, etc., etc. Other days I'm mentally consumed by worries about personal problems, relationship issues, needs of loved ones, or even world problems. This mind-set does me no good and can even damage my health. What a change in attitude when I deliberately choose to fix my eyes on Jesus, meditating on His character and His selfless love for me. Then I find the same joy, peace, and security that little Roman found gazing at the face of the one who loves and takes care of him.

FAITH STEP: *Today use mealtimes, work breaks, or other predetermined times to do a quick mental check. Ask yourself:* What do I have my eyes fixed on?

—*Dianne Neal Matthews*

# TUESDAY, JUNE 17

*So let us come boldly to the throne of our gracious God. There we will receive his mercy, and we will find grace to help us when we need it most. Hebrews 4:16 (NLT)*

I SIT ACROSS THE TABLE from a young woman. She plays with her food on the plate in front of her, pretending that she couldn't care less about our conversation. I ask her about school.

"It's fine." She shrugs.

I ask about her baby. "It must be hard being both a mom and a student."

She acts as if there aren't any problems. That her life is just great. But I know better. What I read in her eyes and hear from her mouth are two different things.

The wall she's placed around her heart is a protective armor, like a turtle's shell. Her slow steps of moving toward our relationship seem at times to be a lack of movement. Her eyes peek out, and then she pulls back in. Everything in her life has changed, and she doesn't know the steps she needs to take to finish school, to keep peace with her parents, to connect with new friends, or to be a good mom. She doesn't know how to handle the responsibility of being a parent when she's still being parented.

I've mentored teen moms for many years. It's easier for a young woman to stay inside her own shell of protection than to risk being hurt again. Yet underneath the armor is real flesh and blood, and a beating heart. There is also the smallest glimmer of hope that dares to risk one more chance.

God's Word tells us to come boldly to the throne of God. Boldness is something that is built through trust. I've worked with many young people, and I've learned that the first step to trusting God is showing them that you can be trustworthy. When they see that someone loves them, then it's possible to believe that God can love them too.

FAITH STEP: *Think of someone in your life with a protective shell. Pray for that person, and also ask God how to reach out to him or her.*

—*Tricia Goyer*

# WEDNESDAY, JUNE 18

*Oh, magnify the Lord with me, and let us exalt His name together. Psalm 34:3 (NKJV)*

HAVE YOU EVER READ ANY of those "Dear God" letters from children? Like those kids, when I was kindergarten age, I had some childish views about Jesus. I loved to play with dolls. I remember whisking away my doll in a box one day to a closet and asking Jesus to turn her into a real-life baby. I closed the door, certain that within a few hours He would grant my request. Pretty foolish, huh? Of course, Jesus's silent "no" answered my request.

At the young age of eight, I discovered who Jesus truly is, and the Son of God became my Savior and my best friend. Through the years I've grown in my relationship with Him and my understanding of Him. Still, there are foolish moments when it seems like I've never moved beyond my kindergarten views of Jesus's character. Times when, without realizing it, I put Him into a predictable box of my own selfish choosing, making Him too small.

I can't whisk away those circumstances with logical explanations. Ultimately, I conclude Jesus's ways are not my ways. And His thoughts are not my thoughts (Isaiah 55:8). But it occurred to me the other day that it's not Jesus who acts unpredictably. He is the same yesterday, today, and forever (Hebrews 13:8). He will always act "otherworldly." That's who He is.

But we, His creation, are the unpredictable ones. Instead of magnifying Him, we misunderstand His power through our own sinfulness and ignorance. And we forget temporarily Jesus's greater purpose and how all of life ends.

As A.W. Tozer once explained, magnifying Jesus is not making Him bigger, but seeing Him bigger. Much bigger.

FAITH STEP: *Take time to magnify the Lord today through praise and thanksgiving.*

*—Rebecca Barlow Jordan*

# THURSDAY, JUNE 19

*Don't love money; be satisfied with what you have. For God has said,*
*"I will never fail you. I will never abandon you." Hebrews 13:5 (NLT)*

ONE OF MY FAVORITE TELEVISION networks is HGTV, where homes and gardens are made over with a limited budget in just a few days. One of my favorite Web sites is Pinterest, where I can not only find what to make for dinner, but also the perfect Mother's Day present for my mother in less than thirty seconds. The problem with both is the more time I spend watching or clicking, the more discontent I become about what I have. Suddenly the couch that I once loved needs to be re-covered and the cabinet that was just fine before needs to be repainted.

Discontentment may seem innocent at first, but it's like a chip in the windshield. Once it starts, it spreads and grows. When we are discontent with things, it's as if we are saying, *God, You haven't provided enough.* When we look for satisfaction from other things, we are saying, *God, You aren't enough.*

Do you want true satisfaction and contentment? Do you want true heart-riches?

"The heart is rich when it is content, and it is always content when its desires are fixed on God," says Miguel Cordero-Munoz. Want a rich heart? Fix it on God. Do you want to be content? Fill your heart with His statutes. As Psalm 119:36 (NIV) says, "Turn my heart toward your statutes and not toward selfish gain."

In this life there will always be more things to obtain or transform. These things may bring us joy for a few minutes, but our greatest gain comes from the only One who will never fail us, never abandon us. The One Who never needs a makeover.

FAITH STEP: *Today when those feelings of discontentment pop up, turn to God's Word and find one thing you're thankful for.*

—*Tricia Goyer*

# FRIDAY, JUNE 20

*But we don't need to write to you about the importance of loving each other,
for God himself has taught you to love one another. 1 Thessalonians 4:9 (NLT)*

I PLAY THE PIANO AT my church. Every week we have a fellowship time during which I play, the choir sings, and everyone else moves around the sanctuary greeting one another. It's many people's favorite part of the service.

Many people are sweet to me during this time. My kids usually come up and talk to me, and others in the congregation will stop by to pat me on the back. There is one lady, Mrs. Betty, who comes up every Sunday, puts her arms around my shoulders, and says gently in my ear, "Love you, hon." Then she walks back down the aisle to her seat.

Over the years I have come to count on Mrs. Betty's hugs. They are an essential part of my church experience. If she misses a Sunday, I know it, because those are the only times she doesn't make her trip up to the piano.

I can't remember the first time Mrs. Betty visited me. At some point the idea must've occurred to her, and she started her routine. What I know is that no human told her to do it. Jesus put it in her heart. Her sensitivity to His Spirit is a continual blessing to the heart of God and to me. I look forward to how Jesus loves me through her every Sunday. Like the verse says, it's so important.

FAITH STEP: *The verse says God Himself teaches us to love one another. Pray He makes you sensitive to His Spirit that you may receive His instruction on whom and how He wants you to love today.*

—Gwen Ford Faulkenberry

# SATURDAY, JUNE 21

*As Jesus was walking beside the Sea of Galilee, he saw two brothers, Simon called Peter and his brother Andrew. They were casting a net into the lake, for they were fishermen. "Come, follow me," Jesus said, "and I will make you fishers of men." Matthew 4:18–19 (NIV)*

MY FATHER PASSED AWAY WHEN I was in my early twenties, and all these years later, I still think of him often. Some of my favorite memories are of the times he took me fishing. The unique scents of sunscreen, lake water, and gasoline from the boat's motor promised adventure. The sound of water lapping in the minnow bucket and the gentle screeing noise of a line being cast invited hours of patient silence.

Sometimes we'd troll into hidden bays of a lake, waiting for any indication that walleye or pike were nearby. Other times we'd cast toward promising stands of weeds. We'd experiment with new lures or switch up the bait we were using. We'd get up early, shiver under plastic ponchos in a cold rain, swat mosquitos, or burn under a hot sun.

Fishing involved finding the fish, attracting the fish, and having enough patience to keep trying.

When I think about Jesus's invitation to teach me to be a "fisher of men," I remember the lessons learned in those old aluminum boats with my dad. As Christians, we always want to join in Jesus's work of drawing others closer to Him. That may mean mission work in a foreign country, or chatting with a coworker who doesn't know Jesus, or nurturing faith in our children through patient repetition and faithful prayer for them. Wherever Jesus calls us to fish, we want to watch for the signs of people hungry for Him, keep experimenting with ways to effectively interest others in Him, and remember that fishing requires plenty of patience.

FAITH STEP: *Ask Jesus to guide you to a new soul to draw in to His kingdom. Tuck their name on a slip of paper in your Bible. Begin praying for that person today.*

*—Sharon Hinck*

# SUNDAY, JUNE 22

*The apostles came up and said to the Master, "Give us more faith."*
*But the Master said, "You don't need more faith. There is no 'more' or 'less' in faith.*
*If you have a bare kernel of faith, say the size of a poppy seed, you could say to this sycamore tree,*
*'Go jump in the lake' and it would do it." Luke 17:5–6 (MSG)*

*CHIA SEEDS?* AS I REREAD the recipe ingredients, flashbacks rolled: "Ch-ch-ch-Chia!" Chia seeds sprout pets and heads and trees like those old commercials sang. At least that's all I thought they were good for until I learned about this diminutive wonder. Now I'm putting them in pancakes and cookies and saying *yum* over them.

They're a nutrient storehouse, chock-full with antioxidants, protein, and Omega-3. And, when mixed with water, they turn into a gel that can replace butter or eggs in baking. All that power in a wee, small seed!

Okay, so you've heard this lesson. But have you ever asked what your sycamore tree looks like? Matthew 17:20 is a similar verse that says a small faith can move a mountain. What does your mountain look like? What miracle do you yearn for?

Most important, how do you unleash your faith's potential, no matter its size?

Even great faith is powerless if its confidence is rooted in anything imperfect. The point of these verses is not to puff up our willpower but to point up our faith to Jesus, the undefeatable Source of strength.

Take a look at who Jesus gave this lesson in faith—to those who sought Him out.

When His children take our little bit to the Savior, He charges His own power in us. *His* power is great, not ours. Don't strive to find more power in your faith; rest your faith in the Source of all power.

**FAITH STEP:** *To grow your faith, stop focusing on the size of that faith and focus instead on the size of your God.*

*—Erin Keeley Marshall*

# MONDAY, JUNE 23

---

*The hour has already come for you to wake up from your slumber, because our salvation is nearer now than when we first believed. Romans 13:11 (NIV)*

---

MY DADDY WAKES EARLY THREE mornings each week to be one of the first to arrive at the local Trade Day, where people sell odds and ends, and the phrase, "One man's junk is another man's treasure," is proven on a daily basis.

Last week, Daddy called at 6:00 AM and said, "They've got one of those Olympic things here, the thing that's leather on top, and the guys run and put their hands on it and flip." My husband is a former All-American gymnast, so even though this was a morning when he could've slept later, I quietly relayed Daddy's information. J.R. jumped out of the bed and was dressed within minutes. The news was important, and he wanted that vault (the actual term for the "Olympic thing").

J.R. was in a sound sleep, but quickly woke for important news. In the verse above, Paul said that we all should wake from our slumber and be alert for what is important. Do you ever have the urge to do something you hadn't planned during the day? Maybe you think about a friend whom you haven't talked to in a while, but you push that urge to call away. Perhaps your checkout clerk is grumpy as you buy your groceries, and you frown back instead of deciding to help their bad day with a smile. Christ said the Holy Spirit is with us, guiding us, helping us. What if those nudges through the day are His way of getting you to wake from your slumber, be alert, notice what's important, and follow through with His desires instead of our own? Why? Because every day brings us closer to the Second Coming of Christ, and He wants us to be alert and ready for His glorious arrival.

---

FAITH STEP: *Don't "sleep" through your day. Wake up, be alert, and concentrate on living for Christ.*

—*Renee Andrews*

# TUESDAY, JUNE 24

*"In this world you will have trouble. But take heart! I have overcome the world."*
*John 16:33 (NIV)*

MY HUSBAND AND I CRINGED at every red light. Our flight was scheduled to leave at 12:30; it was getting close to noon. Richard had gone in to work for several hours that morning, then come home to pick me up. The plan was to grab our bags and hop in the car. But the night before, we had taken our other car to the shop and attended a dinner. So we weren't as prepared as we'd hoped. Ten minutes from home, I discovered that I'd forgotten my driver's license.

Once we reached the airport, I rushed to the ticket counter. 12:05: too late. Fortunately, the agent booked us on a 2:45 flight. Unfortunately, with only a thirty-five-minute layover, the system refused to check our bag.

Following the agent's suggestion, Richard rolled the heavy luggage down the street to FedEx, only to find it would cost $260 to ship it. He trudged back to the airport, and we quickly stuffed a few extra things into our carry-ons; then he took the bag back to the car. Once our new flight arrived a bit late, we ran to make our connecting flight—only to learn it had been cancelled due to weather.

Some days just don't go right. Whether caused by our own shortcomings or by situations beyond our control, Jesus warned that we will have troubles during our life journey. Thank goodness He also reminded us why our struggles won't defeat us. Because Jesus overcame sin and death, I can live in victory through any trials that come my way, knowing that nothing can keep me from reaching my final destination.

FAITH STEP: *Are your troubles getting you down today? Ask Jesus to help you live like the overcomer that He intends you to be.*

*—Dianne Neal Matthews*

# WEDNESDAY, JUNE 25

*When Jesus heard it, he said to them, "Healthy people don't need a doctor, but sick people do. I didn't come to call righteous people, but sinners." Mark 2:17 (CEB)*

ON THE PHONE THE OTHER day, my friend Michelle said something I knew was write-downable. I took notes because her thought struck me as profoundly obvious and profoundly not-so-obvious.

"A hospital is a painful place for a lot of people," she said.

Hospitals are scenes of babies born, children nursed back to health, injuries repaired, cancers removed.

They're also scenes of babies dying, children who can't be nursed back to health, injuries that claim lives, and cancers that can't be removed.

The pain to which my friend referred isn't all related to surgical scars and IV sites and learning to walk again. Hospitals are places where families hear life-altering news and where they say their final good-byes.

One of the things Jesus said that some of us find curious is His statement in Mark 2:17. When some of the legalists who considered themselves religious questioned why Jesus would eat with sinners and swindlers, He said, "Healthy people don't need a doctor *(or a hospital)*, but sick people do."

Asked the same question today, He might answer, "I don't need to convince people who already believe in Me that I can be trusted. I'm here for the spiritually sick, for those who don't yet know Me. And they need a lot of TLC. They're in pain, whether they realize it or not, and I hold the stethoscope, the defibrillator, and the scalpel."

FAITH STEP: *When you pray for those in the hospital, do you pray for the family members who also need mending? For the spiritually sick? For those whose greatest pain isn't from their scars but from the consequences of their actions? Jesus did.*

—*Cynthia Ruchti*

# THURSDAY, JUNE 26

*Let the word of Christ richly dwell within you, with all wisdom teaching and admonishing one another with psalms and hymns and spiritual songs, singing with thankfulness in your hearts to God. Colossians 3:16 (NAS)*

As I STARTED BREAKFAST THIS morning, I stopped to put on a CD. I've always loved to listen to music when cooking. In fact, I enjoy music any time. I started singing the words of a familiar song along with the artist as I stirred the eggs.

"How come we rarely forget the words to songs?" I asked my husband. I've often thought it strange—and unfair—that as we age, our memories naturally begin to fade. *We know those people! We should remember those things!* we try to convince ourselves.

Complicated memory techniques never worked for me. But music? I can remember words set to melody. Maybe Paul knew that secret too. He encouraged Christians to let Jesus's words "richly dwell within you." How? Through "psalms and hymns and spiritual songs." The psalmist David wrote many of the psalms-songs as praise music as he played on his harp. He remembered those "songs in the night" during dark times (Psalm 77:6).

I remember my own "songs in the night" and the comforting words of familiar "spiritual" songs during times like the death of my parents. And I love to create simple tunes and match them with a psalm of praise, singing them back to the Lord in thanksgiving. He loves our praise!

I'm still not sure why the combination of words and notes stick when other things don't. Maybe it's Jesus's way of helping us remember His words and His faithfulness. Whatever the reason, I am confident He created music both for our benefit—and His.

FAITH STEP: *What are your favorite psalms and spiritual songs? Try memorizing a verse of thanks in Psalms this week by setting it to music, using a simple or familiar tune.*

*—Rebecca Barlow Jordan*

# FRIDAY, JUNE 27

---

*Therefore encourage one other and build each other up.* 1 Thessalonians 5:11 (NIV)

---

EVERYONE NEEDS ENCOURAGEMENT. THANK HEAVEN for people who provide it. Ziba is a prime example.

We meet Ziba when David flees from Absalom's attempt to overthrow his kingship. David is emotionally and physically spent. He weeps as he climbs the Mount of Olives. He passes the summit, and there awaits Ziba—with a string of donkeys laden with food and wine.

"What's this?" David asks.

"The donkeys are for the king's household to ride on, the bread and fruit are for the men to eat, and the wine is to refresh those who become exhausted in the desert," Ziba replies (2 Samuel 16:1–4).

Can you feel David's burden lift?

I recall the day someone gifted our family with groceries during a financial crisis. Their kindness relieved my worries about feeding my family, reminded me that God had not abandoned us, and enabled me to persevere in the ministry to which He'd called us.

Busy lifestyles make it easy to overlook other people's needs. But let's embrace God's command to "encourage one another and build each other up." Let's ask God to make us aware of who needs a hug, a prayer, or a listening ear. Who needs groceries, a gas gift card, computer assistance, or child care?

The impact of encouragement, offered even in a small way, cannot be overstated. Recognize its value and become an encourager like Ziba.

---

FAITH STEP: *Name someone who needs encouragement today. Identify an action you can take to provide that encouragement, and then do it.*

—*Grace Fox*

# SATURDAY, JUNE 28

*Jesus answered, "Everyone who drinks this water will be thirsty again, but whoever drinks the water I give them will never thirst. Indeed, the water I give them will become in them a spring of water welling up to eternal life." John 4:13–14 (NIV)*

I PUSHED UP THE PLASTIC airplane shade and looked out the window. My husband and I were flying over Colorado on our way to visit our son. We needed this getaway. Pressures of life had been distracting me and crowding out my worship and devotional life, leading to a perspective on life full of discouragement.

My friend Patti is from Colorado, and she'd mentioned a recent drought affecting the state, but until I saw the land from the plane, her words hadn't made an impact. Acre after acre of dry brown earth stretched beneath us. Most telling of all, I could make out winding riverbeds—bone dry.

I could identify with the bleak, thirsty landscape. Once, those rivers and streams brought life to the land. But without rainfall or snowmelt, soon they had nothing to give. Without regular time with Jesus, my soul is quick to shrivel like those riverbeds. Spiritual drought sneaks up on me. One busy day leads to another, and I don't realize how long it's been since I opened my soul to the River of Life. Too many days slip past without His healing water raining into my life.

As our plane descended toward the runway, I prayed for the area. One good rain would bring new life to the rivers and the land around it. Plants could grow again. I also confessed the dusty, barren condition of my heart and asked Jesus to pour into my life.

I'm so glad I don't have to wait for whims of weather to ease that sort of drought.

FAITH STEP: *How is your spiritual landscape looking today? While you water a house-plant or a lawn today, ask Jesus for His water of life.*

—*Sharon Hinck*

# SUNDAY, JUNE 29

*Above all, keep loving one another earnestly, since love covers a multitude of sins. 1 Peter 4:8 (ESV)*

MY TWO OLDEST KIDS ARE two years apart. They are both overachievers, strong-willed, and competitive. I have tried to teach them how important it is for them to get along. Like my mother before me, I preach the gospel of family and how we are there for one another; we are each other's best friends. Sometimes I get discouraged when it seems like all they do is fuss.

It had been one of those weeks. Grace was especially on edge, and Harper was especially aggravating. Friday morning before school there was a scuffle over sink usage in the bathroom. Breakfast brought a competition over who had the best grades in school, and on the way out of the house Harper stole Grace's hair bow, threatening to ruin the masterpiece she'd carefully curled and styled. "*Harrrpppperrrrrrrrrrr!*" was the last word I heard as they piled into the Suburban with my sister-in-law and her kids. Turning back inside the house, I saw Grace's lunch box sitting on the table. I placed it in the fridge with a sigh.

"Lord, will they ever learn what it means to truly love one another?"

That afternoon, I asked Grace what the cafeteria served that day.

"I don't know. When he saw I forgot my lunch, Harper gave me his."

Harper raised his eyebrows at me, blue-green eyes shining. "They served chicken nuggets." It was as if a halo had suddenly appeared above his head.

"Really?"

"Pretty sweet, huh." Grace nudged him on the shoulder. "My knight in shining armor."

It's true what the Bible says about love covering a multitude of wrongs. We're still working on getting that multitude down to a smaller number, but I believe love is winning out.

**FAITH STEP:** *To whom do you need to show the fervent love of Jesus today?*

—*Gwen Ford Faulkenberry*

# MONDAY, JUNE 30

---

*Do you not know that your body is a temple of the Holy Spirit, who is in you, whom you have received from God? You are not your own; you were bought at a price. Therefore honor God with your body. 1 Corinthians 6:19–20 (NIV)*

---

MY DAUGHTER KIM IS STUDYING to earn her university degree in kinesiology. She explains the marvels of the human body using big words I don't understand, and then she uses simple terms to remind me to care for myself: "Drink more water, Mom. And remember to stretch. Stretches are important."

Kim's right. I have only one body, and I must treat it well. Regular exercise, a nutritious diet, sufficient rest, and annual checkups are important elements of maintaining good health.

I know this is true, but a busy lifestyle makes it easy to slack off. Know what I'm talkin' about? It's easy to wake in the morning and jump into the day's responsibilities, figuring I'll have time for exercise later. Trouble is, that rarely happens.

Our bodies deserve respect. Medical and fitness experts say this is true. So does Scripture. God purchased us through the death and resurrection of Jesus Christ, and, as believers, we're the temple of the Holy Spirit. We're to honor Him by caring for the temple—our body—and treating it with respect.

In context, 1 Corinthians 6:19–20 urges us to flee sexual immorality, saying this behavior is a sin against our own body. But what about habitually consuming unhealthy snacks or drinks? What about forgoing a brisk walk in lieu of answering e-mails, or intentionally staying up too late night after night?

Our bodies belong to God, and caring for them is our responsibility. Let's fulfill it well so we can serve Him effectively for a long, long time.

---

**FAITH STEP:** *Identify a positive health-related change you'd like to make. Thank God that He'll give you the strength to make this change. Ask Him to give you an accountability partner.*

*—Grace Fox*

# TUESDAY, JULY 1

*A life devoted to things is a dead life, a stump; a God-shaped life is a flourishing tree.*
Proverbs 11:28 (MSG)

HOARDERS—TRUE HOARDERS, AS OPPOSED TO those of us with one un-openable closet or a spare room that could use attention—are emotionally incapable of throwing anything away. Anything. Their homes are piled to the ceiling, wall-to-wall, with excess or what others would consider worthless things.

On the TV show *Hoarders*, cameras zoom in on a living room with boxes piled high, barely a foot-wide path through the room to the one chair that's usable for sitting. Every inch of the kitchen counters is covered, stacked—unwashed dishes, years-old takeout boxes, half-used cans of what was once food, and cockroach carcasses. The teen daughter walks a six-inch-wide plank to get over the piles of clothes from her bedroom door to her bed. On the bed are four sleeping dogs and a six-inch space of tangled blankets for the girl.

Those of us who don't fight pathological hoarding may still have hoarding issues. We hang on to many useless or even diseased things—grudges, distressing memories, injustices…We collect all the wrong things and let them pile up until they become tripping hazards, health hazards, spiritual dangers. Or we focus on accumulating good pursuits that become spiritually distracting.

Matthew 6:20–21 (NIV) shows His heart on the matter: "Store up for yourselves treasures in heaven, where moth and rust do not destroy, and where thieves do not break in and steal. For where your treasure is, there your heart will be also."

Jesus doesn't condemn hoarding. He encourages it, as long as it's the right things we're accumulating.

FAITH STEP: *How intentional are you about keeping your earthly storehouses tidy and your heavenly storehouses packed to the rafters? Does Jesus consider you a healthy hoarder?*

—*Cynthia Ruchti*

# WEDNESDAY, JULY 2

*Trust in the Lord with all your heart and lean not on your own understanding; in all your ways acknowledge him, and he will make your paths straight. Proverbs 3:5–6 (NIV)*

THIS SUMMER WE HAD PLANS. For jobs, vacation, and writing. And in the last couple of weeks, it's been like watching a carefully rolled ball of twine unfurl. The summer has come unraveled.

Once again life has thrown us for a loop. Things are nebulous and undecided at best. I find myself thinking things like, *God is not so concerned about us.* And, *We are on our own.* And, *What in the world are we going to do?*

I am a girl who likes to plan…and more than once in the last couple of weeks, I have found myself in tears. Disappointed. Discouraged. Tired. I have thought to myself…maybe this is a test. Maybe if I hang in there and trust God, everything will right itself and be better than I imagined.

Maybe. But here is the thing. We just don't know. And I have been thinking this thought: *Who we are is often defined by our greatest disappointments.* Who are we when we are faced with hardship or trials or summer plans gone awry? Who are we when the things we have banked on are no longer bankable? Are we frantic and wounded, doubtful and anxious…or do we hold firm to what we know to be true?

That Jesus in all of His goodness and mercy and grace, is who He says He is. Father. Provider. Healer. Savior. Friend. And we can remember that above all else, that He is the One we can always bank on.

FAITH STEP: *Write down on a piece of paper, a current situation that has you confused or troubled. Then write next to it: "Jesus is trustworthy. I know that He will see me through this situation." Place it in your pocket and read it throughout the day, each time you start to worry.*

—Susanna Foth Aughtmon

# THURSDAY, JULY 3

---

*But Peter said, "I have no silver and gold, but what I do have I give to you. In the name of Jesus Christ of Nazareth, rise up and walk!" Acts 3:6 (ESV)*

---

THE MAN HAD BEEN LAME from birth. Each day his friends carried him to one of the gates leading into the Temple so he could ask for alms from those going in, just like so many other beggars. Peter and John didn't have any money with them to give him. They knew the man needed something greater than silver or gold anyway. Invoking the name of Jesus Christ, Peter commanded the beggar to get up and walk.

As Peter helped him to his feet, the lame man felt strength surge into his feet and ankles. He began running, leaping, and praising God. Instead of a few coins, this beggar had received something far greater: salvation for his soul and healing for his body through the power of Jesus.

I often feel overwhelmed by the needs around me. I wish I could financially support every worthwhile ministry I read about, and sponsor each hungry child I see in the ads. I think about how great it would be to have the ability to help every needy person holding a sign by the side of the street. Peter's words remind me that although I can't support every cause or solve everyone's problems, I can give those around me a touch of Christ and His healing power.

It's important for me to meet the material needs of others when I have the resources to do so and Jesus calls me to help. But every day people cross my path who need something more. An encouraging word or a loving touch. A few moments of conversation. Or maybe they need to hear the message that Jesus loves them enough to die for them. Those are all things I have with me at any given moment, ready to give away to anyone I meet.

---

FAITH STEP: *Today watch for any opportunity to share Jesus with the people who cross your path.*

—*Dianne Neal Matthews*

# FRIDAY, JULY 4

*Bless your enemies; no cursing under your breath. Laugh with your happy friends when they're happy; share tears when they're down. Get along with each other; don't be stuck-up. Make friends with nobodies; don't be the great somebody. Romans 12:14–16 (MSG)*

"LIFE, LIBERTY, AND THE PURSUIT of happiness" is a well-known phrase from the United States Declaration of Independence. These are considered the unalienable rights our government protects for us. People want to be happy, and they seek it with everything in them, but the truth is that most of the time they don't do a very good job. They put themselves first and wonder why people don't love them. They purchase items for themselves, only to discover it's never enough.

When we bless our enemies, we place our troubles into God's hands. We turn over the people and the problems to Him to take care of. And that burden is lifted. When we laugh with our friends—and cry with them—bonds are created. We have a history together. We have people to turn to when we need someone to laugh with and cry with.

My husband, John, and I purposefully chose to attend a church with people from all sorts of economic and ethnic backgrounds. One week at church we sat next to a woman who was clearly homeless. My heart ached for her, and with each whiff of her odor I sent up another prayer for her. John and I are friends with people whom I'd be scared to meet on the street, but that was before I really knew them. Happiness is realizing that we're all on God's path, and we can walk toward Him together.

When you step out of yourself, you will find true happiness. God knows what works. He knows what will bring true joy and independence to your soul.

**FAITH STEP:** *What does life, liberty, and the pursuit of happiness mean to you in your Christian walk? Write out your own declaration of following God in this pursuit.*

—*Tricia Goyer*

# SATURDAY, JULY 5

*Several days later Felix came with his wife Drusilla, who was a Jewess. He sent for Paul and listened to him as he spoke about faith in Christ Jesus. As Paul discoursed on righteousness, self-control, and the judgment to come, Felix was afraid and said, "That's enough for now! You may leave. When I find it convenient, I will send for you." Acts 24:24–25 (NIV)*

CONVENIENT. FELIX WANTED TO HEAR about Jesus when it was convenient. Those words gave me a cold chill and also convicted me. How often have I put my convenience before Jesus?

I'm so grateful that Jesus isn't convenient.

Grace—free and undeserved—isn't convenient when I've been striving to earn God's favor in my own power.

Surrendering to His Lordship isn't convenient when I'm trying to control everything and everyone around me.

A heart of praise and worship isn't convenient when I'm savoring a time of venting and complaining.

I can choose my pitiful and false convenience, or I can let Jesus gloriously interrupt my life, my thoughts, and my heart.

Poor Felix. When he heard about faith in Christ Jesus, he sensed a major shakeup to the status quo. He gave in to his fear and pushed the truth away. I wonder if he ever found a more convenient time to give Jesus room in his life.

**FAITH STEP:** *Be honest. When has being a follower of Christ led to inconvenience for you? Write about it in your journal. Celebrate the places He has interrupted, shaken up, and changed your life.*

—*Sharon Hinck*

# SUNDAY, JULY 6

---

*Lo, I am with you alway, even unto the end of the world. Matthew 28:20 (KJV)*

---

"I AM GONNA HAVE MY daddy for about three more months."

The text from my friend Sheila entered my heart, weighing it down like lead as I absorbed its meaning. Her father had undergone many tests while we waited for answers, and now the outcome was exactly what we feared: the worst.

How do you respond to something like that? Every word I thought to write back seemed hollow. Instead, my impulse was to go, wrap my arms around my friend, and cry with her. We'd do a lot of that in the coming days.

What do you do when your world falls apart? In those moments when the abyss of darkness opens up? To whom do you go? Where do you look for comfort, for meaning, for hope?

Oswald Chambers writes, "Seeing is never believing: we interpret what we see in light of what we believe."

I saw this principle at work in Sheila as she walked through the valley of her father's death. She grieved, yes. But rather than giving in to despair, she chose to interpret her father's passing in light of her faith. Jesus was with her to the end of the age. Nothing—not even the death of her loved one—could separate her from His love. And she would see her father again in heaven.

---

**FAITH STEP:** *Whatever situation you're facing, Jesus is there. Let Him write it on your heart: I am with you always, even through* _____.
*(FILL IN THE BLANK.)*

—*Gwen Ford Faulkenberry*

# MONDAY, JULY 7

---

*But when he saw the wind, he was afraid and, beginning to sink, cried out, "Lord, save me!" Immediately Jesus reached out his hand and caught him. "You of little faith," he said, "why did you doubt?" And when they climbed into the boat, the wind died down. Matthew 14:30–32 (NIV)*

---

"MAMA, IS *DORA* ON?" CALIANNE followed me into the family room.

"I doubt it, hon."

"Why do you doubt it?"

"Well, *Dora* usually isn't on this time of day."

Confusion filled her face. "Can you undoubt it?"

I love that. As if a little "undoubt" can change reality.

Actually, Jesus's reality says that our undoubt, also known as trust, can make a huge difference. His power unleashed through Peter's belief allowed Peter to walk on water. As soon as doubt set in Peter's mind, though, down Peter went. Jesus still saved him by reaching out to him at Peter's moment of need, but we'll never know how far Peter could have gone if his mind and heart had only latched on relentlessly to the Lord of undoubt.

James, Jesus's brother, obviously learned about the power of undoubt. Here's what he had to say: "But when you ask, you must believe and not doubt, because the one who doubts is like a wave of the sea, blown and tossed by the wind" (James 1:6 NIV).

The word *undoubt* sounds backward, just as trusting in the unseen can sound a little off. Yet, when we get to know whom we're relying on, undoubt becomes simplified.

Take a step of undoubt today, focusing on your Savior, Who promises to walk with you through the impossible.

---

FAITH STEP: *Read John 20:27. Whatever situation is causing you to question Jesus's faithfulness, think of Thomas and Peter and know that Jesus is telling you to stop doubting and believe too.*

—*Erin Keeley Marshall*

# TUESDAY, JULY 8

*The right words will be there. The Holy Spirit will give you the right words when the time comes.*
*Luke 12:12 (MSG)*

FIVE-YEAR-OLD ADELAIDE AND I WERE reading one of her favorite books, *Pinkalicious*. When I mispronounced things on several of the pages, Adelaide looked up at me from where she was nestled in my lap.

"You don't have any words today, do you, Mommy?"

*If only she knew.* Secretly stressed out of my mind, I was way behind on an important deadline. Usually writing flows out of me like water from a faucet, but this time the words were barely trickling. I'd begun to question whether the faucet may have been shut off by an unseen hand. Maybe I was losing it!

The fact is, of course, I never really had "it." The ability to write or do anything else is a gift of His grace, not something we control by our own power. *It* is "not by might, nor by power, but by my Spirit, says the Lord" in Zechariah 4:6.

I didn't intentionally take the gift of words or the opportunity to use them for granted. And I don't believe God was punishing me by turning down the faucet for a season before He let it run free again. However, He did use the experience to remind me of where—and Who—the well is. And, to use a word that's not a word, it *ain't* me.

FAITH STEP: *In what areas of your life do you need to admit you are lacking? Confess those to Jesus, then tap in to His Spirit for whatever you need. He is the fountain of living water that never will run dry.*

—*Gwen Ford Faulkenberry*

# WEDNESDAY, JULY 9

*For every house is built by someone, but God is the builder of everything. "Moses was faithful as a servant in all God's house," bearing witness to what would be spoken by God in the future. But Christ is faithful as the Son over God's house. And we are his house, if indeed we hold firmly to our confidence and the hope in which we glory. Hebrews 3:4–6 (NIV)*

A HUGE CRASH SHOOK THE house. I froze in the laundry room and looked up at the basement ceiling, wondering if it would rain down on my head. My husband was on the main floor beginning a complete remodel of our kitchen. The long back wall had been built with bricks, and when he tackled it, the bricks crashed down in one huge piece.

Each home we've lived in has begun as a "fixer-upper," and the experience has given me an appreciation for the work of a builder. A great deal of thought, planning, love, and perseverance goes into creating a new kitchen, or adding on a patio, or finishing a basement.

Since I know what we put in to the work of building, it reassures me that Jesus is putting even more care and effort into building my life, building the household of faith, and building all of human history. And unlike the projects my husband and I have tackled, Jesus will complete His work on schedule, and the budget has already been paid with the price of His holy, precious blood.

**FAITH STEP:** *Look at several different buildings today, and think about the work that went into forming them. Thank Jesus for being the builder of your life.*

—*Sharon Hinck*

# THURSDAY, JULY 10

*I pondered the direction of my life, and I turned to follow your statutes. I will hurry, without lingering, to obey your commands. Psalm 119:59–60 (NLT)*

THE MORNING DIDN'T GO AS planned. I dashed outside, headed for an eye appointment with no time to spare. To my dismay, a van with a flat tire blocked our carport.

The van's owner strolled from her apartment. "You can get out," she said. "No problem."

Her casual approach irked me. Couldn't she see I was in a hurry?

I started the engine and inched forward until it appeared I'd take the carport's support post with me. "No, I can't," I said. I backed the car into its original position.

"Go, go," she insisted.

"No," I said. "I'll just cancel my appointment." Afraid of being charged for a no-show, I blew past her and ran inside for my phone.

I felt less frazzled after rescheduling, but I also felt convicted about my attitude. Psalm 119:59–60 came to mind. The words compelled me to ponder my attitude, turn to follow Scripture's command to respect others, and hurry to obey it by issuing an immediate apology.

How might these Scriptures apply to your life? What direction are you headed with your marriage? Your response to your kids when they try your patience? Your thought life? Your conversation with your friends?

Ponder the direction you're headed with your words, thoughts, and actions today. If you're not walking as Jesus walked, then turn to follow His commands. Do it without lingering.

**FAITH STEP:** *Write Psalm 119:59–60 on a recipe card and post it where you'll see it often. Doing so will provide a constant reminder of the need to walk as Jesus did.*

*—Grace Fox*

# FRIDAY, JULY 11

*All this is from God, who reconciled us to himself through Christ and gave us the ministry of reconciliation: that God was reconciling the world to himself in Christ, not counting people's sins against them. And he has committed to us the message of reconciliation.*
*2 Corinthians 5:18–19 (NIV)*

I AM TERRIBLE WITH PLANTS. I do not have a green thumb but a black one, and I kill almost everything I try to grow.

Now's the time for my confession. I am not like those peace lily plants. Sometimes I have a difficult time forgiving. You could say I hold a grudge, even nurture it at times. I forgive more easily if I'm the one who's been wronged, but mess with my children, and I don't find anything easy about it.

When my oldest son was in the six-year-old pee-wee football league, he weighed in at forty-six pounds. The largest player weighed in at ninety-two pounds. I remember, because it was at hearing that difference that I began to rethink allowing our son to play. But he wanted to so badly that we let him continue playing. Then to let the bigger kids practice their tackling, the coach put them up against the smaller ones. And that large boy knocked our son to the ground so hard I didn't know whether he would get up. I've forgotten many of the boys' coaches' names over the years, but I'll never forget that one. Nor will I forget the name of the child who did the tackling. I still have a hard time even typing the story out, because it upset me so badly.

But Christ tells me to forgive, *commands* it, and therefore, I am striving to follow that command. I pray for His help and know that He listens. And it's amazing how I feel myself perk up like that plant when I slowly but surely find my way to forgive. By the way, that football league established teams based on weight after that year. Maybe they saw my look of disapproval from the stands.

FAITH STEP: *Buy a peace lily plant. When it forgives you, remember you should forgive too.*

—*Renee Andrews*

# SATURDAY, JULY 12

*Do everything without grumbling or arguing, so that you may become blameless and pure,*
*"children of God without fault in a warped and crooked generation." Then you will shine among*
*them like stars in the sky as you hold firmly to the word of life. Philippians 2:14–16 (NIV)*

REALLY, JESUS, NOT ONE LITTLE gripe? I thought the goal is to grow in maturity, not achieve it every moment everywhere. Are we never allowed to have any negative ideas or behaviors?

Rest assured, we have an understanding Savior who knows our weaknesses and the failings of this world that leave us feeling not very shiny like stars, as the verse says. I think the point of today's verse is once again to encourage us to look toward Him instead of focusing on the negativity. He knows that this battle for our focus is beyond our abilities many times. So, ever true to Himself and to us, He is ready to help. Look at what the following verses say about His Spirit's readiness to help us:

The moment we get tired in the waiting, God's Spirit is right alongside helping us along. If we don't know how or what to pray, it doesn't matter. He does our praying in and for us, making prayer out of our wordless sighs, our aching groans. . . . That's why we can be so sure that every detail in our lives of love for God is worked into something good" (Romans 8:26–28, MSG).

Instead of condemning us for grumbling, Jesus takes the more positive approach of *freeing us* from a complaining heart. When we entrust our troubles to Him, He can lift our spirits above the desire to gripe. But make no mistake, He does want us to take Him up on that better offer.

Shine without grumbling as you hold firmly to Him.

FAITH STEP: *Put a note on your bathroom mirror that says "Freedom!" Each morning be reminded to enjoy Jesus's freedom from a complaining spirit.*

—*Erin Keeley Marshall*

# SUNDAY, JULY 13

*"I brought glory to you here on earth by doing everything you told me to do." John 17:4* (NLT)

ARCHERY WAS A FAVORITE ACTIVITY at the Christian camp where my family worked. Campers knew the goal was to hit the bull's-eye on the target. Those who listened to their instructors and practiced diligently often achieved the goal before the week ended. Those who lacked patience and focus failed.

Archery provides a great parallel to the Christian life. Our bull's-eye, as believers, is to accomplish our life's purpose and thereby bring God glory as Jesus Christ did.

Sadly, some believers miss the target altogether by viewing their Christian faith as fire insurance. They want a ticket to heaven but they're not interested in being Christ's disciples on earth.

Others begin their faith journey with good intentions but allow distractions to blur their focus. Sometimes those distractions are spiritual activities—serving Jesus requires so much energy that we no longer have time to develop friendship with Him.

The secret to hitting our spiritual bull's-eye—accomplishing everything God's given us to do—is to keep our relationship with Christ our foremost priority.

"Remain in me, and I will remain in you," Jesus said (John 15:4, NLT). Remaining in Christ requires intentionality. We spend time regularly with Him, read His Word, obey, pray, and practice His presence. Knowing Him intimately enables us to discern what He wants us to do and then do it.

Jesus said, "I brought glory to You here on earth by doing everything You told me to do." He hit the bull's-eye. Let this be true of us too.

**FAITH STEP:** *Draw a picture of an archery target on a recipe card. Write "John 17:4" on the bull's-eye. Use it as a bookmark for this book.*

*—Grace Fox*

# MONDAY, JULY 14

---

*Jesus answered, "It is written: 'Man does not live on bread alone, but on every word that comes from the mouth of God.'" Matthew 4:4 (NIV)*

---

I OPENED MY LAPTOP AND skimmed through the Twitter feed. My eyes caught on occasional posts by friends, but I didn't have time to read everything. I opened my e-mails. I subscribe to several writing groups, so dozens of messages filled my inbox. I surfed through the subject lines, stopping only when I noticed a topic I was interested in. Later that evening, my husband and I watched a home remodeling show. Because of our recording device, we were able to forward quickly through commercials, but also forwarded through repetitive or boring parts of the show. It took about ten minutes to watch a thirty-minute show.

My habit of skimming has trickled into other areas, as well. Today when I sat down to do the homework for a small group Bible study, I raced through the lesson, glanced briefly at the verses in my Bible, and checked that off as another task accomplished.

Yet when Jesus confronted temptation, He made a declaration that makes me want to slow down. He proclaimed the importance of every word that comes from the mouth of God. When God speaks to us in His Word, each truth is valuable—the warm and fuzzy passages, the difficult and confusing verses, and even the stories that seem so familiar we think we can rush past because they have nothing new to teach us.

---

FAITH STEP: *Read a section of Scripture slowly, drawing sustenance from every word.*

*—Sharon Hinck*

# TUESDAY, JULY 15

---

*Remember Jesus Christ, who was raised from the dead, who is from the family of David.*
*This is the Good News.* 2 Timothy 2:8 (NCV)

---

I WAS IN THE DENTIST's office the other day, along with two of my children. We were all assigned to separate rooms, waiting for our teeth to be cleaned. As I walked down the hall to check on Grace and Harper, I noticed there were flat-screen televisions on the walls in every room. They were all tuned in to news stations like CNN, Fox News, and MSNBC.

On every screen was a story of bad news. Bombings in Syria, death in Afghanistan, economic distress across Europe and the United States. The dentist agreed with my observation and commented, "Almost makes you depressed, just looking at it."

Sometimes life can feel akin to the daily news. It's no fun receiving a mailbox full of bills. And just glancing through the prayer list at my church, I'm reminded of how many people I know who are battling disease or grieving a loss.

How are we to keep from being overcome by the bad news that surrounds us? Timothy offers this advice: "Remember Jesus." Remember that He was raised from the dead. Remember that He is with us, and through Him we have resurrection life. That's the good news we need to remember no matter what bad news comes our way.

---

**FAITH STEP:** *Are you discouraged by bad news today? Take heart. Remember that Jesus has overcome the world.*

*—Gwen Ford Faulkenberry*

# WEDNESDAY, JULY 16

*Your word I have treasured in my heart, that I may not sin against You. Psalm 119:11* (NAS)

I HAVE A VIVID MEMORY of perching on a metal chair on a hot July night during vacation Bible school, chanting, "Without faith it is impossible to please God. Hebrews 11:1." I got a sticker for my memorization skills.

At the time, I had no idea I was tucking away Scripture for further use. I was just really into stickers. But I have found through the years that Scriptures I memorized in my early years have come back to me during times of prayer or stress or in line at the grocery store. Scriptures like, "Trust in the Lord with all your heart, and lean not on your own understanding; in all your ways acknowledge Him, and He shall direct your paths. Proverbs 3:5–6," and of course, "For God so loved the world, that he gave his only begotten Son, that whosoever believeth in him should not perish, but have everlasting life. John 3:16," We loved the King James Version back in the day.

But the King's English aside, the truths of these verses have shaped me. They have marinated all these long years in the corners of my memory, and they remind me on a regular basis of who Jesus is and Who He created me to be. "Thou shalt not covet" pops into my head every time I pick up a decorating magazine. "Be ye kind one to another" surfaces each time my boys start swinging at each other. "Shout to the Lord all the earth" comes to my mind as I sit in church surrounded by the praises of His kids.

Sometimes I forget that Scripture is alive. That its words are transformative and powerful. I think it might be time to learn some new verses. Even if I don't get a sticker.

FAITH STEP: *Pick a favorite Scripture and put it up on your fridge. Each time you see it, say it out loud. Once you have memorized it, put up a new one.*

—*Susanna Foth Aughtmon*

# THURSDAY, JULY 17

---

*I pray that out of his glorious riches he may strengthen you with power through his Spirit in your inner being, so that Christ may dwell in your hearts through faith. Ephesians 3:16–17 (NIV)*

---

A WORD HEARD OFTEN IN my businesswomen's circles is *empowerment*. The source of that empowerment varies based on one's personal beliefs.

Some feel it comes from having a good education. Others believe it's from a goddess within oneself. Some think it comes from discovering one's life purpose as revealed in our fingerprints. Others think the body's energy currents influence empowerment levels. But God's Word says otherwise.

Scripture teaches that true empowerment flows from the Holy Spirit's presence in the lives of those who have trusted Jesus Christ for salvation. He's our indwelling Counselor, Teacher, Comforter, and the strongest spiritual force ever.

Jesus said, "I will ask the Father, and he will give you another Counselor to be with you forever—the Spirit of truth. The world cannot accept him, because it neither sees him nor knows him. But you know him, for he lives with you and will be in you" (John 14:16–17, NIV).

Imagine! The Holy Spirit's power raised Christ from the dead, and this power lives in us. He enables us to parent our children well, understand our spouses, and forgive our offenders. He gives us everything we need to teach a Bible study, make wise work-related decisions, speak truth to a friend who's making foolish choices, break bad habits, and share our testimony with an unbelieving coworker. We can say no to temptation and live as more than conquerors.

We, of all people, know what it means to be empowered. Let's live as though we believe it.

---

FAITH STEP: *For what do you need empowerment today? Pray, "Father, I need Your power for _____. Please fill me to overflowing. Thank You in advance. Amen."*

—*Grace Fox*

# FRIDAY, JULY 18

*He treated us as equals, and so made us equals. Through him we both share the same Spirit and have equal access to the Father. Ephesians 2:17–18 (MSG)*

THROUGHOUT OUR ADULT LIFE (AND probably growing up), my mom must have made "treating kids equally" the eleventh commandment—at least with gift-giving. I never felt like she preferred one child over the other.

Evidently I "caught" her habit, only my fairness policy with my own children bordered on the ridiculous. By the time my little equaling game finished, I had spent much more than I ever intended. For the most part, my motive was harmless. I just wanted the girls to know I loved them both equally.

Apparently Jacob and Rebekah could have used some of that philosophy, because they made no attempt to treat their children equally (Genesis 25:28). In fact, Rebekah resorted to deceit in order to reverse her husband's gift of blessing to their older son, Esau. She clearly wanted Jacob to receive that gift (Genesis 27:1–40).

In the end, Rebekah's actions resulted in a painful sibling rivalry that lasted for years. I've often wondered how things could have changed if Rebekah had only listened to God's words at childbirth (Genesis 25:23).

My over-the-top attempts of equal treatment didn't really make much difference. In reality, Jesus is the only One Who loves and treats all His children the same. In His plan, there's no room for preferential treatment and no reason ever for jealousy among His children. He's the perfect parent. As God's children, we would all benefit by simply listening to His words.

FAITH STEP: *If you have children, let them know this week that you—and Jesus—love them equally. If you don't have kids, ask Jesus to show you those this week who need to know how much Jesus loves them.*

*—Rebecca Barlow Jordan*

# SATURDAY, JULY 19

*The faithful love of the Lord never ends! His mercies never cease. Great is his faithfulness; his mercies begin afresh each morning. Lamentations 3:22–23 (NLT)*

*DEAR LORD, SO FAR I'VE done all right. I haven't gossiped, haven't lost my temper, haven't been greedy, grumpy, nasty, selfish, or overindulgent. I'm really glad about that. But in a few minutes, God, I'm going to get out of bed. And from then on, I'm going to need a lot more help.*

I've seen that humorous prayer on plaques and on Web sites. It always reminds me of a quote spoken by Anne Shirley in a L.M. Montgomery book: "Isn't it nice to think that tomorrow is a new day with no mistakes in it yet?" I can really relate to both messages. I start each new day with only the best of intentions. To use my time wisely. To be a blessing to those who cross my path. To be the loving, godly person Jesus wants me to be. But it doesn't take long for that mistake-free day to be marred by a blunder, a bad habit, an unkind thought, or a word that I wish I could take back.

That's why I'm so thankful that Jesus is the Lord of second chances. Just as fresh manna rained down each morning for the Israelites as they wandered in the wilderness, Jesus offers me a fresh supply of love, grace, and mercy each day. And boy, do I need an outpouring of those things every single day!

Each morning dawns with new opportunities to honor and obey Jesus and to reflect His character to others as we go about our day. Since we're imperfect human beings, each day also brings the chance to experience His mercy and forgiveness anew. We may not know what challenges the day will bring, but we can trust Him to supply whatever we need to make a fresh start with each dawn.

**FAITH STEP:** *In what ways do you need a fresh start today? Ask Jesus to supply whatever you need to live this day in a way pleasing to Him.*

*—Dianne Neal Matthews*

# SUNDAY, JULY 20

*And we know that in all things God works for the good of those who love him, who have been called according to his purpose. Romans 8:28 (NIV)*

LAST NIGHT I STOOD UP in front of our church and recounted a time in my life when I was in a tailspin.

Deciding I could do better on my own than following Jesus, I was failing my college classes, struggling with an eating disorder, and caught in the throes of an unhealthy relationship. I was a mess. But in the midst of my wreck of a life, Jesus stepped in and showed me grace. He lifted me up out of the pit, as it were.

Life is often messy at best. A hodgepodge of decisions and circumstances, some that are our own and some that have been visited on us. We usually can't see our way clear when we are in the mess. How in the world could Jesus make any sense of our poor decisions or the heartache that others have visited on us? It makes no sense. But last night at church we sang together, "You work all things together for my good."

And it is true. At twenty-one, I would have said, "I am a train wreck . . . I don't see how any good can come of my life." Twenty years later I have walked a path of grace, forgiveness, joy, and restoration, and Jesus is not yet done. He is still working things together for my good.

And for yours. All of our mess-ups. Our failures. Our disappointments. Our heartbreaks. They are not beyond His touch or His redemption. As long as we keep handing over our hearts to Jesus, He will keep on mending, healing, overhauling, and revamping us into the person He created us to be. This is our great hope, and we can rest in it.

FAITH STEP: *Look back over the last ten years and write in your journal the ways that Jesus has worked things together for your good. Thank Him for His work of redemption in your life.*

—Susanna Foth Aughtmon

# MONDAY, JULY 21

---

*Take my yoke upon you and learn from me, for I am gentle and humble in heart, and you will find rest for your souls. Matthew 11:29 (NIV)*

---

MY SWEET KIDS ARE HOME sick for the second day, and along with a bit of renewed perkiness has come a greater dose of demands.

I've been hard-pressed to fill requests for juice, no not *that* juice, just water, yes water for both, and toast with jelly but only for one, the other wants hot cereal (cue whiny voice). How about a DVD? Stick it in the player, then off to wash bedding, pjs, and towels; check temperatures; give medicine; give baths; give more water; answer the door—it's the icemaker repairman; answer the phone—it's the doctor's office; help with activity books; back to answer the phone—it's the hubby . . . hold on, let me catch my breath. NOPE, sorry! Back to the kitchen for a banana, no make that applesauce, but only if it's the regular kind in a bowl not the strawberry kind in the pouch.

Right now my daughter is sitting on me on the sectional as I'm leaning sideways under her weight while trying to finish paying some bills before one of them needs more juice. My children are hurting and I love them, so hither and yon I go. Honestly, they're reminding me of the needy soul I am with Jesus. And I know *He* remains the image of calm as I fall apart before Him.

Even when I'm way behind on sleep and pushed to my limits as a mother, I still need only to look at my kids and the energy to meet their needs somehow rises through my weariness. Jesus's care is even more faithful, His endurance never-ending. He holds me, no matter how needy I feel.

You know what I have to say to that today? *Ahhh* . . . rest time!

---

**FAITH STEP:** *Admit your neediness to Jesus and thank Him that He isn't exasperated or disappointed by it. He's committed to meet your deepest needs.*

*—Erin Keeley Marshall*

# TUESDAY, JULY 22

*But my God shall supply all your need according to*
*His riches in glory by Christ Jesus. Philippians 4:19 (KJV)*

WHEN I WAS PREGNANT WITH Stella, we decided to turn our playroom into a bedroom for Adelaide and her new baby sister to share. Adelaide and I had fun browsing catalogs and searching the Internet for ideas. In time, the room was pretty much transformed according to her specifications.

She got a new bedspread, pink with roses, and a bedside table with matching lamp. A wonderful carpenter built lots of new cabinetry that would become her closet, dresser, and bookshelf. The only problem when he delivered and set it was that the white cabinets looked bare. She needed some knobs and drawer-pulls.

Adelaide found some pink crystal butterflies from Pottery Barn Kids that were adorable, perfect, and way out of my budget. I explained we just couldn't get those right now. We had to save money for the new baby. She was angelically good about this, which made me want to get them for her even more, but I just didn't feel I could. We both decided to be content without them.

About a week later, I got a writing assignment I was not expecting. Guess what it paid? The exact amount of the butterflies. I told Adelaide we could get them now, that I believed God had provided the money.

When she opened the box and examined the butterflies, she squealed as though they were pink diamonds. She clutched me around the neck, and I expected her to say, "Thank you, Mommy!"

But her thoughts went in a different direction. "That was so sweet of God, wasn't it Mommy? To get me these butterflies?"

Now every time I pass that room, I'm reminded of His sweetness, and how He truly provides for our every need.

FAITH STEP: *Is there something your heart desires today? Trust the Lord to provide everything you need in Jesus.*

—*Gwen Ford Faulkenberry*

# WEDNESDAY, JULY 23

*I have loved you with an everlasting love; therefore, I have continued to extend faithful love to you. Jeremiah 31:3 (HCS)*

SINCE I LIVE SO FAR from my grandchildren, I cherish the notes I receive from my eight-year-old granddaughter. Last summer Lacey sent me a sheet of stationery folded in half. On the front, she had drawn three colorful flowers and labeled them: You, Me, and PawPaw. The inside of the note had a red heart at the top around the words "Good luck charm. Good luck!" The note itself opened with "I love you so much" and ended with "I miss you so much." The P.S. instructed me to "Read the back." When I turned it over, I read, "I couldn't think of anything to draw here so I put this."

Lacey wanted to fill up every space on her note with love and good wishes. Just like God has filled up every part of the Bible with His love. Some verses are obvious, like Jeremiah 31:3 and the familiar "For God so loved the world…" in John 3:16. But really, every page is an integral part of His love letter to us. The history of Israel warns us to avoid mistakes they made. The Ten Commandments are designed for our own protection and well-being. Even the tedious lists of names in the Old Testament demonstrate how God cares for individuals.

When we get to the New Testament, we read about Jesus, God's Living Love Letter. As God in human form, Jesus brought healing to the sick, comfort to the hurting, and light to those living in darkness. He taught people how to find meaning and purpose in life through a relationship with their Creator. Then He gave the ultimate demonstration of love by dying on the cross. If I'm ever tempted to doubt God's love, all I have to do is read about Jesus in the greatest love note ever written.

FAITH STEP: *If you haven't read the Gospel accounts of Jesus's life lately, why not get reacquainted with God's Living Love Letter to you?*

*—Dianne Neal Matthews*

# THURSDAY, JULY 24

*Then everyone deserted him and fled. Mark 14:50 (NIV)*

DURING JESUS'S THREE YEARS OF ministry, men, women, and children of all ages followed Him, seeking His help, listening to His teaching, and singing His praises. Many of them had seen or heard about Jesus's miracles. Some even experienced them. Mesmerized by His wonder-working power, they wanted to be near Him, wherever He went.

I wonder how many of those same worshippers stood at the crucifixion watching Him die. Perhaps only a few silent ones. Perhaps none. Many had turned their backs on Him when things went sour. Had I been there, how would I have responded? Do I offer thanks to God only when things are going well, when I'm a direct recipient of His divine blessings?

When Jesus was arrested, the Bible says His disciples deserted Him and fled. A few watched from a distance. Maybe Jesus's foreknowledge of their rejection and wimpy discipleship contributed to the stinging tears in Jesus's eyes and heart as He looked over the city of Jerusalem earlier and wept, adding, "How often I have longed to gather your children together, as a hen gathers her chicks under her wings, but you were not willing" (Matthew 23:37, NIV).

To their credit, Jesus's disciples returned, all but one, and became strong followers of Jesus after His resurrection, even to their own deaths. Many more believed. But I wonder how many of those seekers among the early multitude still watched from afar.

True worshippers of Christ will follow Him even in the most difficult circumstances.

**FAITH STEP:** *In what areas is it hardest for you to give thanks to Jesus? Is there a difficult situation in your life right now? Praise Jesus today for allowing it to come into your life, and ask Him to use that circumstance for His glory.*

—*Rebecca Barlow Jordan*

# FRIDAY, JULY 25

*Your word is a lamp before my feet and a light for my journey. Psalm 119:105* (CEB)

AFTER MANY MONTHS' ABSENCE, I saw a friend the other day and couldn't help notice there was less of her to notice. Her energy level was even higher than normal for her. She seemed happier with herself.

I knew better than to ask, but it's tradition, isn't it? "How did you do it? How did you lose the weight and get healthier?"

I could have guessed her answer. It's the one I've heard most frequently, no matter what the exercise routine, supplement, or even surgery that accompanies dramatic weight loss when the goal is to get healthier. Lower the carb intake.

How often have we heard another bit of wisdom? "If you want to grow closer to Jesus, up your intake of the Word of God. Read, study, meditate on, and apply what the Bible has to say, and you will not only know Jesus better, but you'll find yourself empowered to follow Him."

That basic counsel never changes. But have we changed to match its wisdom, to adopt the advice into our daily lives? Or do we listen and nod—*Yes, great idea*—but go back to ingesting a diet of things that aren't spiritually healthy for us and do nothing to help our soul's health or energy?

"The pounds melted away," my friend told me, "when I started to get serious about eating smart and applying myself to the right kind of exercise."

"The fears and doubts melted away," she could have said, "when I started to seriously pursue knowing Jesus better through His Word."

FAITH STEP: *Feeling spiritually sluggish? Start with the basic, age-old sage advice—get more of God's Word into your daily diet. Followed faithfully, it can't help but yield results.*

—Cynthia Ruchti

# SATURDAY, JULY 26

*Let us run with endurance the race that is set before us, looking unto Jesus, the author and finisher of our faith, who for the joy that was set before Him endured the cross, despising the shame, and has sat down at the right hand of the throne of God. Hebrews 12:1–2 (NKJV)*

ONE SUMMER MY DAUGHTER, GRACIE, was invited to a basketball camp at John Brown University. She was to stay with Bethany, a good friend of ours who played basketball there in her college days. On the way, the van was full of excited chatter about how much fun it was going to be.

When we walked into the gym, however, Gracie grew quiet. There was a picture of Bethany on the wall in the lobby, and a list of her accomplishments. I looked around for our friend, but Gracie hoped she wouldn't come to watch.

"Why?"

"Because I'm not very good!"

Her hand felt icy as she handed me her bag. We sat down in the bleachers while she laced up her high-tops.

"You know, Gracie, you don't have to be able to play on the college level in fifth grade."

I could so relate Gracie's feelings about basketball to my own about faith.

Sometimes we get really down on ourselves when we make mistakes, or compare ourselves to others who seem to be a lot better at the Christian life. In those times we must remember how Jesus works in our lives to grow us, and bring us to maturity in His perfect timing. The same One Who started us on the path of our faith will lead us onward and upward, all the way home.

FAITH STEP: *If you can, go on a little walk today. Meditate on where Jesus has taken you so far, and ask Him to give you a vision for where He wants you to go.*

—*Gwen Ford Faulkenberry*

# SUNDAY, JULY 27

---

*"I know all the things you do, that you are neither hot nor cold. I wish that you were one or the other! But since you are like lukewarm water, neither hot nor cold, I will spit you out of my mouth!" Revelation 3:15–16 (NLT)*

---

SWEAT RAN DOWN MY FACE and neck. My T-shirt felt plastered to my back. I hadn't meant to walk so far up the mountain trail. I also hadn't realized how stifling the heat would be in the upper part where thick trees blocked the breeze. Opening the car door, I grabbed my big plastic container of water and took a gulp. Then I resisted the urge to spit it out. The water had been sitting in a hot car in the sun too long.

In a letter to a church, Jesus used tepid water as an illustration for the people's spiritual condition. Laodicea was located near famous hot springs and also a city known for its cold, pure water. Whichever source they piped water from, it would have been tepid by the time it reached the city. Jesus warned that the believers had become lukewarm in their faith: complacent, indifferent, not willing to take a stand one way or the other.

To maintain spiritual health, I need to regularly check the "temperature" of my heart. Is it on fire for Jesus, burning with a desire to honor and obey Him, to tell others about Him? Or has it grown cold toward spiritual things? The third possibility is harder to detect—and more dangerous. Have I grown too comfortable, stagnant, and self-satisfied, no longer realizing my need for Jesus? If so, it's time for serious self-examination and prayer. I need to ask Jesus to help me make the needed corrections in my attitudes and behavior. I don't want to ever make Him feel like spitting me out of His mouth.

---

FAITH STEP: *Spend some time in prayer examining your own spiritual condition. Ask Jesus to help you if you sense that your faith has grown lukewarm.*

—*Dianne Neal Matthews*

# MONDAY, JULY 28

---

*He who was seated on the throne said, "I am making everything new!" Then he said, "Write this down, for these words are trustworthy and true." Revelation 21:5 (NIV)*

---

THIS PAST WEEK I VISITED my friend Katie, who had recently had a baby. He was small and sweet and perfect. He made my heart hurt a little with the joy of him. The smell of a new baby does something to the mother's heart.

For a moment, I started thinking, *Maybe I could have one more...* Then Katie told me that her sweet boy had been up every half an hour during the night. I was able to remind myself why I am doing just fine with three children.

But I was a little jealous of the small bundle sleeping in his swing. Everything about him was new. New is so beautiful. So full of hope. So full of expectation. His whole life is stretching before him, full of promise. Sometimes I feel old. Then my back starts hurting and I know I am old.

But I love the thought of new beginnings, new chances, and new starts. Even though I am not new. And I believe that is a hope that Jesus has buried in my soul. The promise of a new life and a new kind of living. It is this promise that drives me to know Him more. I get a new start each day that I offer my life up to Him, and then there is also the hope of heaven within me.

One day, I will get to be the person that I was originally created to be. I will get a new body and a new way of thinking in one fell swoop. Jesus said so. And that is something I can look forward to.

---

**FAITH STEP:** *Jesus says that in Him we are new creation, the old has gone and the new has come. Think about some of the ways that He has made you new. Write a prayer in your journal, thanking Him for His new beginnings in your life.*

—*Susanna Foth Aughtmon*

# TUESDAY, JULY 29

*But these things I have told you, that when the time comes, you may remember that I told you of them. John 16:4 (NKJV)*

A FEW YEARS AGO, A young woman approached me for help with her marriage. I gently encouraged her to remember how their relationship began.

She smiled weakly as she shared their dreams and the promises they'd made to each other. But the joy quickly faded as she began to describe the broken promises and unmet expectations that had snowballed in their relationship.

King David, the "man after God's own heart," made a remarkable statement after his sin with Bathsheba. He confessed to God, "For I know my transgressions, and my sin is always before me" (Psalm 51:3, NIV). If God forgives us completely, why would David choose to remember his painful sins constantly?

Perhaps the answer lies in grace. Remembering what we are capable of—and what God has delivered us from—can make us extremely grateful. David's prayer continued: "Then I will teach transgressors your ways so that sinners will turn back to you" (verse 13). A picture of grace.

Jesus also told the disciples to "remember" His death. Painful memories. But after His resurrection and ascension, Jesus empowered them with the Holy Spirit to move forward in victory. They would always keep His death—and their sinfulness—"before them." But those events would also remind them that Jesus's grace was stronger.

Just like the young woman, we all need to place "grace" beside the painful memories of our lives, and with grateful hearts, let Jesus keep moving us forward.

**FAITH STEP:** *Take time today to remember Jesus's painful sacrifice for you. Then celebrate—and thank Jesus—for all the times when His grace covered your own sinful behavior.*

*—Rebecca Barlow Jordan*

# WEDNESDAY, JULY 30

*For this light momentary affliction is preparing for us an eternal weight of glory beyond all comparison.* 2 Corinthians 4:17 (ESV)

ON A DAY WHEN CAREGIVING consumed me and threatened to capsize my small, leaky craft, I clung to the chewed-up life preserver emblazoned with the word *Temporary*. The caregiving was temporary. My husband would get better, stronger, maybe even back to near-normal someday. He would heal. Eventually.

My empathy meter peaked for those whose caregiving responsibilities were poured out for loved ones whose illness or disability meant every day would get a little worse. The next day, a little worse than that. To what life preserver did they cling when they felt the waves washing over the gunwales?

"This present suffering," Jesus said through the apostle Paul, "is not worthy to be compared to the weight of glory in the world to come." The *weight* of glory? It's the suffering that feels like poundage, isn't it? How can glory weigh anything? What did the biblical writer mean?

He may have meant it's like comparing apples and oranges—the difference between our temporary afflictions and the forever glory that lies ahead for those who follow Jesus.

We may not see the end of what we're enduring. It's around the corner. Over the next hill. Over the next dozen hills. But it is limited.

I'll take a stronger grip on that truth today.

FAITH STEP: *Take a fresh inventory today. Two lists—Forever and Not Forever. What's overwhelming you today? Does it fit on the* Forever *list or the* Not Forever? *Does it help to see it in black and white?*

—*Cynthia Ruchti*

# THURSDAY, JULY 31

*You prepare a table before me in the presence of my enemies.* Psalm 23:5 (NAS)

"OH, I'M SO SORRY. I didn't mean to interrupt your dinner."

My friend had come to pick up a beauty product I had ordered for her. One glance at my kitchen table had brought her quick apology. At first I was confused about her statement, because there was no food on the table. And then it dawned on me.

I keep my table "prepared" all day long, with a place setting at each chair. I've been doing that for years, probably because I admired the look in model homes or in magazines. My friend saw the dishes and thought it was dinnertime.

When I was reading the Twenty-Third Psalm recently, I remembered that day's scenario. In David's analogy, the Lord was His Shepherd. One of the blessings He prepared for David was a "table in the presence of his enemies." In Eastern hospitality, the pursued could find a safe refuge and a hearty meal prepared by his host, even while his enemies waited outside the door. They could never barge in and interrupt the meal.

Jesus, our Shepherd, does the same thing for us today. Only His table is always prepared and ready for us. Piled high with spiritual blessings, He has conquered our enemies. But even when they try to threaten us, Jesus invites us to sit down with Him anytime and enjoy His feasts in security and peace. And regardless of the "interruptions" in our life, Jesus never has to scramble to make up for lost time or to apologize for cold meals. His table is always set.

Now every time I look at my kitchen table, I smile. The place settings remind me to stop, sit, and enjoy the good things Jesus has waiting for me. He continues to prepare a wonderful place for us someday (John 14:2).

But for now, the sweetness of His presence is all I really want.

FAITH STEP: *Take time today to enjoy Jesus's presence and all the good things He has prepared for you.*

—*Rebecca Barlow Jordan*

# FRIDAY, AUGUST 1

*And as the Spirit of the Lord works within us, we become more and more like him and reflect his glory even more.* 2 Corinthians 3:18 (NLT)

A FRIEND'S KITCHEN AND LIVING room are being remodeled. What a job! Workers have removed cupboards and doors. They've ripped out flooring, walls, and windows. Eventually they'll install new cabinets, countertops, carpet, French doors, and light fixtures.

This process hasn't been easy for my friend's family. They disposed of their old appliances, placed their belongings in storage, and moved into a rental for five months. A hassle? Yes, but worth it because the makeover will result in a more comfortable home.

Sometimes the Holy Spirit performs a makeover on us. He surveys our attitudes and behaviors and says, "Hmmm. That pride's gotta go. So must the grumbling and the gossip." Then He sets to work.

Slowly, He strips the characteristics that grieve Him and then builds new qualities into our lives. Qualities such as love, joy, peace, patience, and kindness—the familiar ones listed in Galatians 5.

Sometimes the makeover feels painful, embarrassing, or downright annoying. But the Spirit is the pro. He knows what He's doing, and it's smarter to let Him work than to argue.

Letting the Holy Spirit work in us as He wishes results in greater Christ-likeness, and we'll reflect His beauty to those around us.

**FAITH STEP:** *Be honest. What attitude needs a makeover—impatience? Pride? Envy? Invite the Lord to strip away any attitude He finds offensive and replace it with one that honors Him.*

*—Grace Fox*

# SATURDAY, AUGUST 2

*Those who sow with tears will reap with songs of joy. Those who go out weeping, carrying seed to sow, will return with songs of joy, carrying sheaves with them. Psalm 126:5–6 (NIV)*

MY HUSBAND, J.R., IS A former All-American gymnast who now co-owns a cheerleading and gymnastics company. To improve their strength for tumbling and jumps, his athletes occasionally wear ankle weights while they work out. The weights make the skills more difficult to accomplish; however, when they are removed, the athletes find new strength and obtain increased power and height.

Occasionally we endure struggles in life because we are Christians. Our sons traveled across the country to share the importance of bearing witness for Christ. Sometimes no one wanted to hear their message, and they were left disheartened and discouraged. But then they would meet an individual (or a large group) eager to hear what they wanted to share, and they found themselves joyous for the opportunity in spite of the struggles along the way.

Christ never said living the Christian life would be easy (Matthew 7:13–14). In fact, He told us we would endure storms along our journey; however, He also promised that with Him, we can survive all storms (Matthew 7:24–27).

When those athletes strap on the weights and endure the difficulties of performing the skills with additional pressure, they are preparing themselves to soar once the burden is lifted. Our struggles in life do the same thing: prepare us to soar with Christ once our burden is lifted.

**FAITH STEP:** *If you have access to weights, walk around your house today for ten minutes carrying medium-sized dumbbells. If not, use something heavy enough to feel, such as your laundry detergent container. Then put the weight down and walk again, realizing how much easier it is once you've endured the storm.*

—*Renee Andrews*

# SUNDAY, AUGUST 3

*Work from the heart for your real Master, for God. . . . Keep in mind always that the ultimate Master you're serving is Christ. The sullen servant who does shoddy work will be held responsible.*
*Colossians 3:23–25 (MSG)*

"Aw Mom, cleaning up our toys isn't fun!" The morning had been riddled with tasks my kids saw as reasons to threaten a strike.

I rolled my eyes. "Well, Fun Mom didn't show up for work today, so you're stuck with me. Now go clean your rooms."

That eye roll? It's habitual. My shoddy response to the less-than-fun task of listening to whining as I enforce rules and good habits with my kids. A bright and shining example that the apples don't fall far from the tree!

I need to help them learn to do everything with an attitude of gratitude, to take care of what they've been given. But if I don't want to be a hypocrite, then I can't be too judgmental of them. After all, I can be guilty of a bad attitude, too, when work I don't care for casts a dreariness over the day.

I've been feeling Jesus's conviction about those eye rolls. They're the non-verbal equivalent of an "Aw, kids! Your whining isn't fun for me!" It's a sure bet Jesus doesn't roll His eyes *ever* when He sees me roll mine, even though it's a fairly exasperating habit I have.

While my children and I are learning to work with good attitudes, it's help-ful to imagine Jesus taking pride in seeing us live to please Him. The least fun tasks provide great opportunities to bring glory to our Savior simply because we're His and that's a reason for gratitude. Our fun is secondary; but because He's such a great Savior, He in turn fills us with the joy of knowing we're do-ing our best for Him.

FAITH STEP: *What tempts your bad attitude? Commit to a new response that shows a heart of gratitude.*

*—Erin Keeley Marshall*

# MONDAY, AUGUST 4

*With men this is impossible, but all things are possible with God. Matthew 19:26 (AMP)*

THE GOD OF IMPOSSIBLE SITUATIONS. That was the topic cropping up everywhere I turned. In lots of books. In lots of life.

Gideon. David. A starving woman. A dead daughter. A man whose eyes had never seen one sunrise, not one sunset, or the faces of his parents. A hillside auditorium of thousands and no concession stand.

A woman with a twelve-year history of pain and distress, ostracized, exhausted, bankrupt, with a medical file many inches thick. No answers. Worse problems than before. Weak. Helpless. Alone. The poster child for pathetic.

Until she met Jesus. And everything changed.

The Bible tells us Jesus not only healed her when she reached out for the hem of His garment, but He called her "Daughter."

What a tender term of endearment for a woman whose problem—twelve years of constant hemorrhaging—makes pastors blush when they preach from the passage!

Impossible situation? To anyone except the God of Impossible Situations.

**FAITH STEP:** *What life circumstance have you labeled "Impossible"? Write it on a piece of paper. Then take a cloth or a larger piece of paper and write the words, "The God of Impossibilities." Lay the opaque piece of fabric over the circumstance you thought had no answers. Now what do you see?*

*—Cynthia Ruchti*

# TUESDAY, AUGUST 5

*"Anyone who listens to my teaching and follows it is wise, like a person who builds a house on solid rock." Matthew 7:24 (NLT)*

THAT WEEK DID NOT GO well. On Monday the dermatologist's office squeezed me in after a miserable weekend, my body covered with itchy bumps. That afternoon I backed out of a parking space. I was about to pull forward when I heard a noise. A young man had backed out after me and scraped paint off my new car. Visibly upset and apologetic, he gave me his insurance information.

The next day I took my car for an estimate as his insurance company had instructed. On Wednesday I had an emergency dental appointment and discovered that I needed a root canal ASAP. On Thursday I learned that the young man who scraped my car had changed his story, insisting that we backed out at the same time. His insurance company denied responsibility. During my root canal on Friday, a chunk of a tool broke off in the cavity. The dentist recommended leaving it there and filled up the tooth. I later learned that was not the best way to handle it.

The events crammed into that week served as a powerful reminder that people are fallible. No matter how well-intentioned, anyone can make a mistake that impacts our life in a negative way. Then there are people who deliberately lie or break promises. Relationships are important, but if we're basing our life on another person, sooner or later we'll be disappointed.

Jesus is the only One worthy to be the center of my life. He will never fail me, lie to me, or let me down. He always seeks my highest good, and He never makes mistakes. If I build my life on Jesus and His teachings, I will never be disappointed.

FAITH STEP: *The next time someone lets you down, remind yourself that you can always depend on Jesus. Make sure He is the foundation of your life.*

—*Dianne Neal Matthews*

# WEDNESDAY, AUGUST 6

*Therefore, brothers and sisters, in all our distress and persecution we were encouraged about you because of your faith. 1 Thessalonians 3:7 (NIV)*

NOTHING WAS WORKING. THE WEB connection had broken; my brain took a vacation; and my body felt like a flat tire in bad need of repair. Unwritten assignments taunted me with a deadline looming. "Help!" I cried to Jesus. Not much improved that day. In fact, I felt more and more unproductive, and increasingly discouraged. I discarded the day like a throwaway milk carton, determined that I really had nothing helpful to write about, anyway.

Later that evening, I checked my e-mail. My Internet provider had restored the needed connection, so I scanned my inbox hastily before bedtime. One message blinked at me like a neon light:

> *Rebecca, you are a joy to my life. I love reading your Encouragement every day.... I wish there was a way I could capture them all in my thoughts every day because they [are] such a joy to read. I share them with my daughters and friend, and when my granddaughter is older I will share them with her.*

Jesus used that e-mail and some words from Paul's writings to lift my spirits that day and remind me that our efforts are never in vain. Paul encouraged the Thessalonians: "Never tire of doing what is good" (2 Thessalonians 3:13, NIV).

Yet there were times when the encourager (Paul) needed encouragement. Paul had been through multiple trials, persecutions, and yes, imprisonment. But when Timothy visited him and related how the body of Christ had been prospering, Paul felt encouraged. Their faith had grown! The ones Paul had previously taught and encouraged subsequently encouraged him.

FAITH STEP: *The next time you feel discouraged, remember that your work is not in vain. Thank God for the ones He is reaching and will continue to bless through your faithfulness.*

—*Rebecca Barlow Jordan*

# THURSDAY, AUGUST 7

*"Therefore go and make disciples of all nations, baptizing them in the name of the Father and of the Son and of the Holy Spirit, and teaching them to obey everything I have commanded you. And surely I am with you always, to the very end of the age." Matthew 28:19–20 (NIV)*

NANNY LANKFORD, MY MATERNAL GRANDMOTHER, was an outstanding cook, particularly when it came to desserts. No one wanted to miss out on a taste of her apricot fried pies or six-layer chocolate and divinity cake. But whenever anyone came in her kitchen, she stopped cooking and waited until the person left before continuing, because her recipes were "her secrets."

Unfortunately, Nanny never shared her recipes. Those secrets would have been treasured by all of us, her children and grandchildren, but we didn't receive the gift.

Every day we are around people who may not know our most valuable gift, the fact that Jesus Christ is Lord of our life and died for our sins. We are around others who may be as eager to learn about Him as our family was eager to learn Nanny's recipes. How sad would it feel to arrive at Judgment Day and realize that you had the opportunity to share Christ with so many people, and yet you never found the time or the courage? They may be yearning, hungry to know that He died for them, and they may remain hungry if you don't share His Good News. I yearned to know Nanny's recipes, and I feel saddened every time I wish I could bake one of those chocolate cakes for my own children.

FAITH STEP: *When someone asks how you're doing today, don't say the traditional, "I'm fine." Tell them the truth: "I'm blessed." And then tell them why. Share your amazing secret with the world!*

—*Renee Andrews*

# FRIDAY, AUGUST 8

*I have set before you life and death, blessings and curses. Choose life.*
*Deuteronomy 30:19 (NRSV)*

ONE OF OUR ALL-TIME FAVORITE movies to watch as a family is *Megamind*. We love the blue villain, played by Will Ferrell, and his best friend, a fish named Minion. From the music, to the one-liners, to the epic battle between good and evil, the movie is hilariously entertaining. But there's a redemptive twist in it that, I believe, teaches a great lesson.

Megamind seems destined to be a bad guy. Everything about his young life has set him up for this, in direct opposition to Metroman, who is the superhero. The problem is that about two-thirds through the story, Megamind realizes he doesn't want to be bad anymore. In a flash of insight, he utters, "Our destiny is not the path we are given but the one we choose for ourselves."

This moment makes me want to stand up and cheer. I know that God is sovereign, but the magic of our relationship with Him is that He gives us the choice to follow Jesus or not. That can be terrifying and wonderful all at once. We have to choose—and we get to.

That means that no matter where I come from, no matter what circumstances are out of my control, it's still my choice to live my life in Christ.

FAITH STEP: *What would it look like for you to live your life in Christ today?*

*—Gwen Ford Faulkenberry*

# SATURDAY, AUGUST 9

*The amazing grace of the Master, Jesus Christ, the extravagant love of God, the intimate friendship of the Holy Spirit, be with all of you. 2 Corinthians 13:14* (MSG)

IN THE PAST YEAR I'VE had a couple of disappointments in relationships that left me feeling down on myself, doubting that my good intentions were ever noticed or appreciated.

My unsettled feelings kept me up at night and often brought me to tears. I could tell Satan was kicking me while I was down because my thoughts were filled with negativity about myself.

Sometimes when relationship troubles emerge, it's hard to discern whether the problem is someone else's or our own, or simply what is. After struggling for a while, I turned to a trusted mentor. She let me talk for a couple of minutes and then halted me by firmly saying, "You need to let this go. This condemnation is from Satan, not Jesus."

Maybe I made mistakes, maybe not. The losses I felt were not ones I could go back and try to fix; they were in the past, done. I needed to leave them for Jesus to heal, whether by healing my hurt or the relationships. I was ready to ask forgiveness if He brought to my attention any wrong I'd done; I was ready to talk honestly with those friends if they were open to it. Until that day comes, if ever, it is time to move on.

Human relationships sometimes end or leave us unfulfilled. Perhaps Jesus makes good use of those losses by showing us His ever-faithfulness. Even though we can't see Him or physically feel His arms around us, we can know and feel in our spirits that He still calls us friends. He is the Friend Who will never leave us confused about where we stand with Him.

FAITH STEP: *Ask Jesus to deepen the friendship you share with Him in the coming months.*

—*Erin Keeley Marshall*

# SUNDAY, AUGUST 10

*But the Advocate, the Holy Spirit, whom the Father will send in my name, will teach you all things and will remind you of everything I have said to you. John 14:26 (NIV)*

"MOM, DID YOU FINISH WRITING your chapter this morning?" My daughter poked her head into my room.

"Not yet. But thanks for the reminder," I answered. She was home from college for Christmas vacation, and I'd asked her to help hold me accountable for the writing work I needed to accomplish. I had a checklist on my bulletin board and my goals marked with yellow highlighter in my "to-do" list. But when she checked in with me, she did more than prompt me to remember to do my work. She offered encouragement.

"You can do this, Mom."

The older I get, the more I need reminders…for appointments, for goals, and for the location of important things like my glasses.

I'm so glad that Jesus has given us the gift of the Holy Spirit to remind us of everything He has taught us. When we're preoccupied with selfish plans, the Spirit reminds us to seek Jesus first. When we're stressed by problems, He reminds us to cast our cares on Jesus. When we're crushed by pain and loss, He reminds us of Jesus's love and His promise that He is preparing a place for us.

As we invite the Holy Spirit to remind us of the truth each day, we may even hear a whisper of encouragement. "I'm with you. You can do this."

FAITH STEP: *Thank Jesus for the gift of the Holy Spirit, and listen for His reminders today. Whenever you notice His encouragement or guidance, jot the thought on a Post-it Note. At the end of the day, review them all.*

—*Sharon Hinck*

# MONDAY, AUGUST 11

*"Here I am! I stand at the door and knock." Revelation 3:20 (NIV)*

YESTERDAY I WAS IN THE Los Angeles airport, traveling home with my husband and oldest son. Our seats weren't together, and I waited in line at the gate to ask if they could be reassigned.

A young soldier in army fatigues stood in front of me in line. Several people looked at the soldier, but no one spoke to the young man. When he glanced in my direction, I said, "Thank you for your service." A huge smile broke across his face. "You're welcome, ma'am." Then he proceeded to tell me that he was on his way home to meet his first child, that he'd been called because his wife was in labor. I congratulated him and shared in the new daddy's excitement.

Thinking about the scene, I wondered if some people don't know what to say to soldiers. Maybe they don't feel worthy to have someone risk their life for their freedom. I've felt that way, but because I found the courage to speak to the young man and thank him, I was able to share in his blessed news. Jesus is like that soldier. We aren't worthy for Him to give His life for us, but He did. It would be so easy to look the other way and act like we don't see the soldier, or act like we don't see Christ, right there in front of us. But He doesn't want us to feel ashamed because we feel unworthy. He wants us to feel blessed for everything He has done to save us from our shame.

FAITH STEP: *Don't be afraid to talk to the One Who saved you. Thank Him, like I thanked the soldier, and you will have the opportunity to share in His glorious news.*

—*Renee Andrews*

# TUESDAY, AUGUST 12

---

*The steps of the godly are directed by the Lord. He delights in every detail of their lives.*
*Psalm 37:23 (NLT)*

---

DAVID DELIVERED HIS BROTHERS' FOOD to their battle camp. He didn't intend to become a giant-slayer and national hero that day.

Moses was watching his father-in-law's flocks. Seeing a burning bush and being appointed exodus executive director hadn't crossed his mind.

Gideon was hiding in a winepress. Meeting an angel and becoming a mighty warrior weren't in his plans.

Mary was going about her usual teenage girl business. Conceiving God's Son was the furthest thing from her mind.

My husband and I were working at a year-round Christian camp. Establishing a ministry that involved hosting evangelistic summer camps in Eastern Europe was nowhere on our radar. Then the phone rang.

Isaiah 55:9 is indeed true—"As the heavens are higher than the earth, so are my ways higher than your ways and my thoughts than your thoughts." We may think we've mapped our lives, but God can change our direction in a second. That's His prerogative. He's God; we're not.

What might your future hold? Only God knows. Your responsibility is to remain faithful and flexible—faithful in your walk with God, and flexible to go wherever He calls you.

---

**FAITH STEP:** *Determine now to say yes if God suddenly changes your direction.*

—*Grace Fox*

# WEDNESDAY, AUGUST 13

*Let the one who boasts boast in the Lord.* 1 Corinthians 1:31 (*NIV*)

WHEN I FIRST STARTED SELLING greeting card verses to companies years ago, I was so excited to receive the card samples from them with "my" verses on them.

But I soon wondered at my real motives. One day a friend commented about receiving some of my greeting cards in the mail. Without thinking I boasted, "Did you see my name on the back?" Immediately, Jesus pricked my conscience, and I was extremely embarrassed. I knew what I would be doing as soon as I returned home. The next day I took down the clothesline and tucked the cards away in a box. I continued sending my card samples to people during times of illness, family loss, or birthdays—whatever the occasion warranted.

There's a difference between feeling the pride of a job well done and boasting about that work. Sometimes we don't even recognize our own motives. In the end, nothing we do is of ourselves. Jesus gives us our ability and gifts, but He asks something in return: that we give the glory to Him.

I still include greeting cards among the other things I write. Except for longer, inspirational verse, most of those card companies publish only the artist's name, not the writer's. Like everyone else, I still love to receive a byline. We all like to feel important.

But Jesus constantly teaches me that it's His name that counts, not mine. Anything done for reasons other than His glory has little value (1 Corinthians 10:31, NLT). My constant prayer is, "Lord, if I boast about anything, let it be about You—for Christ alone."

**FAITH STEP:** *Today list all the reasons why you can boast in Christ—alone.*

*—Rebecca Barlow Jordan*

# THURSDAY, AUGUST 14

*And then he told them, "Go into all the world and preach the Good News to everyone."*
Mark 16:15 *(NLT)*

I HAVE HUNDREDS OF CHRISTIAN blogger friends who are sharing Jesus Christ on a daily basis, right from their living room.

These women are kindred spirits with Hudson Taylor, George Mueller, and Amy Carmichael. They want to share Jesus and help people…but they're not packing up their bags and heading to Africa to do it. (Well, not always.) They're sitting at home, pouring a cup of coffee, and then pouring out their hearts into blogs while their children play in the yard or tumble on the crumb-covered couch. (At least mine is crumb-covered.) A missionary heart is not hindered by ten loads of laundry, piano lessons, and a bad hair day.

What does it take to reach out like this? Just like missionaries of old, it takes giving away your heart. It also takes courage. Courage to "put yourself out there." Courage to be transparent. Courage to turn your back away from other important tasks to focus on writing about how Jesus impacts your daily life.

"Courageous people are still afraid, they just obey God anyway," writes Jennie Allen, and I agree. Why do we blog? Partly because it's an outlet for our daily thoughts, but mostly out of obedience. We take Jesus's command to "Go ye into all the world…" seriously.

I'm sure Christians from generations past never pictured the impact generations today make. How about you? You may not be interested in starting a blog, but is there someone who needs to hear the Good News of Jesus coming from your lips with transparency and passion?

**FAITH STEP:** *If you read a great faith-based blog, take a moment to write and thank the blogger for sharing his/her life. Or, if you aren't a regular reader, search for a good blog to read and follow.*

—*Tricia Goyer*

# FRIDAY, AUGUST 15

*We share in his sufferings in order that we may also share in his glory. I consider that our present sufferings are not worth comparing with the glory that will be revealed in us.*
*Romans 8:17–18 (NIV)*

MY FRIEND WENDY SCHAY WAS visiting the other day. Her two daughters are close to the ages of my oldest two, and we've watched as they've all grown up way too fast.

"I miss mine being babies," Wendy said, "even though it was so hard in those days." She went on to reminisce about when her husband and she were both in school, their girls were tiny, and money was as scarce as sleep.

Looking at them now, it's hard to believe. He's a psychiatrist, and she's a registered nurse who stays home, volunteering at her girls' school and leading Bible studies at their church. They just moved into a new house, and the whole family is vibrant and flourishing.

After Wendy left, I thought about what an inspiration she is, how successful she and Johnny have been at weathering life's difficulties. Many couples I know might not have made it through those hard days. But Wendy and Johnny were able to take the long view, knowing their situation was temporary, and fulfillment was ahead.

The long view also applies to the Christian experience. Not only because we are promised heaven after death, but also as we learn and grow through life's trials, fulfillment comes. Our hearts can be at peace. We become more and more like Jesus. And we see that following Him is worth it.

FAITH STEP: *Is it hard for you to see a light at the end of your present tunnel? Keep on trusting, obeying, and putting your hope in Jesus, the Light of the world.*

—*Gwen Ford Faulkenberry*

# SATURDAY, AUGUST 16

*For I can do everything through Christ, who gives me strength. Philippians 4:13 (NLT)*

"YOU'LL HAVE TO GO ON without me," I told my husband. "I'll never make it." We had driven to this scenic area north of Salt Lake City to celebrate our thirty-eighth anniversary. After spending the night in a historic bed-and-breakfast, our first stop on the Logan Canyon Byway was the Wind Cave Trail, a 1.3-mile hike to see "remarkable wind-sculpted 'caves' 980 feet above the canyon floor." But I hadn't realized how steep and rocky the trail would be, or how it would aggravate my spinal problems. Plus, the high altitudes made me struggle with shortness of breath.

After finally convincing Richard to go on without me and get pictures of the formations, I slumped down on a rock. After a few minutes, my exhaustion was replaced by disappointment—and annoyance that physical problems were interfering with our special day. Besides, I really wanted to see those wind caves. I got back on the trail, praying for divine strength in my back and breath in my lungs. After a few minutes, I gave up again. This scenario repeated itself several times, until I finally reached the top of the mountain and saw Richard's surprised face.

The apostle Paul lived a victorious life and accomplished great things for God despite unbelievable hardships. He had learned the secret that through Christ, a believer has all the power and strength needed to live each day. That doesn't mean I can do whatever I want; I do need to consider my physical limitations. But as long as I'm following His will, I can draw upon Christ's strength to carry me through. And sometimes that divine strength will carry me to the top of a mountain just to see beautiful scenery.

FAITH STEP: *If you face a difficulty today and feel like giving up, remember the promise of Philippians 4:13. Ask Jesus to give you divine strength so you can keep going.*

*—Dianne Neal Matthews*

# SUNDAY, AUGUST 17

*Very early in the morning, while it was still dark, Jesus got up, left the house and went off to a solitary place, where he prayed. Mark 1:35 (NIV)*

JESUS HAD ONLY THREE YEARS to accomplish His life's purpose. His days were filled with activities such as healing the sick, restoring sight to the blind, and preaching in the synagogue. He taught to the masses, fed thousands, dined with society's outcasts, ministered to individuals, comforted the grieving, and raised their dead to life.

Jesus had much work and little time. He could have crammed activity into every spare moment, but no. He made time for prayer, and He made it a priority.

Scripture tells us that Jesus spent time alone in prayer very early in the morning. He got up, left the house, and withdrew to a solitary place, where He conversed with His heavenly Father. He did so at night too.

Martin Luther said, "I have so much to do that I shall spend the first three hours in prayer." Seems he understood Jesus's heart and the importance of seeking God's help for the tasks on his to-do list.

Do we value prayer, or are we so bent on completing our work that we're too busy to withdraw for conversations with the Father?

Our life's work is important, but prayer is the real work. Engaging in it invites our Father to direct our steps, guide our conversations, and make divine connections. It ensures we stay on task and thereby accomplish the work He's given us to do.

FAITH STEP: *Purpose to spend five minutes in specific prayer each day and track the results.*

—*Grace Fox*

# MONDAY, AUGUST 18

*In the beginning was the Word, and the Word was with God, and the Word was God. He was in the beginning with God. All things came into being through Him, and apart from Him nothing came into being that has come into being. John 1:1–3 (NAS)*

MY SON ADDISON WAS GIVING me a hard time the other day. Telling me that he didn't need my help anymore. He is six, after all. There is the slight possibility that he is getting too big for his britches.

I asked him, "Did you forget who makes you all your meals?" I always take it back to food with my boys. It is their love language. Addie looked at me, a little nervously. Jack piped, "We love you, Mom!" They wouldn't want to miss out on an upcoming snack.

It made me chuckle. I know that someday my boys will not need me like they do now. But for now, we are intertwined. They depend on me for their care, their food, and their clean underwear.

Sometimes I forget Who it is I am dependent on. I think I have a handle on living. But I am fooling myself. I am getting a little too big for my britches. Because in reality, everything that I am, from the brain that is between my ears to my pinky toes, has come into being through the One Who loves me best. From the One Who has been since the beginning of time. From the One Who speaks galaxies into being with a word. Jesus. Sometimes I forget who it is Who makes all my meals. Who gives me life and breath and hope for new tomorrows. Without Him I have nothing. And really, without Him, I am nothing.

It might be a good time to start telling Jesus how much I love Him.

**FAITH STEP:** *Think of all the ways that Jesus has blessed you with the life He has given you. Nothing comes into being except through Him. Tell Jesus how much you love Him and why.*

—*Susanna Foth Aughtmon*

# TUESDAY, AUGUST 19

*But God demonstrates his own love for us in this: While we were still sinners, Christ died for us.*
*Romans 5:8 (NIV)*

J.R. AND I ARRIVED HOME late last night after traveling for a week. We were exhausted and ready to finally relax. Upon entering the kitchen, we found an abundance of dirty dishes in the sink. A faint odor filled the air that turned out to be soured milk in a dish that hadn't been rinsed. Boxes were scattered around the kitchen floor, and practically every spot on the counter was filled with something (a giant cookie, a bowl of gold-wrapped chocolates, gum wrappers, etc.).

Our youngest son had stayed at the house while we were gone. Consequently, his twenty-second birthday occurred while we were away, which explained the odd items around the kitchen. My husband went upstairs, found our son, and told him to waste no time cleaning up the mess.

I couldn't say anything. We'd missed his birthday, and I'd missed him dearly. In spite of the mess, I couldn't wait to hug him. And within a few minutes, he and my husband were laughing about the scene and picking it up together.

Don't you think Christ is the same way? He sees us choosing to do something that is going to leave our lives in a mess, that will cause us time and energy when we have to go about trying to clean it up, and He would rather us not make the mess at all. But He also isn't surprised when we do. He who knows the very number of hairs on our head (Matthew 10:30) obviously knows when we say "yes" to something when we should say "no."

However, when we make a mess, although He is disappointed, He still loves us, still wants to hug us, and, like my husband, will often step in to help us clean up.

FAITH STEP: *Ask Christ to help you clean up your messes today.*

*—Renee Andrews*

# WEDNESDAY, AUGUST 20

*"My thoughts are nothing like your thoughts," says the Lord. "And my ways are far beyond anything you could imagine. For just as the heavens are higher than the earth, so my ways are higher than your ways and my thoughts higher than your thoughts." Isaiah 55:8–9 (NLT)*

Do you DARE TO HOPE? Before answering, consider your deepest need. Maybe it's for healing for yourself or someone else. Maybe it's for financial security or for someone to love you no matter what. Maybe it's to know that your children will be okay. What if those needs are not met?

In *The 90-Day Novel*, author Alan Watt comments that "it is only in surrendering our idea of the way we believe things ought to be that we begin to glimpse the nature of the way things actually are." Although he's talking about developing a story, his comment got me thinking about the disconnect that often occurs between our view and Jesus's view—a disconnect that affects our hope.

Those who take the "risk" of faith in Jesus have taken the first step in letting go and learning to see life with His vision instead of our finite human vision. His vision is much farther reaching, whereas ours is limited to the here-and-now of earthly life.

Hope appears to disappoint us when our vision doesn't happen, when our child suffers without healing, when our home is foreclosed on, when the love of our life decides to love someone else. Yes, those bring horrible, even horrific pain. Jesus would not ask you to deny that. In fact, He aches deeply with you.

Hope's branches reach higher, to the heights of heaven, where Jesus anticipates for us the joy He knows we'll experience when we're united with Him forever. We can't see all He's doing in another person's life, and we have no idea how good things will be for believers when this life is over.

FAITH STEP: *Ask Jesus for stubborn hope that sees with His vision.*

—*Erin Keeley Marshall*

# THURSDAY, AUGUST 21

*Trust in the Lord with all your heart, and lean not on your own understanding; in all your ways, acknowledge Him, and He shall direct your paths.* Proverbs 3:5–6 (NKJV)

MULTIPLE VOICES CAN CRY OUT to us daily, offering bits and pieces of so-called wisdom. "If you try this, you'll find the answer." "This happened because of what you did last week." "Everyone knows you won't find success that way." "Why don't you just give up? You're not going to make it."

That advice may come from friends as well as enemies. And sometimes, we are our own worst enemy, as we try to figure things out through our own faulty reasoning. Who hasn't drawn the wrong conclusions at one time or another?

Some of Jesus's brothers tried to tell Him how He should conduct His ministry. I can just hear them now: "You need to go into Judea and announce who You are. None of this hiding in the shadows or false humility. How are people going to respect You and know who You really are if You don't tell them?" (John 7:2–4).

But I can also see Jesus smiling, shaking His head, and ignoring their faulty reasoning. Later when the others had left, He did go into Judea—quietly, according to His own Father's plan (John 7:6–10).

Each time we try to make excuses, provide reasons, or listen to others' wrong advice without consulting the One Who already knows it all, we will come up short. There is only One Who is wise, only One Who has all the answers. When we trust in Him completely, relying not on our own faulty reasoning, but on His faultless wisdom, we will find the answers close by. Jesus is ever ready to "direct our paths."

When He chooses the direction, it will always be the right way.

FAITH STEP: *Is there a decision you need to make? Tell Jesus you trust Him completely, and ask Him to direct your paths.*

—*Rebecca Barlow Jordan*

# FRIDAY, AUGUST 22

*For in him all things were created: things in heaven and on earth, visible and invisible, whether thrones or powers or rulers or authorities; all things have been created through him and for him. He is before all things, and in him all things hold together. Colossians 1:16–17 (NIV)*

I TURNED UP THE VOLUME on my laptop, and then wished I hadn't. I was watching the live streaming of a government advisory meeting. The committee was of great interest to me since they were working to advance understanding and research into an illness that has had a large effect on my life and that of several friends.

Yet the committee members seemed to talk in endless circles, buried in bureaucracy, unable to put any teeth behind a recommendation. I despaired of any progress being made.

Hopelessness flooded me as I turned away from the screen, wanting to cry. Instead, I prayed. *Lord, I can't put my hope in these institutions. Not entirely. It looks like there will be no answers, no agreement, no commitment to finding solutions in my lifetime.*

As I prayed, my focus shifted. *But I can put my hope in You. You can grant answers in various ways. If You choose to work through science, medicine, and government agencies, You are able to move those institutions in the right direction.*

Powers or rulers or authorities can feel daunting. I love this reminder in Colossians that Jesus is undaunted. He is big enough and wise enough to steer, guide, and shape every part of creation.

**FAITH STEP:** *Is there a place where you feel powerless or overwhelmed? Next time you watch the news, ask Jesus to show you a glimpse of His ability to hold everything together.*

—Sharon Hinck

# SATURDAY, AUGUST 23

*Jesus matured in wisdom and years, and in favor with God and with people. Luke 2:52* (CEB)

MY GRANDKIDS CAME TO VISIT yesterday—a delightfully noisy, loving, laughing time. When one of the youngest threw a minifit, it was his seven-year-old cousin who appointed herself minicounselor. You didn't get your way this time. But you might the next time."

The advice came from a little girl who had been given the same lecture the day before following her own meltdown. But she was maturing. Baby steps.

Jesus wasn't born fully mature. I reread a familiar verse the other day in a passage of Scripture that hasn't always been clear to me: "Jesus *grew* in wisdom and stature and in favor with God and man."

It's the story of Jesus at twelve years old, when He lingered behind in the Temple, talking to the religious scholars even though his family's caravan—the biblical equivalent of a minivan—had already left for home.

He was—according to His parents—not where He was supposed to be. His mom said, "How could You worry us like that?" when He was reunited with the family. "What are You trying to do? Give us heart attacks?"

Luke 2 ends with this moment in history. Jesus responded to their angst by going to Nazareth with His earth parents and "was obedient to them" (Luke 2:51, CEB). And Jesus "matured in wisdom and years, and in favor with God and with the people."

In the wisdom category, there's hope for all of us! Even Jesus had room to grow.

FAITH STEP: *Consider in what realms you're wiser than you were a year ago. Does that encourage your heart? In what area would you like to make the same claim a year from now? Mark your calendar with a reminder to check on your progress.*

—*Cynthia Ruchti*

# SUNDAY, AUGUST 24

*Call on Me in a day of trouble; I will rescue you, and you will honor Me.* Psalm 50:15 (HCS)

I STRUGGLED TO PUSH BACK the rising panic. *How in the world do I get myself in these messes?* I groaned. I'd gone to the department store that evening to shop for a dress; it had been years since I'd bought one, and two weddings were coming up. I finally found a pretty peach dress with a side zipper. Figuring I could wear a smaller size dress than pants, I pulled one off the rack and headed for the dressing room.

As soon as I pulled the dress over my head, I saw that the sides of the zipper wouldn't even come close to each other. So I tried to pull the dress off. It wouldn't budge. I tried pushing it down over my hips. No chance. Several times I grabbed the bottom edge and pulled upward. I was stuck.

My husband was on a job assignment out of the country. My daughter had recently moved away. Should I call a friend to come to the store with a pair of scissors? Should I stick my head out of the dressing room and call a salesperson? Then I thought about praying for help. And I'm not sure how, but I finally got out of that dress.

I often find myself in situations that would be hilarious if they were scenes in a television sitcom, but in real life—not so much. If the circumstances are the result of my own foolishness or poor choices, I don't immediately think of praying for help. Yet I wouldn't hesitate to call out to Jesus if I were in a serious emergency. Since Jesus loves me unconditionally, I should trust Him to respond to my cries anytime I need Him, whether I'm in mortal danger or just stuck in a too-small dress in a department store.

FAITH STEP: *This week watch for any feelings of panic or helplessness that arise. Regardless of the situation, immediately recite Psalm 50:15, then ask Jesus to rescue you. Trust that He will answer.*

—*Dianne Neal Matthews*

# MONDAY, AUGUST 25

*Jesus, who offered himself in exchange for everyone held captive by sin, to set them all free.*
1 Timothy 2:6 (MSG)

WHEN WE MOVED TO OUR first full-time church after seminary, my husband's salary was tight with our growing family. When I opened the mail one day and found a $400 late fee bill from a car dealership we had formerly done business with, I was devastated.

A few months before we had paid off our first new car and celebrated our "debt-free" status. The bill might as well have read $4,000! As far as we knew, we had always made our payments on time. Apparently the dealership had never notified us of any late payments until after they had received our last check.

After praying, we finally decided to send them an honest appeal letter, explaining that we were unaware of any late payments while in seminary and had worked hard to keep a good credit rating. The debt would be extremely hard on our family. We were hoping for more time or at least small monthly payments. Finally a letter arrived, which offered neither option. Instead they forgave our debt—erased the entire amount!

God sent us a personal letter called the Bible. Those who read it carefully discover they owe Him a tremendous debt caused by sin. No amount of money, good credit ratings, or emotional appeals can reduce or ever remove the debt. How devastating!

But in that same letter God revealed a way for us to be debt-free. He gave His own Son, Jesus, to die on a cross and take our penalty. Our part? Only believe, and receive that one-time payment for ourselves—for eternity. How could we not accept His offer?

FAITH STEP: *Have you ever received Jesus's gift of "debt-free" status personally? If so, describe how that feels.*

—*Rebecca Barlow Jordan*

# TUESDAY, AUGUST 26

*But the fruit of the Spirit is love, joy, peace, patience, kindness, goodness, faithfulness, gentleness, and self-control. Against such things there is no law. Galatians 5:22–23 (NIV)*

LATELY, MY KIDS HAVE BEEN into mastering the art of making smoothies. I am thrilled. Anytime they opt for fruit as a snack food, I feel I have won a small nutritional victory. They put in any kind of fruit we have on hand. Peaches. Pineapple. Strawberries. Blueberries. Bananas. Everything is dumped in the blender.

It is interesting to me how the smoothie tends to taste better with each subsequent fruit. Strawberry and banana is lovely. But strawberry, banana, and orange juice? Even better. And strawberry, banana, orange juice, and blueberry? Stupendous!

It is no different when it comes to the fruit of the Spirit, the fruit that is yielded in our lives when we are following Jesus and letting Him shape our character. Love is so attractive. I will spend hours with someone who is loving, basking in the warmth of their care. But being with someone full of love and joy? Even better. And a person overflowing with love, joy, and kindness with a splash of goodness? Fantastic!

When we invite Jesus into our lives, we become more like Him. He is the embodiment of the fruit of the Spirit. When we are full of His presence, we become more attractive to those around us. Who wouldn't want to spend time with us when we are overflowing with love, joy, peace, patience, kindness, goodness, faithfulness, gentleness, and self-control? The more we are like Jesus on the inside, the more the people on the outside get a taste of Who He is. And that is good stuff.

FAITH STEP: *Eat your favorite piece of fruit. Or better yet, make a smoothie chock-full of different fruits. Enjoy its sweetness. Ask Jesus to keep producing the fruit of the Spirit in your life.*

—Susanna Foth Aughtmon

# WEDNESDAY, AUGUST 27

*Because of our God's deep compassion, the dawn from heaven will break upon us, to give light to those who are sitting in darkness and in the shadow of death, to guide us on the path of peace.*
Luke 1:78–79 (CEB)

THE PHYSICAL THERAPIST EXPRESSED SURPRISE at how far my husband had advanced since his hospitalization following a near-fatal fall, and asked us, "To what do you attribute this remarkable recovery?"

Without stopping to think about it, I responded, "Time, love, and tenderness," remembering a song title from decades ago.

As soon as the words were out of my mouth, they bounced back to jolt me. That was how we'd survived. We accepted that it would take time. We determined to love strong even when pain or frustration threatened to weaken that bond—even when neither of us liked the roles into which we'd been thrust. And we made a commitment to be tender with each other's hurts: his back and leg and dignity, my schedule and creative energy and loss of freedom.

Time. Love. And tenderness. That's what it takes. It's a divine combination that sets the stage for healing or coping. Either one.

As with everything good, Jesus set the precedent millennia ago. How did He put up with thick-skulled, fickle, disobedient, faithless, unfaithful disciples? Time. Love. Tenderness.

He waited—time. He kept loving. And He "remember(ed) that we are but dust," as the Old Testament tells us—tenderness.

Time and love are great healers. Throw tenderness in the mix, and you have a powerful cocktail for difference-making. Jesus knew it, modeled it, and taught it to the rest of us who would desperately need it.

FAITH STEP: *You may have a lock on patience and unwavering love. Is your serving marked by tenderness? Like me, do you need to invite the Lord's help in gaining better balance in the tenderness department?*

—*Cynthia Ruchti*

# THURSDAY, AUGUST 28

*Open their eyes and turn them from darkness to light, and from the power of Satan to God, so that they may receive forgiveness of sins and a place among those who are sanctified by faith in Me. Acts 26:18 (NIV)*

ONE OF MY FAVORITE SHORT stories, *Cathedral*, by Raymond Carver, is about a blind man who comes to visit a couple in their home. He's friends with the wife of the couple, who used to work for him, and the husband is none too keen on his visit. As the story evolves, the husband reveals that he's a pretty big jerk; he's rude to his wife, and prejudiced against people with physical limitations.

One night, it's just the husband and the blind man together after the wife has gone to bed. They have an experience in which they draw a cathedral and the blind man shows the husband how to see with his heart instead of his eyes.

It's a beautiful story of spiritual awakening. This man, who was so absorbed in himself and blind to the beauty in life, learns to see beauty, ironically, when a blind man shows him how.

That's what Jesus does when He comes into our lives. Like the old hymn says, I "was blind, but now I see." And that's our role in the lives of others, to bear His light that they may see Jesus and find His way in the darkness.

FAITH STEP: *Who needs you to share the light of Jesus today? Pray for God to bring them to mind. When He does, send a card, call, do whatever you can to bear His light.*

—*Gwen Ford Faulkenberry*

# FRIDAY, AUGUST 29

*God proves to be good to the man who passionately waits, to the woman who diligently seeks.*
*Lamentations 3:25 (MSG)*

LAST YEAR I WAS AT a women's retreat, and the organizer gave us two whole afternoons with nothing on the schedule.

I couldn't be happier. As a mom of one toddler, I was happy if I got fifteen minutes of quiet time with God each day. With a smile I plumped up a pillow, stared out at the ocean view, opened my Bible, and pulled out the journal. It was a sweet time with God, and as I read His Word one thing came up over and over in the Scriptures I read: "Care for the orphan."

This couldn't be a coincidence. On the plane ride to the retreat I'd read the book *Kisses from Katie*. It's about a young woman who moved to Uganda to care for orphans, and now it seemed like every Scripture verse that God led me to spoke about the same thing.

"God, what are You asking us to do?" I thought of my husband. Sure, God could put something on my heart, but what would my husband say?

I asked a few friends to pray for me, and that night I called my husband. As the phone rang I was unsure if I should bring it up. My mouth dropped open in surprise when one of the first things John said to me was, "Have you ever considered adopting children from the foster care system?"

"Yes," I told him. "Yes, I have."

It's amazing what happens when we seek God. There may be times when He has a plan for our lives, and we simply need to be quiet enough—take the time—to listen and seek.

**FAITH STEP:** *Look at your schedule and find a block of time—even two or three hours—where you can spend time seeking God, reading His Word, and praying.*

—*Tricia Goyer*

# SATURDAY, AUGUST 30

*For the Son of God, Jesus Christ, who was preached among you by us—by me and Silas and Timothy—was not "Yes" and "No," but in him it has always been "Yes." For no matter how many promises God has made, they are "Yes" in Christ. And so through him the "Amen" is spoken by us to the glory of God. 2 Corinthians 1:19–20 (NIV)*

I SAT AT MY DESK, running my pen down the list of names. It was only a few days until Saturday. We had invited friends to a party celebrating the release of a new novel, asking folks to RSVP so we'd be able to prepare things like door prizes, snacks, and enough chairs.

But my list was a mess. Some people had called or e-mailed to tell me they were coming, but later said they couldn't. Others hadn't responded, but when I followed up they said they planned to be there. Plenty of "maybe" answers filled my page with question marks.

I certainly understood. Life is overwhelming and busy for everyone. On top of that, unexpected events interrupt: a car breaks down, a child gets chicken pox, a business crisis calls us in to work. Our plans often swing between yes and no.

Getting a firm "yes" or "no" wasn't of major importance for the party. We had fun with the folks who could come. But there are some questions where the answer is vital. Does God keep His promises? Is there a way of salvation? Does He truly love me? Does my life have value to Him? Do I have a purpose?

What a joy that Jesus is the resounding and unchanging "yes" to the important questions of life.

FAITH STEP: *Have you been wavering between a "yes" and "no" on a decision lately? Ask Jesus for guidance, and thank Him for being the resounding "yes" to life's important questions.*

—*Sharon Hinck*

# SUNDAY, AUGUST 31

*"Be careful that you do not forget the Lord, who brought you out of Egypt, out of the land of slavery." Deuteronomy 6:12 (NIV)*

I HAVE AN EARLY 1900s Singer treadle sewing machine table sitting in my foyer. I have fond memories of learning to sew with my Granny Bowers on that sewing machine. I inherited the treasured piece when she passed on to her reward, and I think of her often when I see it in our home.

There are other things that remind me of Granny. The smell of cold cream, because she kept a big pink jar of Pond's cold cream in her vanity. The sight of yellow roses, particularly growing in a large bush, because Granny loved the huge yellow rosebush that framed one side of her house. An old-fashioned single-seat swing tied to a large tree with rope, because Granny often pushed me on a swing like that.

It doesn't take a lot for me to be reminded of Granny, because I associate her presence with so many things. Likewise, I associate Christ's presence in my life with little reminders, as well. A song on the Christian radio station. A cross on a necklace. The sight of a rising or setting sun. So many reminders to keep me aware of my Lord. Like those reminders of my granny, the reminders of Christ give me peace and comfort, letting me know that He is everywhere.

FAITH STEP: *Find three things today that remind you of your Lord.*

—*Renee Andrews*

# MONDAY, SEPTEMBER 1

*Just as a body, though one, has many parts, but all its many parts form one body, so it is with Christ. For we were all baptized by one Spirit so as to form one body—whether Jews or Gentiles, slave or free—and we were all given the one Spirit to drink. Even so the body is not made up of one part but of many. 1 Corinthians 12:12–14 (NIV)*

MY FAMILY HAS A LABOR Day tradition. The entire gang gathers at my parents' home on the river for jet-skiing, swimming, good food…and homemade ice cream. My mother makes the *best* homemade ice cream. This Labor Day we were waiting for the ice cream, but the ice-cream maker just kept spinning. Then my dad remembered that he accidentally tossed the tiny part in the bottom out (and into the river, no less). That one little part ended up being important, and without it, the ice cream took much longer to get firm.

Like that tiny part in the ice-cream maker, each part of Christ's body is important to the livelihood of Christ's church. We may not feel like our tiny part matters, but in the entire scheme of things, we could be the reason the church doesn't stand firm. He needs our part.

For me, I sometimes feel I don't offer anything overly impressive to the growth of the Kingdom. I can speak, but I'm sure not great at it. I can sing, but it's nothing to write home about. And it took me *years* before I gathered the courage to pray out loud. But I do have a few things I can do and enjoy doing. I can write and share God's message with my readers. I can teach the preschoolers at church and help start their growth in the Lord. I can do my part servicing the nursery so new moms can fully enjoy the sermon. I can be willing to attribute my good mood to my good Lord whenever asked why I seem particularly happy. I can also let others know that God will see me through when I'm having hard times.

FAITH STEP: *Eat a bowl of ice cream today and think about all of the parts that were necessary for that delicious taste, and then thank Jesus that you can be a tiny part in His Kingdom.*

—*Renee Andrews*

# TUESDAY, SEPTEMBER 2

*"There is more to life than food and more to the body than clothing." Luke 12:23 (CEB)*

A CRISIS AT HOME HELPED put "things" in perspective, as crises often do. So does the Word of God, but we humans too often wait for the crisis to remind us what the Bible already had been saying to our hearts.

We lost a lot of minor things in a fire. The insurance inventory took several pages to print out, but some were as small as "lemon pepper, vegetable peeler, spatula, toast tongs, cereal..."

The remediation team scrubbed and rubbed some of the decorations I'd had sitting on top of the cupboards. At one point, I asked them to stop. They were just things. Nothing precious about them. I'd grown tired of them years ago, but hadn't the heart to toss them. Now I could. I saw them in a clearer light. Clutter.

Jesus isn't the typical picture of a homeless man. But He somehow managed to survive three years of ministry—travel included—without owning anything except the clothes on His back, for all we know. He enjoyed good food during feast times, created it at others, fished to feed His friends, appreciated the beauty of the Temple, felt blessed when invited to stay in a nice home. He and His Father were accustomed to providing things for those who needed them.

But He lived and taught that life does not consist in the accumulation of things (Luke 12:23).

It's a lesson that sometimes gets burned into the soul with flames.

I only have one spatula now. It's enough.

But I must say I'm grateful the fire didn't reach the dishwasher.

FAITH STEP: *Not for the sake of more cupboard space, but as an exercise in perspective, empty a cupboard today. Thank the Lord for what He's given. Donate anything of worth and toss the insignificant. You may be surprised how large a garbage bag you need.*

—*Cynthia Ruchti*

# WEDNESDAY, SEPTEMBER 3

*The Lord is my shepherd, I lack nothing. He makes me lie down in green pastures, he leads me beside quiet waters, he refreshes my soul. He guides me along the right paths for his name's sake.*
*Psalm 23:1–3 (NIV)*

WHEN SCHOOL STARTS UP AGAIN after any break, I go through several days of chasing my tail. After I drop the kids off, I'm eager to tackle the to-dos that I've put off while my young ones are home.

However, a curious thing happens as I walk through my door. My brain freezes and I lose all ability to prioritize. I stare at my list feeling useless about where to begin.

This phenomenon doesn't throw me as much as it used to. I've learned to sit down and pray first, asking Jesus to focus me on His action plan.

Ernest Hemingway is credited with saying "Never mistake motion for action." Based on how Jesus lived, I think He'd advise us to sit still more often than not, rather than scurry around wasting time. This advice can seem backward to our motion-driven culture; someone who looks busy must be accomplishing a lot, right?

Read carefully today's verses from Psalm 23, and notice what the Lord does first for the writer, King David. After David acknowledges that he lacks nothing (including the ability to accomplish his God-given tasks), he writes that the Lord makes him lie down in green pastures. Rest is the first task the Shepherd gives David. After that, the Shepherd gently nudges him to action, leading him first by quiet waters to refresh his soul. Once David is refreshed, Jesus knows he's ready to be guided along the right path for the day.

Never feel like you're wasting time by pausing to listen for Jesus to speak to you. In fact, prioritize that over the to-do list. You'll be much better prepared for what the day throws at you.

FAITH STEP: *Read Luke 5:16 to remind yourself that Jesus paused with His Father in order to refill for the coming demands.*

—*Erin Keeley Marshall*

# THURSDAY, SEPTEMBER 4

*When Jesus spoke again to the people, he said, "I am the light of the world. Whoever follows me will never walk in darkness, but will have the light of life." John 8:12 (NIV)*

WHEN I WAS FIVE YEARS old, I was invited to be part of a study at my school. Students from the nearby university were doing research about kids being afraid of the dark.

The day of the study, the student leading it told me, "We are going to leave you in this room with the lights out. At any time, you can turn them back on. But why don't you see how long you can go without turning them on." I said, "Okay." Piece of cake. The student proceeded to turn the lights off and walk out the room closing the door behind him. Five seconds later I proceeded to turn the lights back on. The student returned and said, "Why did you turn on the lights so quickly?" "Because I wanted to."

Most of us don't like sitting in the dark. We are made for light. Light is clarifying and warm and reveals the truth to us about our surroundings. We need it to function and to be able to see. We need it so that we are not afraid. It is no different when it comes to our hearts. We need the light of Jesus to come in and give us life, reveal the truth of our need for Him, and help us to grow.

There can be moments when we feel trapped in the darkness of real living, but the truth is that when we are following the One Who loves us most, He can take away our fear. He surrounds us with His warmth. And He gives us new life. There is nothing better than that.

**FAITH STEP:** *Sit in a dark room for five minutes. Think about what living life without Jesus is like. Then turn on the light. Think about the difference that Jesus brought into your life when you decided to follow Him.*

*—Susanna Foth Aughtmon*

# FRIDAY, SEPTEMBER 5

*But to all who did receive him, who believed in his name, he gave the right to become children of God. John 1:12 (ESV)*

LIKE SO MANY WOMEN, I struggle with feelings of inadequacy. I still remember the first time I felt like I didn't quite measure up. On my very first day of school, the teacher asked us to take out our tablets and chunky pencils and draw a page of straight lines and *O*s. I felt so excited and proud of my accomplishment—until I looked over at the tablet of the girl next to me. Suddenly my own page looked sloppy, with crooked lines and lopsided *O*s.

Those feelings of inferiority only worsened as I grew up, especially during the teen years. Now I have to admit that even at my age (gasp!) the problem hasn't completely gone away. Too many times I find myself thinking that I'm not quite good enough, whether in the area of intelligence, talent, or appearance. Or I use my background and past life experiences as an excuse to shy away from stretching myself and trying new things.

That's why I so appreciate Jesus's condensed genealogy in the opening verses of Matthew. Although genealogies didn't normally include women, God recorded the names of four. They include Tamar, who disguised herself as a prostitute so she could have sex with her father-in-law, and Bathsheba, who committed adultery with David. Rahab was a prostitute from Jericho, a city destroyed by the Israelites. Ruth came from Moab, a country despised by Israel.

In spite of these women's moral failures and questionable backgrounds, God gave them the privilege of being physical ancestors of the Savior of the world. What a great reminder that faith trumps any inferiority on my part. God's arms are open wide to any who are willing to believe in Jesus. And that relationship is where my true worth comes from.

**FAITH STEP:** *The next time you catch yourself feeling like you don't measure up, remember your identity as God's dearly loved child and someone whom Jesus died for.*

—*Dianne Neal Matthews*

# SATURDAY, SEPTEMBER 6

*Be still, and know that I am God! Psalm 46:10 (NLT)*

HAVE YOU EVER BEEN STUCK in a rut? I have—a literal one. One year our family camped together in the Oklahoma mountains. Our older daughter, who had already graduated from college, joined us for the adventure.

For some reason, she and I had each driven a car down the hill to the small store in a central area. My daughter left to go back first. I told her I knew the way and would soon follow. But as I drove up the hill I must have taken a wrong turn. The road began to ascend, twisting and turning like a pretzel. I hadn't remembered that coming down.

To make the scene worse, no lights flickered in the area. It was pitch-dark. Where was I? I crept slowly around a curve, desperately trying to avoid the edge, which I couldn't see. *Wham!* All of a sudden I felt the car drop into a shallow crevice on the right side. I couldn't move forward, and I couldn't move backward. The car was riding on high center. I tried every way I knew to get out, but nothing helped. I was stuck.

I began honking my horn, and then stopped. What if someone—or something—sinister lurked nearby? Finally I mustered the courage to open my door and peer through the darkness. I heard faint voices! Apparently my family was directly below and heard the horn. "*Larrryyyyy!*" I yelled into the blackness.

"Stay where you are!" I heard the swift but familiar voice. Within five minutes, my knight in shining armor arrived in the other car and pulled me to safety.

Whenever we're stuck in the ruts of perfection, fruitless work, or unyielding circumstances, we can struggle until we're bone-weary. But nothing helps, until we learn to be still, cry out to Jesus, and wait for the familiar, reassuring voice of our Rescuer.

**FAITH STEP:** *Are there any ruts in your life? This week, practice "being still" so you can hear Jesus's voice and get to know Him better.*

—*Rebecca Barlow Jordan*

# SUNDAY, SEPTEMBER 7

*No eye has seen, no ear has heard, no mind has conceived what God has prepared*
*for those who love him.* 1 Corinthians 2:9 (NIV)

AS A SPEAKER, ONE OF my favorite things to do is encourage the audience to "dream big." Too many times we put God in a box. We're afraid to step out of our comfort zones. We forget that God created the universe, so surely He can help us with our small dreams. There are many dreams God has helped me fulfill: starting a crisis pregnancy center, leading a mission team to Europe, and writing books for a living, to name a few. So I like to encourage others to dream big since I've seen dreams come true in my life. Yet lately I've been adding a P.S. to my message. Why? Because in my good intentions, I may have led people to become discouraged instead.

One of the problems with the message "dream big" is that we let our human minds measure what "big" is. We think it has to be fame or success or a huge blog. We think it has to involve starting a ministry or sharing Christ in an atheistic country. This doesn't always have to be the case. What is "big" to God?

The "big" thing to God is obeying what He asks you to do. You could become famous, make it big, and become well-known—and it would amount to nothing. Or you can ask God what *big* is to Him. You might be surprised.

Last year, my husband and I felt God telling us to walk away from some of our ministry opportunities in order to adopt two children from the foster care system. I will not become famous wiping noses, playing mommy, or pushing a swing, but to God this is a big thing.

What is big to God in your life? It's a question you need to ask. It's wonderful to dream big . . . just as long as you are sure you know that the direction of your dream was inspired by your loving heavenly Father.

FAITH STEP: *Take a minute and think about the dreams God has been speaking to your heart. Write them down, even though they may not seem big to the world's eyes. Now, what is one step you can take toward them? Write that down too.*

—*Tricia Goyer*

# MONDAY, SEPTEMBER 8

*The first thing Andrew did was to find his brother Simon and tell him, "We have found the Messiah" (that is, the Christ). And he brought him to Jesus. John 1:41–42 (NIV)*

OUR OLDEST SON'S NAME IS John Rene. He has my husband's name, because having a John Rene Jr. was very important to him; he wanted his name to be passed down. So, since he picked the oldest child's name, I picked our youngest child's name: Kaleb Andrew. The "Andrew" in his name was given because I knew our boys would be close in age (only eighteen months between them), but I also wanted them to be close spiritually. And Andrew in the Bible brought his brother, Simon Peter, to Christ. Peter, whom we hear about as giving the first Gospel sermon. Peter, who walked on water to get to his Lord. Peter, upon whose confession Christ said He would build His church.

Today our boys are closer than ever. They lived together in college. They have served in ministries together. They preach together. They hang out together. They love each other. And, in fact, I have witnessed our boys bringing several others to Christ.

Who knows what will happen from the new Christians who heard the Good News through Rene and Kaleb? They could have planted the seed in a future preacher, or a young father who will now raise his family in the Lord, or a teen who may have traveled the wrong path in life. Who knows what would have happened to Peter if Andrew hadn't felt compelled to share his great news with his brother?

Yes, we learn a lot about Peter and those like him, who stand out in the world for their spirituality. But in order to have Peter, we need Andrew. And in order to build Christ's Kingdom today, we need to be like Andrew. We need to bring our brothers—and our sisters—to meet our Lord.

FAITH STEP: *Ask someone today if they know who brought Peter to Christ. Then ask yourself if you've ever been an Andrew to someone else. If you haven't, today is a great day to start!*

—*Renee Andrews*

# TUESDAY, SEPTEMBER 9

*Your beauty should not come from outward adornment, such as elaborate hairstyles and the wearing of gold jewelry or fine clothes. Rather, it should be that of your inner self, the unfading beauty of a gentle and quiet spirit, which is of great worth in God's sight.* 1 Peter 3:3–4 (NIV)

IN ONE OF THE CLASSES I teach, we talk about gender roles in society. I usually show a video called *Killing Us Softly*, which examines advertising's image of women and how that influences our thinking about beauty and what it means. The message of the video, and its challenge, is that we must think critically about popular culture, and make choices to reject unhealthy stereotypes as we define what beauty means to us.

It's a great conversation starter. And I am all for critical thinking. What I would add is that we should look to Jesus to define what it means to be beautiful. First, it has nothing to do with anything outward—not our size, age, the color of our skin, our clothes—none of that. Instead, it has everything to do with what's inside. What have we allowed Him to cultivate in our inner selves?

The Bible says a gentle and quiet spirit is of great worth to God. We also want to display the fruits of the Spirit. There's nothing wrong with looking good, but rather than spending too much time in front of the mirror, we need to focus on the time it takes with Him to develop character.

**FAITH STEP:** *Is it time for a spiritual makeover? What might you need to change in order to look more like Jesus?*

—*Gwen Ford Faulkenberry*

# WEDNESDAY, SEPTEMBER 10

*Dear friends, carefully build yourselves up in this most holy faith by praying in the Holy Spirit, staying right at the center of God's love, keeping your arms open and outstretched, ready for the mercy of our Master, Jesus Christ. This is the unending life, the real life! Jude 1:21–22 (MSG)*

DO YOU APPROACH JESUS WITH the "arms" of your heart outstretched, sure of the blessing and mercy He's waiting to lavish on you?

If not, why not? It's right there in His Word that we're to approach Him just that way, staying in the center of His love, keeping (as in consistently, not just every now and then) our arms open and outstretched, ready for His mercy.

Our lives are in Jesus's hands, it's true. The more we know Him, the more we know how much we truly depend on Him.

Yet we still have our part to do. We must take an active role in building up our own faith, in seeking Him out with a heart that lives to be filled by Him. Notice the focus isn't on getting every behavior correct, never ever messing up. Sure, it's important to obey Him consistently. Yet the focus of these verses is about soaking Him up, not showing Him how perfectly we can act.

*I love that!*

Can we breathe a collective sigh of relief? Oh, such good news that His direction to us about building our Christian faith is first about soaking up all that good love He has for us.

He tells us to talk to Him, to stay right in the center of His love, and to run to Him for bountiful doses of mercy.

Today is the perfect day, right now is the perfect time, to head to Him for some of that abundant life.

**FAITH STEP:** *Ask Jesus to lavish you with Himself. Then get ready; He loves to fulfill that request!*

*—Erin Keeley Marshall*

# THURSDAY, SEPTEMBER 11

*Therefore, since we are surrounded by such a great cloud of witnesses, let us throw off everything that hinders and the sin that so easily entangles, and let us run with perseverance the race marked out for us. Let us fix our eyes on Jesus, the author and perfecter of our faith, who for the joy set before him, endured the cross, scorning its shame, and sat down at the right hand of the throne of God. Hebrews 12:1–2 (NIV)*

MY FRIEND JENN AND I are training for a mud run that we will run with a group of our friends.

It is a 5K run with an obstacle course. We may die trying to complete this race. Our first obstacle is a mud pit that we will have to wade through. The mud is waist-high. The other obstacles include a climbing wall, a net wall, a mud crawl, and a tire run. This is why we are going to die.

But we are also going to have fun. Because we will thoroughly enjoy seeing our friends crawl through a pit of mud too. We will be cheering them on, rooting for them, and hoping they don't get too much mud up their noses.

This is not unlike life and following Jesus. It is challenging and messy. But one of the best parts of following Jesus is that we don't have to go it alone. We have banded together with our fellow Christ-followers, throwing off what holds us back, shaking loose from the sins that try and hold us and looking toward the One Who loves us most—Jesus. We may make mistakes and fall all over ourselves, but we have each other's backs.

We are witnessing each other become more like Jesus each step of the way. And that is a beautiful thing. Even if we get mud up our noses.

**FAITH STEP:** *Go for a walk with a friend. Tell them that you love them and that you are so glad that you are on this journey of following Jesus together, even when it gets messy.*

—Susanna Foth Aughtmon

# FRIDAY, SEPTEMBER 12

*For our struggle is not against flesh and blood, but against the rulers, against the authorities, against the powers of this dark world and against the spiritual forces of evil in the heavenly realms. Ephesians 6:12 (NIV)*

LIKE A WOMAN DUMPING THE contents of her purse on the table so she could sort through the mess, a friend dumped her family issues on the table between us.

Only one verse came to mind. She was in no mood to hear it that day, but I'm watching for the opportunity to share its comfort.

Jesus knew the concept well. When He asked His Father to forgive the men who spat on Him, pierced Him, drove nails in His hands and feet, He was living out the truth of it.

"For we wrestle not against flesh and blood."

I've skipped past that verse with, "Oh. Right. It's not *humans* who are our ultimate enemies." But now, because of the frustrations of people like my friend and her dysfunctional family, I'm seeing its deeper meaning.

"My own flesh and blood," my friend might say. Those are the spears that hurt the most—when they're hurled by our own loved ones.

Jesus, having felt it all to the depth of His marrow, reminds us they're not the enemy. Through Him and like Him, we can hold our flesh and blood close and see that the heart of the trouble isn't with who they are, but with the greed or selfishness or irresponsibility that grips them at the moment.

FAITH STEP: *If your own flesh and blood sometimes drives you crazy, take a step back and filter their actions or attitudes through the one Jesus used with those who hurt Him: "Father, forgive them, for they know not what they do."*

—*Cynthia Ruchti*

# SATURDAY, SEPTEMBER 13

*And there was a widow in that town who kept coming to him with the plea,*
*"Grant me justice against my adversary." Luke 18:3 (NIV)*

"MOM, IT'S GONE. MY WHOLE semester of work, over one hundred hours...gone." Kaleb was in his fourth year of college, and as an art major, he depended on that portfolio at the end of the semester for his final grade. But every piece of art he'd created was on a jump drive that he'd left in the university's computer lab. He'd returned to find it was gone, and he hadn't thought to produce a backup. "I might as well not even finish the semester."

"Have you prayed?" I asked, and he answered he had. "Then we'll pray too." And I called others to pray, as well. We all prayed our hearts out, and the next day another student brought the jump drive back to the lab.

Right now, my husband and I have two houses for sale. Do I need two houses? No. Am I certain that Christ knows I do not need two houses (or want two house payments)? Yes, I'm sure He knows, because my husband and I keep asking Him for guidance and for help with either or both of the homes selling. It would be easy to say, "Well, He doesn't want us to sell the houses. Let's rent them out and wait a few years." But we've decided not to give up and instead, to turn it over to Christ...again and again.

In the parable of the persistent widow, Jesus showed that it never hurts to keep asking. For Kaleb's work, we kept asking through prayer, and He answered with a "yes" that made Kaleb's day. Consequently, Kaleb now has a backup of all of his artwork...just in case. And we'll keep praying about the houses and remain hopeful that He will say "yes."

**FAITH STEP:** *Do you feel like you're wearing out Christ's ear with your requests? Do you assume He said no if you pray once and don't see results? Repeat that prayer, then repeat it again. Maybe what He wants from you...is persistence.*

—*Renee Andrews*

# SUNDAY, SEPTEMBER 14

*Peter, an apostle of Jesus Christ, To God's elect, exiles scattered throughout the provinces of Pontus, Galatia, Cappadocia, Asia and Bithynia, who have been chosen according to the fore-knowledge of God the Father, through the sanctifying work of the Spirit, to be obedient to Jesus Christ and sprinkled with his blood: Grace and peace be yours in abundance. 1 Peter 1:1—2 (NIV)*

WHEN I WAS IN GRADE school, I was often chosen last for teams at recess. My response to a ball flying toward me is to close my eyes and duck. Not an effective approach to baseball, kickball, or basketball. Even though I acknowledged my lack of skill, it still hurt. Waiting to be chosen. Hoping this time I'd be second-to-last instead of last. Feeling unwanted.

We all long to be chosen in some way. A single young man wonders if the sweet woman he's dating will choose him as a spouse one day. A woman applying for a job wonders if this time she'll be picked over the hundreds of other applicants. A high school senior wonders if his favorite college will accept him.

What a blessing to know that Jesus has chosen to love us. To rescue us. To die for us. We don't have to wait at the sidelines feeling unwanted. He calls us to Himself in a loud and eager voice.

FAITH STEP: *Think of a time when you weren't chosen. Invite Jesus to heal that hurt and embrace the joy of being chosen by Him.*

—*Sharon Hinck*

# MONDAY, SEPTEMBER 15

*When the Red Sea saw you, O God, its waters looked and trembled! The sea quaked to its very depths... Your road led through the sea; your pathway through the mighty waters—a pathway no one knew was there! Psalm 77:16, 19 (NLT)*

IMAGINE THE TERROR AND HOPELESSNESS the Israelites felt as they stood on the Red Sea's banks. Behind them approached the Egyptian army. Before them lay a vast body of water. With no visible escape route, doom seemed inevitable. But God was on their side, and that changed everything.

The people panicked, but the Red Sea looked at God and trembled to its core. Then the waters parted to reveal a path—a dry path, nonetheless. A way of escape known by no one but God.

Sometimes *we* face a Red Sea too. When International Messengers USA asked me and my husband to launch its Canadian office, we hadn't a clue how we could afford to leave our ministry, where accommodation was provided, and reenter the housing market. For months we prayed, "God, the date of our departure fast approaches, and a financial Red Sea lies before us. We can't see a way through this, but You are God. We trust You to make a way."

We cried out to God in our distress, and He parted the waters to reveal the path He knew existed all along. He provided a Christian Realtor and mortgage broker, and He used them to lead us to an affordable townhouse. The deal closed the day before we moved.

You might be facing a Red Sea today—a situation that looks impossible. Don't let it intimidate you. It sees God and trembles to the core. God already knows the path through it, and He will part the waters for you.

**FAITH STEP:** *Read Psalm 77:13–20 out loud as an act of worship and praise. Thank God for being sovereign over the Red Sea you face today.*

—*Grace Fox*

# TUESDAY, SEPTEMBER 16

*The wise are glad to be instructed, but babbling fools fall flat on their faces. Proverbs 10:8 (NLT)*

SOME PEOPLE WEAR PEDOMETERS TO record the miles they walk each day. With all the gizmos available, surely there's one to record the number of words we speak. If not, we ought to invent one.

Let's call it a word-o-meter. We'll program it to limit us to 25,000 words per day. It blinks a red light when we hit 23,000. It buzzes a warning at 24,000. At 25,000, it slaps duct tape across our mouths.

The word-o-meter's hypothetical, of course. Too bad the talk-too-much issue is reality. Not for everyone, but for many. And those who struggle with it know what troubles it can cause.

Talking too much means we say things we probably shouldn't. We share a piece of our minds. We gossip, or we share confidential information. And we do it without considering our words' hurtful impact on others.

Talking too much may also mean we're not allowing others to speak, or we're not really hearing what they say because we've engaged our mouths but not our ears or our hearts.

Proverbs 10:19, (NLT) says, "Don't talk too much, for it fosters sin. Be sensible and turn off the flow!" Saying fewer words leaves smaller margin for error. And less chance of eating duct tape.

**FAITH STEP:** *Consciously pay attention to how many words you speak today. How many are unnecessary? How many are hurtful or critical? Compare that to how many are encouraging. Ask the Holy Spirit to put a guard over your mouth so the words you speak bring life to others.*

*—Grace Fox*

# WEDNESDAY, SEPTEMBER 17

*We know how troubles can develop passionate patience in us, . . . keeping us alert for whatever God will do next. In alert expectancy such as this, we're never left feeling shortchanged. Quite the contrary—we can't round up enough containers to hold everything God generously pours into our lives through the Holy Spirit! Romans 5:3–5 (MSG)*

"IF HE ASKS YOU TO put something down, it's because He wants you to pick up something greater." Someone recently posted that quote on Facebook. It's the promise of a better tradeoff coming for those who feel shortchanged by something they feel Jesus is asking them to let go of in this life.

Read today's verses again in light of that hope.

I think a major reason for our culture's crazed drive to acquire is because of the underlying terror of knowing we will lose everything earthly at the end of this life. Without the eternal hope of Jesus to anchor us, we go nuts to think that we could lose all that is most precious here.

However, from Jesus's perspective, life on earth is about loss and letting go. From the first sin in Eden, we have been unable to save this world. Along with sin comes more loss. Even when we do our best for Him, we still are vulnerable to sin's effects.

Sometimes in living for Jesus, He asks us to let go of something we care for deeply so that He can do a greater work. Sometimes He allows terrible things because those things are part of this failing world. However, He promises to "repay you for the years the locusts have eaten" (Joel 2:25, NIV).

Jesus knows eternity with Himself and our heavenly Father will far, far, far surpass all that we lost on earth. In fact, it will wipe away all those losses and disappointments.

That hope doesn't completely remove our pain today, but it offers a glimpse into glory that we need to keep going.

**FAITH STEP:** *What (or whom) have you lost in this life? What hope does God offer for eternity that lifts your heart in the here and now?*

—*Erin Keeley Marshall*

# THURSDAY, SEPTEMBER 18

*"Everyone brings out the choice wine first and then the cheaper wine after the guests have had too much to drink; but you have saved the best till now." John 2:10 (NIV)*

FOR AS LONG AS I can remember, I've eaten my food one item at a time, and I save my favorite for last (not necessarily dessert, since I love vegetables). I do the same thing with many aspects of life. If I see an e-mail that I know I'll enjoy, I open it last. When I get the mail, if I see a royalty check is in the batch, I save it for last.

When I read the story of Jesus turning the water into wine and then the Master's comment about saving the best for last, I think of my own method of savoring the things I love most, saving them for last. And then I realize that the ultimate "best for last" scenario is the one that is to come, because our Lord truly saved the best for last when He promised us heaven.

He knows we will have several amazing moments in life. Graduation from high school or college. Our wedding day. The birth of a child. That first job. A big anniversary. All of those are wonderful, but not one (or all combined) compare to the "best" that our Lord saved for last, an eternity to spend with our loved ones and with our Lord and Savior. How awesome is that best for last?

FAITH STEP: *Today when you eat a meal, save your favorite item until the end. Then think about how the true end will be when you're reunited with your loved ones in heaven…and when you finally meet your Savior face-to-face. Definitely saving the best for last!*

*—Renee Andrews*

# FRIDAY, SEPTEMBER 19

*David, ceremonially dressed in priest's linen, danced with great abandon before God.... I'll dance to God's glory—more recklessly even than this. And as far as I'm concerned... I'll gladly look like a fool.* 2 Samuel 6:14, 21 (MSG)

CERTAIN ACTIVITIES CAN EVOKE BOTH positive and negative emotions from us, like when our favorite sports team is winning or losing. Ordinary reserved fans can transform into animated fools. After all, who wouldn't express great enthusiasm when your team just made the winning touchdown?

King David had just rescued the coveted Ark of God, the symbol of God's presence, and was bringing it back to Jerusalem, where it belonged. Enemies had waged a battle over it, and David's "team" had won! He was ecstatic.

Others had tried to transport the Ark without following God's precise instructions and had died. So David took his time, reviewing God's words with great caution. As he drew near Jerusalem, he could contain his joy no longer. David cut loose and "danced with great abandon" after shedding his customary royal robe. About that time his wife Michal looked out the window and saw David's antikingly behavior. She accused him and his actions as undignified and indecent. Michal failed to see the joyful motive in David's heart. Her criticism cost her a great deal.

It's easy to misjudge another's expression in showing our love to Jesus. He is the only One Who truly knows our motives. King David's joyful abandonment to the Lord was both appropriate and pleasing to the Lord.

While we may express our deep joy to Jesus in different ways, He knows us thoroughly. If it's done for Him, that's what matters.

FAITH STEP: *Think about what Jesus means to you. In the way that fits you best, express it to the Lord with "great abandonment" today.*

—*Rebecca Barlow Jordan*

# SATURDAY, SEPTEMBER 20

*"But when you give to the needy, do not let your left hand know what your right hand is doing, so that your giving may be in secret. Then your Father, who sees what is done in secret, will reward you." Matthew 6:3–4 (NIV)*

As my husband and I walked off the plane, we could barely hold our heads up. Both of us had been terribly sick the night before. Driving home, we thought about how cold the house would be with the thermostat turned down to fifty-eight degrees. Seeing almost a foot of snow on the ground, Richard felt even worse when he pictured our driveway. How would we manage to clear a path feeling so weak and achy? A half hour later we turned down our street—and saw our driveway neatly shoveled. Later, I wondered which of our neighbors had done such a kind deed.

I also remembered a different approach to giving that I'd witnessed during my college days. As I arrived in the psychology office one morning to make coffee, I noticed a box lying on a table with this humorous note: "Help yourself to a doughnut. And don't forget who gave it to you." Then the professor had signed his name.

In Matthew 6 Jesus listed three ways that we can reap rewards: giving to the needy, praying, and fasting. He also explained that we have a choice of whether we want to be rewarded by people or by God. If we make sure that everyone knows we're giving, or if we do our praying in public in a showy way, then we may win admiration from others. But if we do these things in secret with no thought of glorifying ourselves, God will reward us Himself.

There's a special feeling that comes from doing something for others anonymously, without expecting thanks or anything in return. But the best part? Knowing that God saw our actions and promises to reward us Himself.

**Faith step:** *Whom can you bless today with an anonymous kind deed? Ask Jesus to help you be alert to opportunities.*

—Dianne Neal Matthews

# SUNDAY, SEPTEMBER 21

---

*Do not be anxious about anything, but in everything, by prayer and petition, with thanksgiving, present your requests to God. And the peace of God, which transcends all understanding, will guard your hearts and your minds in Christ Jesus. Philippians 4:6–7 (NIV)*

---

THE OTHER NIGHT I COULD not go to sleep. I tossed and turned. I flipped my pillow over seventeen times. I was thinking about all the things that needed to be done in the morning.

When I finally drifted off, it seemed like it was mere minutes later that it was time to get up and face the day. I was exhausted and cranky. Even coffee couldn't help. The children gave me a wide berth. They seemed to know by the wild look in my eyes that this was not a good morning to push any of Mom's buttons.

Anxiety tends to lend itself to...more anxiety and some worry with a large side of irritability. It makes sense that the Scriptures say, "Do not be anxious for anything." Anxiety flies in the face of what Jesus came to earth to do. He came so that we might have life and have it more abundantly.

It is hard to live an abundant life when you are constantly worried. Instead we get the choice of offering our worries to the One Who can do something about them. And in return He will give us an incomprehensible peace and will protect our hearts and minds, which will actually keep us from being anxious. It seems like a good deal to me. I think I'll take Him up on it.

---

FAITH STEP: *On a piece of paper, write down three things that are making you anxious. Offer them up to Jesus in prayer and thank Him in advance for His peace and the protection of your thoughts. Toss the piece of paper in the trash, reminding yourself that you have given your worries to Jesus.*

—Susanna Foth Aughtmon

# MONDAY, SEPTEMBER 22

*And since I, your Lord and Teacher, have washed your feet, you ought to wash each other's feet. I have given you an example to follow. Do as I have done to you. John 13:14–15 (NLT)*

DURING A DIFFICULT TIME IN one of the churches where we served, my husband agreed to become interim pastor, in addition to his other roles. The temporary position lasted less than a year, but the church overwhelmed us with their gift of gratitude: a trip to "anywhere we wanted."

We chose Hawaii, our first cruise. The night before we left, our travel agent called and told us we had been upgraded to a "penthouse suite." No way! But when we boarded the ship and found our room, we stood with mouth agape. The huge, beautiful room had too many amenities to list! Within the hour a "butler" appeared to offer her services. "I am here for you," she said.

She reappeared several times during the week. Wasn't there anything we needed? We explained to her that in the ministry we were used to serving others, not being served. We felt a little uncomfortable. We did finally agree to a couple of breakfasts on the balcony. And we thoroughly enjoyed the beautiful room upgrade all week, realizing our "trip of a lifetime" as God's gift to us.

A worship song we sing regularly at our church is, "We Are Here for You." I thought about our Hawaii experience the other day as I was singing that song. Sometimes we may unconsciously say to Jesus: *You are here for me.* And other times, though He grants undeserved blessings and promises, His goodness may even make us feel uncomfortable.

A fine line exists between "acting like a King's kid" and choosing servanthood. Jesus wants us to enjoy His gifts. But He is not "here for us"—not as a butler who will satisfy our every whim or craving. His supreme example reminds us that we are here to love and serve Him and others, any way we can.

FAITH STEP: *How can you serve others this week?*

*—Rebecca Barlow Jordan*

# TUESDAY, SEPTEMBER 23

*I praise you, for I am fearfully and wonderfully made. Wonderful are your works; my soul knows it very well. Psalm 139:14 (ESV)*

MY DAUGHTER AND I SHARE a love of handmade pottery. At a high-quality art fair, we'll head for the pottery booths every time.

One of her husband's most romantic gifts to her was a kiln he found at a garage sale. Now, that's love.

The footed pitcher-like pottery bowl I use to make pancake batter is a little off. Its handle droops like a left arm after a stroke. The rim isn't what one would use as a standard for something "level." The glaze is uneven in one spot. But I love that footed bowl because a friend made it. Its supposed flaws are what make it unique, one of a kind. It was made and given with heart.

The amateur potter apologized for how misshapen it is, compared to the perfect picture in his mind.

But its charm is in its imperfection.

Why do we have such a hard time adopting that attitude toward ourselves and others? Jesus still holds the world record as the only perfect human to have lived, and even He was noted as not being particularly attractive on the outside. Isaiah says it wasn't His appearance that drew people, but the Spirit of God within Him. "He had no form or splendor that we should look at Him, no appearance that we should desire Him" (Isaiah 53:2, HCS).

We were handcrafted for Him and by Him. His workmanship. Even with our droopy handles, He thinks we're charming.

**FAITH STEP:** *They say every woman has an instant answer to the question, "What one thing would you change about your looks?" Is today the day to start seeing that feature through the eyes of an appreciator of the unique?*

*—Cynthia Ruchti*

# WEDNESDAY, SEPTEMBER 24

*Teach the older men to be temperate, worthy of respect, self-controlled, and sound in faith, in love and in endurance. Likewise, teach the older women to be reverent in the way they live, not to be slanderers or addicted to much wine, but to teach what is good. Then they can urge the younger women to love their husbands and children, to be self-controlled and pure, to be busy at home, to be kind, and to be subject to their husbands, so that no one will malign the word of God. Titus 2:2–5 (NIV)*

IN SEPTEMBER, OUR MATURE PECAN tree sprouts new growth. The new, shiny light green leaves stand out even more prominently against the older, deep emerald leaves. And the older, darker leaves seem even more intense, even deeper in color, when next to the new growth.

In the verses above, Paul commands the older women to teach the younger women what is good. We all learn from example, and we should strive to learn from the examples of our elders. Growing up, I'd often attend what we call "Ladies' Day" at church. This was a day for women only, where the older, wiser women in God's Word would share their life experiences with the younger women, letting them know what they had learned regarding strengthening their relationships with their husbands, their families, and their Lord. Those days were invaluable to me, as were those precious women who were so willing to share.

I don't hear of that many "Ladies' Days" anymore, and that is bothersome. If both parties, young and old, would follow their portion of Paul's command, then based on the verses above, no one will malign the Word of God.

**FAITH STEP:** *Do an Internet search for "Ladies' Day" and "Women's Day." Locate a one-day event near you and attend. Then, as you feel led, determine whether you can help organize a similar event at your local congregation.*

—*Renee Andrews*

# THURSDAY, SEPTEMBER 25

*Set your mind on the things above, not on the things that are on earth. For you have died and your life is hidden with Christ in God. When Christ, who is our life, is revealed, then you also will be revealed with Him in glory. Colossians 3:2–4 (NAS)*

TODAY MY FIVE-YEAR-OLD DAUGHTER ASKED me to come outside to sit with her. I did, and when she sat on my lap on the lawn chair, we laid back our heads and looked at the sky. A cool wind blew on our faces, and we looked at the clouds drifting by. In fifteen minutes' time we watched three flocks of birds and saw four airplanes fly overhead.

My plan was to finish folding laundry and cleaning the kitchen. I'm so glad she talked me into her plan. By stepping away from my busywork, and taking time to "look up," I was able to connect with God's creation. I found joy in marveling at clouds, at the flight of birds, and at the wonder of airplanes!

So many times in our lives we forget to look up. We focus on the daily tasks and forget the marvel of Jesus, Who will one day descend in the clouds. We forget to ponder God's amazing design of all creatures. We forget to appreciate how we humans are made in God's image and are able to create and explore. We get so busy with what is seen, that we forget that we are hidden with Christ in God. We forget that this world is only temporary, and what matters most—our life in God—has yet to be revealed.

It only takes fifteen minutes of stillness to help you remember . . . and sometimes a five-year-old to encourage you to stop and look at the sky!

**FAITH STEP:** *Take fifteen minutes today to sit outside, stare at the sky, and marvel at the wonder of God.*

*—Tricia Goyer*

# FRIDAY, SEPTEMBER 26

*Just as a body, though one, has many parts, but all its many parts form one body, so it is with Christ. 1 Corinthians 12:12 (NIV)*

IT SEEMS THERE ARE MANY ideas out there as to what a Christian woman should be. People frequently cite Proverbs 31 as the model we should all aspire to (and the woman in that passage *was* pretty awesome). There are other great characters like Ruth, Esther, Mary, and Lydia, who provide examples for women of today to follow. And some churches will point to specific verses on topics like submission, child-rearing, hair-covering, and teaching in order to guide women to a better knowledge of true femininity.

I meet a lot of women who are exhausted by trying to be what they think God wants. Many become discouraged when they see others who are better at cooking for potlucks, home-schooling their children, or caring for the sick. What's ironic is that some of those ladies wish they were better at singing, or writing, or teaching a class.

I believe Jesus's answer to what a Christian woman should be is much simpler: *Be who you are. Who I created you to be.* The body of Christ, like a human body, needs all of its parts to function correctly. We can't all be the mouth or the ears or the hands. All of us, with our unique gifts, are needed, in order to bring about the Kingdom of heaven here on earth.

FAITH STEP: *Consider what makes you unique in the body of Christ, even if it seems like something small. Ask the Lord to show you how to be who He has made you to be, for His glory.*

—Gwen Ford Faulkenberry

# SATURDAY, SEPTEMBER 27

*Jesus replied: "'Love the Lord your God with all your heart and with all your soul and with all your mind.' This is the first and greatest commandment. And the second is like it: 'Love your neighbor as yourself.'" Matthew 22:37–39 (NIV)*

IT HAD BEEN A LONG day. But when my son approached me in the kitchen and meekly said, "Mom, I'm sorry to bother you again. . . ." my heart sank. Was I making him feel like an interruption? The kids and I have been working on showing respect for others' time and how to interrupt politely, but what got me was the meekness in his expression, his uncertainty of my time for him.

I'm constantly checking myself about my interruptability. I tried all day to sit down and outline my next project. To be honest, now that I'm finally parked at the computer I'm feeling bent out of shape that the pressure's on to make the creativity flow before the next crisis.

Fortunately, Jesus has worked me through this experience before, so I'm ever hopeful that He is still Lord of this day and this project. Hallelujah that inspiration is not limited by me!

Once His Spirit convicts me about my snarky heart, I'm always so glad that Jesus is bigger than me. He's allowed to interrupt me and to send others to do it too. He's allowed to show me that His priorities may be vastly different from my to-do list. He has the power to grace me through the tyranny of the urgent so I don't become a tyrant in urgent need of a time-out.

If I'm sending people the message that *they* are interruptions, I've got some changes to make in my approachability and priorities. The second greatest commandment Jesus gives is to love other people as ourselves. That means being interruptible and respecting their hearts.

I'm so glad Jesus can turn my shortcomings into lessons learned.

**FAITH STEP:** *Determine now to show grace and patience when people interrupt your day, because it's a given they will! Jesus may have beautiful detours for you through them.*

—*Erin Keeley Marshall*

# SUNDAY, SEPTEMBER 28

*Peter turned and saw that the disciple whom Jesus loved was following them. (This was the one who had leaned back against Jesus at the supper and had said, "Lord, who is going to betray you?") When Peter saw him, he asked, "Lord, what about him?" John 21:20–21 (NIV)*

ONE OF THE MIXED BLESSINGS of modern culture is that we know (or know of) so many people. We move from place to place, communicate across the globe through the phone and the Internet, and have opportunities to make large numbers of acquaintances. Even if we live in a tiny community, we hear about the lives of many people through the media.

As my address book bulges, I have more and more opportunities to ask Jesus, as Peter did, "Lord, what about him?" I see families that seem to be the perfect model of love and closeness, and compare that to the relationships that feel too cool and distant in my life. I see friends with health and vigor taking on physical adventures or active mission trips and new ministries while I struggle to find a way to serve. I see writers I once helped and encouraged achieving success while I long to reenter my career as a novelist.

Comparisons are a terrible trap. When I observe someone else's blessings, I'm not privy to the full reality of their experience. Their unique road may include many sacrifices and challenges that I can't see.

There's a moment in *The Horse and His Boy* by C. S. Lewis when Shasta asks about Aravis. "Child," said the Voice, "I am telling you your story, not hers. I tell no one any story but his own." I've begun to realize that it is a mark of Jesus's tender love that He has a unique story for each of us.

FAITH STEP: *Have you recently pointed out to Jesus that someone else's story looks a lot better than your own? Confess the temptation to compare, and thank Jesus for what He is writing in your life.*

—Sharon Hinck

# MONDAY, SEPTEMBER 29

*Contend, Lord, with those who contend with me; fight against those who fight against me. Take up shield and armor; arise and come to my aid. Brandish spear and javelin against those who pursue me. Say to me, "I am your salvation." Psalm 35:1–3 (NIV)*

As SOON AS OUR FAMILY spotted the black-purple water moccasin invading our "river day," we sent the kids inside. My mother, sister, and I hovered on the back porch and watched as our respective husbands all headed for their weapons of choice to combat the venomous snake. My brother-in-law grabbed the first thing he spied on the back porch, a broom, and headed toward the moccasin. My husband went to the garage and got a hoe, then also made his way to face the thing, now striking at my brother-in-law. My father went in the house, got his shotgun, and was soon ready to face the enemy.

Like that snake, the devil is often hovering near our families and hoping for a chance to strike. And like the men in our family, we can choose our weapons for battle. Immersing ourselves in the Bible. Surrounding ourselves with Christian friends. Placing ourselves in Christian environments. Will we still face the enemy? Yes. But will we be prepared for battle? Definitely, because Christ is right there with us, ready for a victory.

**FAITH STEP:** *Become more familiar with at least one of your Christian weapons today.*

—*Renee Andrews*

# TUESDAY, SEPTEMBER 30

*Now the body is not made up of one part but of many . . . God has arranged the parts in the body, every one of them, just as he wanted them to be. 1 Corinthians 12:14, 18 (NIV)*

MY HUSBAND AND I LEAD short-term mission teams to Eastern Europe each summer.

One group recently headed to Romania to minister among HIV-infected young adults. As always, the team represented a variety of skills and personalities.

One fellow was a salmon farmer. His wife taught a community program for parents and tots. One gal, a rancher's wife, was a foster mom. Another, a mother of six young kids. The mix included a nineteen-year-old girl, a school principal and her husband—an expert in inseminating cattle—and a nurse and her husband, a retired teacher.

Each person added a unique dimension to our group, and watching them exercise their gifts made me smile. The cattle expert led singing during team devotions. The teen played guitar for worship services. Several taught Bible lessons and crafts. Others served behind-the-scenes, bathing the program with prayer. Each played a vital role in making the mission trip successful.

The same principle holds true in our churches. God has created His children with unique personalities and gifts. We're diverse, and we're all needed. Individually, we're like pieces of stained glass. Collectively, we form a beautiful window through which the world can see Christ. Let's fulfill our role with excellence and without comparison, and let's encourage others to do the same.

**FAITH STEP:** *Name three people who are different from you and thank God for them today.*

*—Grace Fox*

# WEDNESDAY, OCTOBER 1

*I will answer them before they even call to me. While they are still talking about their needs,*
*I will go ahead and answer their prayers! Isaiah 65:24 (NLT)*

"Mom! Mom! Mama! Mommy! Look, Mom! Mom, look! *Mom!*"

Although my children can utter that whole line in 1.87 seconds, by the intensity in their voices you'd think they rarely have my attention, or that I need to be shouted to across the country rather than across the kitchen island.

If only they'd stop to breathe, maybe I could have a chance to answer. However, they couldn't hear me if I tried because their own (unnecessary) panic would drown me out.

I'm thinking Jesus can relate. Only in His case, I'm the one bombarding His ears with my anxieties.

Perhaps my tendency to fret explains why I read such freedom in today's verse. He already knows what I'm feeling undone about, and amazingly He's already on the move on my behalf. It's not like I ever need to shout to get Him to pay attention to me.

Really. Think about that for a minute. He's all eyes and ears for you, so calm down.

I'm trying to practice acknowledging to Him that I believe He already knows my concerns. I begin by praising and thanking Him for seeing the whole picture and wasting no time acting on it. Since worry says that I don't truly believe He'll come through for me, I refocus my emotions by asking Him to amaze me once again with His presence and provision.

Today, swap your anxiety for belief that Jesus has been on the move for you. You might actually hear Him when your spirit is quiet.

**Faith step:** *What threatens your sense of calm? Believe Jesus is already working on it. Ask Him to grow your belief in Him so you can rest easier.*

*—Erin Keeley Marshall*

# THURSDAY, OCTOBER 2

*Don't get sidetracked; keep your feet from following evil. Proverbs 4:27 (NLT)*

I CAN FOCUS WELL; YET I get easily sidetracked. When I'm doing something enjoyable, I lose all sense of time. But if I'm facing an unpleasant task, interruptions become close friends. But that's not the only time I can get sidetracked.

In reality, anything that promises a pleasant diversion can sidetrack us from the more important things of life. I've experienced that too. Intended to make life easier, some tools or activities can actually steal time from family, from our productivity, and from God's purpose for our lives, if we let them. Some things may be good and harmless in themselves, but we need Jesus's help to stay on track.

Some people try to do that by following the old adage, "Idle hands are the devil's workshop." But meaningless activity can produce the same results as no activity at all.

Jesus knew His identity. And nothing could sway Him from accomplishing His divine purpose, though many, including His disciples, tried unknowingly to do so at times. Beginning with His earliest temptations in the wilderness, Jesus could have been sidetracked. He could have yielded to selfish power or other whims that would have prevented and short-circuited His true mission in life. But as the Son of God, He declared His purpose: "to accomplish the will of the One Who sent Me." And throughout His ministry He allowed nothing and no one to deter Him.

That's my prayer: to constantly stay on track, asking Jesus for wisdom to accomplish His will alone.

**FAITH STEP:** *If you've never done so, write down a "mission statement," or Jesus's purpose for your life. In light of that, ask Jesus to order your activities this year to keep you on track.*

—*Rebecca Barlow Jordan*

# FRIDAY, OCTOBER 3

*Every good gift and every perfect gift is from above, coming down from the Father of lights with whom there is no variation or shadow due to change. James 1:17 (ESV)*

I READ RECENTLY THAT THE Templeton Foundation is investing six million dollars to study the practice of gratitude, including its effects on health and child development. It seems to me they should save their money and read the Bible instead. After all, according to Proverbs 17:22 (NIV), "A cheerful heart is good medicine."

As a mom of six—including three preschoolers—one of the things I say dozens of times a day is, "Say thank you." Yet the truth is, there are times when I do better at prodding it, than living it. It's easier to remind your child to thank the nice lady at the grocery store, than to remember to do it myself.

More than that, I forget to thank God for the goodness He provides during the day—for my life, my health, my ability to work, and the chance to enjoy the good world around me. I forget to thank my family members, friends, and even strangers for small, thoughtful deeds. Yet gratitude makes a difference, doesn't it? Gratitude not only brightens our day, but it lightens our hearts.

When we are thankful, it's easy to be cheerful. When I look around at the beauty of a blooming tree, watch in awe the wonder of a small ladybug, or appreciate the taste of a crisp apple, my mind should turn to God with gratitude. If we are to invest anything, we should invest in sharing a kind word, in offering thanks, and in sending up prayers of appreciation to God Who makes all things possible. Gratitude makes us cheerful. It also displays how a follower of God should live before a seeking, investigating world.

FAITH STEP: *Think of one way to show gratitude to a family member, one way to show gratitude to a friend, and one way to show gratitude to a stranger . . . and then see if you can complete your plans before bedtime!*

—*Tricia Goyer*

# SATURDAY, OCTOBER 4

---

*He went away again the second time, and prayed, saying, O my Father, if this cup may not pass away from me, except I drink it, thy will be done. Matthew 26:42 (KJV)*

---

I BELIEVE THE SCENE IN the Garden of Gethsemane when Jesus prays is one of the greatest glimpses we have into His humanity. The Bible says He is sorrowful "even unto death" and "very heavy." He asks His friends to watch and pray with Him, and even though they care as much as they can in their own humanity, they fall asleep. Soul-weary, He seems vulnerable here. So utterly alone.

Zoom in. Note the drops of blood He sweats. He's omniscient. He knows what's coming. But He's also human, so very human. He's begging on His face before God. *O My Father . . .* This scene is there, I believe, for all of us in hospital waiting rooms. Or divorce courts. Or funerals. Or any other place where our dreams go up in smoke. *Thy will be done.*

Elisabeth Elliot writes, "I realized that the deepest spiritual lessons are not learned by His letting us have our way in the end, but by His making us wait, bearing with us in love and patience until we are able to honestly pray what He taught His disciples to pray: Thy will be done."

I always want the easy thing. The quick fix, the simple solution, the least painful route. And sometimes it happens. But for deep spiritual growth I'm with Elisabeth. It only comes through the cross, through death to self that He may live His resurrection life in me. *Thy will be done.*

---

FAITH STEP: *Ask God to draw back the veil from your eyes that you may see into the deep mystery of His mercy, even as you wait on Him. Make it your mantra: O Jesus, Your will be done.*

—*Gwen Ford Faulkenberry*

# SUNDAY, OCTOBER 5

*Commit your way to the Lord; trust in him and he will do this: He will make your righteousness shine like the dawn, the justice of your cause like the noonday sun. Psalm 37:5–6 (NIV)*

I SPENT MOST OF MY growing up years in Santa Cruz, a beach town on the coast of Northern California. A distinct love of the ocean is in my blood, but I love the sun even more.

I love the feeling of its rays permeating my skin and the warmth that it gives off on a hot day. I love its brightness and how when it is out, everything just seems better. I love when it lingers late into a summer's evening and you can sit outside sipping lemonade and watching the kids play past their bedtime. Nothing is better than a sunny day.

And apparently, when we are trusting Jesus and committing our path to Him, He makes our lives feel like a sunny day to those who are around us.

Usually, I think about how following Jesus affects me and how I live my life. It is amazing to know that when we offer our lives over to Him, when we ask Him to shape our thoughts and direct our paths, that others reap the benefits too. He makes us shine. Our character and the things we care about reflect His glory to those around us like a bright, warm, lovely summer day. And that is beautiful.

**FAITH STEP:** *Spend some time in the sun. As it warms you, remind Jesus again that you are committing your life to Him and that you would like Him to make you shine.*

—*Susanna Foth Aughtmon*

# MONDAY, OCTOBER 6

*The grace of our Lord Jesus Christ be with all of you.* 1 Thessalonians 5:28 (CEB)

IN SOME DOG-EARED GRANDPARENTING MANUAL are pages devoted to the toddler game "Chase Me." The beautiful chime of toddler giggles accompanies a little one learning to run, chased by a smiling, tickle-threatening, intentionally slow-motion grandparent. As the child's gait grows steadier, the tables are turned. The child becomes the one chasing, in pursuit of a theatrically skilled grandparent always just out of reach.

Each of our grandchildren teaches us something priceless. Our oldest grandchild is named Grace. She's the one with whom we first engaged in grandparent/grandchild peek-a-boo, tickle hugs, tummy raspberries, and Chase Me. We were chased by Grace.

*Ahh.* Chased by Grace. The win came when we slowed down enough to be caught in Grace's loving embrace.

And there's the Gospel. There's life with Christ. Pursued by a loving God with an overflow of grace for us, we run the other direction until the day we realize that the real win lies in stopping to let grace overtake us.

I'm fascinated by the verses of Scripture that are benedictory prayers for the grace of Jesus to be "with" us, as if the prayer is, "May the grace of Jesus chase you down!"

Galatians 6:18 (CEB)—"Brothers and sisters, may the grace of our Lord Jesus Christ be with your spirit."

It's the race in which true joy comes from being outdistanced, outrun.

**FAITH STEP:** *In what area of life have you been running away from what Jesus wants? A misplaced affection? An addiction? A tough decision? Let His grace catch you. It's the only way you'll win that race.*

*—Cynthia Ruchti*

# TUESDAY, OCTOBER 7

*Enoch walked with God. Genesis 5:24 (NIV)*

THREE-LEGGED RACES CAN BE A lot of fun, especially for spectators. Two racers, joined at the knee and ankle, must master a stride that lets them run as one person. Defeat's inevitable if either pulls ahead or lags behind.

The depth of our relationship with God depends on our ability to fall into stride with Him. Developing that stride takes time, and we usually experience a few tumbles in the process.

Sometimes we rush ahead of Him despite His warnings to wait. "C'mon, let's go!" we say. "Not yet," He replies. But we don't listen. We pull ahead of Him and take a nosedive.

Sometimes we lag behind. "It's time to move," He says. But fear or selfishness grips us and we refuse to budge.

Falling into stride with the Lord takes time and intentionality. It requires learning to recognize His Spirit's voice and obeying Him without question. He says, "Go visit so-and-so," and we go. He says, "Speak encouragement to that sales clerk," and we speak. He says, "Give $100 to that charity," and we give.

Oswald Chambers writes, "Getting into God's stride means nothing less than oneness with Him. It takes a long time to get there, but keep at it.... Before long you will find that you have a new vision and a new purpose."

Enoch walked with God. He got into stride with Him, and it showed. One Bible translation (NLT) says, "He enjoyed a close relationship with God throughout his life."

Let's get into stride with the Lord that we might become one with Him and enjoy intimacy as Enoch did.

FAITH STEP: *Pray, "Father, reveal to me anything that hinders my walk with You today. Grant me the ability to walk in stride with You, perfectly in step as one. Amen."*

—*Grace Fox*

# WEDNESDAY, OCTOBER 8

*"So in everything, do to others what you would have them do to you, for this sums up the Law and the Prophets." Matthew 7:12 (NIV)*

THE OLDER GENTLEMAN STOOD BEHIND the chain-link fence separating the football players from the fans. Known as "Papa" to everyone on the team, he was the coach's father-in-law and an avid supporter of the group on the field.

"Attaboy, you've got this," he'd say. "You're the man, son!" he'd call out.

One by one, the boys would glance his way, then turn and face the field without acknowledging the man's praise. Then one of the younger players, a sophomore named Mason, came off the field after making a good play.

"You're the man, Mason!" Papa called.

Mason grinned from behind his helmet, stepped to the fence, and shook Papa's hand. Papa continued wishing him luck and then Mason returned to the team.

After the game, Papa's daughter found Mason's mother and asked her to please let Mason know how much it meant to her that Mason acknowledged the older man.

Christ looked for opportunities to show kindness. He commanded us to treat others the way we want to be treated. In Luke 8, Christ showed compassion on the woman who touched His cloak believing that by merely touching the Savior, she would be healed. Even when Jesus was in sorrow over the death of John the Baptist and retreated to a solitary place, He had compassion on the crowd that followed Him and healed their sick. Christ knew the importance of showing kindness.

Mason followed Christ's example that day, and I have no doubt that Papa—and Christ—were both touched by the young man with the big heart.

FAITH STEP: *Make a point to say "thank you" at least three times today.*

—*Renee Andrews*

# THURSDAY, OCTOBER 9

*Again, the kingdom of heaven is like a merchant looking for fine pearls. When he found one of great value, he went away and sold everything he had and bought it. Matthew 13:45–46 (NIV)*

"I KNOW WHAT I'D BUY if I were wealthy." I was enjoying the store clerk's amusing commentary and continuous chatter as she scanned my grocery items.

Before I could ask her what she would buy, the woman answered herself without missing a beat. She had preceded her statement with a tale of cell phone disasters and her frustration with each phone. "Yes, sir! I'd buy one of those smartphones that can do everything!"

She paused and looked up for a split second, then reached for the next item. "But I'll never be rich, so I'll never get to buy one."

On a recent television show I watched one couple equate wealth with their newly built $7,000,000 home. But their expensive collections had outgrown the house, so they were designing a bigger and better home.

Jesus encountered numerous views of wealth: the man whose crops had increased so much that he decided to tear down his barns and build bigger ones (Luke 12:16–21). One sinful, but grateful woman used her "wealth," an expensive alabaster bottle of perfume, as an extravagant love gift for Jesus (Luke 7:37–38).

Jesus emphasized the dangers of wealth. Some could use it selfishly and miss God's purposes for it entirely (Luke 8:14). Accumulating things had little value in the Kingdom of God, compared to Jesus's standards. Perhaps one of the most poignant ways Jesus defined wealth was in His parable about the man who found an expensive pearl and sold everything he owned to buy that pearl.

Who is really rich? The one who has found Jesus, the Pearl of Great Value.

**FAITH STEP:** *What makes you feel wealthy? Bless someone this week with an unexpected gift.*

—*Rebecca Barlow Jordan*

# FRIDAY, OCTOBER 10

---

*I pray that out of his glorious riches he may strengthen you with power through his Spirit in your inner being, so that Christ may dwell in your hearts through faith. And I pray that you, being rooted and established in love, may have power, together with all the saints, to grasp how wide and long and high and deep is the love of Christ. Ephesians 3:16–18 (NIV)*

---

WE LIVE IN A LARGE city, so light pollution makes it difficult to enjoy a starry sky at night. Last summer my husband and I stayed at a bed-and-breakfast in a remote area far from the city. We made a point to go outside at night and turn our gazes upward. Back home we could enjoy a full moon, find the Big Dipper, and spot the North Star. But here, the constellations were endless. I'd never seen so many stars.

I tried to imagine the amount of space and time between those distant points of light and our planet. I tried to comprehend the vastness of galaxies and universes. Pretty soon my temples throbbed, and my brain felt the size of a peanut. My human mind couldn't fully absorb the vastness of the night sky.

I confront the same struggle when I try to understand the love of Christ. I can't fully absorb the vastness of Jesus's love. The Word Who was present at creation, Who set the huge universe into motion, also came to earth to save us, and also longs to fellowship with us. It's too much to grasp. Yet as Christ dwells in our hearts through faith, He helps us at least begin to glimpse the depth, constancy, and power of His love for us.

---

FAITH STEP: *Go outside tonight and look at the stars. Let your mind strain to grasp the vastness of infinity. Thank Jesus that His love for you is every bit as infinite.*

*—Sharon Hinck*

# SATURDAY, OCTOBER 11

*Keep a close watch on how you live and on your teaching. Stay true to what is right for the sake of your own salvation and the salvation of those who hear you. 1 Timothy 4:16 (NLT)*

I HAVE A CONFESSION TO MAKE. Even though I write about parenting, it's easy for me to become a lazy mom. It's easier for me to flip on a movie, rather than pick up a board book to read. It's easier to say a quick prayer than to teach my child to pray. It's easier to fold the laundry myself, than to teach my preschooler how to join in the family team. Yet even though some of these shortcuts would make my life easier *now*, I know that a lazy mom leads to lazy kids . . . God's been speaking to me about this.

Recently, I wrote a book about parents as leaders, and this is the premise: "Any time you choose to influence the behavior, thinking, or development of another person, you are a leader." It sounds like a parent, doesn't it? In God's Word we are told to keep a close watch on how we live . . . because our children are watching. We are told to keep a close watch on our teaching . . . because others are learning by seeing what we do and how we respond.

God wants us to live righteous lives not only for our sakes, but also for the sake of all those who follow us. Every day you are leading someone somewhere . . . the question is where. The question is, does your leading guide another toward God, toward salvation?

First Timothy 4:15 (NIV) says, "Be diligent in these matters; give yourself wholly to them, so that everyone may see your progress."

When we lead our children, God doesn't expect perfection, but He does desire progress. Everyone has a lazy day now and then, but the journey of our lives should be toward God and right living . . . for His sake and the sake of those who follow us.

FAITH STEP: *Write out ways you've become lazy in your walk and take those things to God as prayer requests. He is there to listen and to help!*

—*Tricia Goyer*

# SUNDAY, OCTOBER 12

*Salvation is found in no one else, for there is no other name under heaven given to mankind by which we must be saved. Acts 4:12 (NIV)*

I HAVE AN AGNOSTIC FRIEND who recently adopted a child. She brought her little boy to spend the day with my kids, and we sat in the yard and drank coffee and talked while they all played. That night, I invited them to go with us to vacation Bible school.

My friend is a worker, so while her kid went with his class to the various stations (music, crafts, storytime, games), she helped me with snacks. We made about eighty hot-fudge sundaes and distributed them to each class as they came through our station. A girl who is a former drug addict helped us too.

Later, my friend commented on how much fun she had. She especially liked the girl, who, according to my friend, had a sweet way about her.

"You're always asking me why I'm a Christian, how I can believe all of the stuff about Jesus." I grinned at her. "That girl is the reason."

"Why?"

I told her what I knew of the girl's story, what she was like when she first started coming to Sunday school, and how much she had changed as she began to grasp her Savior's love for her. "When you distill Christianity down to its purest form, that's what it's about. And there's nothing else like it in the world."

**FAITH STEP:** *Have you begun to grasp how much your Savior loves you? No one will ever know you better—or love you more—than Jesus.*

*—Gwen Ford Faulkenberry*

# MONDAY, OCTOBER 13

---

*Listen for God's voice in everything you do, everywhere you go; he's the one who will keep you on track. Proverbs 3:6 (MSG)*

---

LIFE SOMETIMES FEELS LIKE A swirling vortex of plastic rubber duckies at a kids' carnival. Pick the right one, and you win a valuable prize. Pick the wrong one, and you win an undesirable future. Or a goldfish that won't live through the weekend.

Life forces us to pick something from the swirling vortex. Job. Location. Service opportunities. Neighborhood. Friends. Parenting styles. Time use.

How do we ever know the wisest choice? How do we reach out with confidence into uncertainty? How do we know the "duck" we pick doesn't have "You've won a goldfish!" written on the bottom?

At every decision-making point in His life, Jesus sought wisdom from His heavenly Father. One of His followers later wrote down His perspective about a starting point for wise decisions. "But anyone who needs wisdom should ask God, whose very nature is to give to everyone without a second thought, without keeping score. Wisdom will certainly be given to those who ask" (James 1:5, CEB).

Jesus was well-acquainted with the Old Testament teaching that the knowledge of God is the beginning of wisdom. Is my starting point a list of pros and cons of the decision? Or is it plunging in to know God more deeply and hear Jesus more clearly?

---

FAITH STEP: *Are you facing a tough decision today? Lay your list of pros and cons on the table. Then lay your open Bible on top of the list. Don't look at the list again until you can "see" it through the pages of Scripture and its definition of wisdom.*

—Cynthia Ruchti

# TUESDAY, OCTOBER 14

*"Come to me, all you who are weary and burdened, and I will give you rest."*
Matthew 11:28 (NIV)

"Grandma, I want to snuggle with you," said my three-year-old grandson, Luke. I hoisted the feverish tyke onto my lap, and he placed his head on my chest. There he dozed for the next hour. And there I sat, cuddling my precious cargo.

After months of constant go, go, go, I relished this hour as an unexpected gift. I felt sorry that Luke was ill, but rocking him provided guilt-free rest for my weary body and soul. For that, I felt thankful.

Psalm 23:2–3 (NIV) says the Lord's aware of our needs. "He makes me lie down in green pastures, he leads me beside quiet waters, he restores my soul." As a shepherd cares for his flock, so Jesus cares for us. He knows when we're weary, and He knows how to refresh us.

Sometimes He provides rest through an extended getaway or sabbatical. Other times He provides minivacations—an overnight escape or a relaxed evening with a spouse or close friend. Most often, He sends soul-refreshing snippets—a cup of tea sipped on the back deck, a stroll around the block, or a few minutes to read undisturbed.

Are you weary today? Jesus knows. Acknowledge Him as your Shepherd and ask Him for green pastures and quiet waters. Ask Him to restore your soul.

**Faith step:** *Sometimes choices we make cause weariness. Ask yourself if this is true in your situation. Are you getting enough sleep? Can you delegate some of your work? Do you need to learn to say no to others' requests for your time and energy?*

*—Grace Fox*

# WEDNESDAY, OCTOBER 15

*But if we hope for what we do not yet have, we wait for it patiently. Romans 8:25 (NIV)*

BEN, MY FRIEND'S YOUNG SON, suited up in his football gear, helmet and pads and all, and informed his mom that he was going out to play. After a few minutes, she looked out the window and saw him standing in the backyard alone. Feeling sorry for her little boy, Jana went outside. "Do you want to play something else?" she asked. Ben turned and grinned from within his helmet. "Nope, I'm playing football." Confused, Jana asked, "You are?" Ben nodded the bulky helmet. "Yep, I'm offense. The defense is on the field now."

Jana couldn't see the game Ben visualized, the one obviously still entertaining him while he waited for his turn. But Ben knew that part of playing football involved waiting patiently on the sidelines. He also had the ability to hope for what he didn't yet have, a chance to play.

Often we are the little boy on the sidelines wanting a chance to play. We want to shine for Christ. We want to be needed, have purpose. However, every now and then we need that reminder that contentment may also be found in letting someone else have their time on the field. We should try to be like Ben, quite happy waiting his turn.

**FAITH STEP:** *Remember what Christ said in Luke 14:10 and find Ben's joy in waiting your turn.*

—*Renee Andrews*

# THURSDAY, OCTOBER 16

*Youth may be admired for vigor, but gray hair gives prestige to old age. Proverbs 20:29* (MSG)

I ENTERED A NEW DECADE a few months ago. I'm now part of the new thirties, which is a more palatable way of saying I'm forty.

When I turned thirty I told my husband, whom I was dating at the time, that people had to start taking me seriously. When I turned forty, *I* felt a new seriousness about my age. Nostalgia and introspection, some regrets, and a greater sense of purpose have commingled in my thoughts in recent years, leaving me with the overwhelming wonder, *How did I get to be forty already?*

Although forty is not old, it isn't very young anymore, either. No previous age has ever struck me that way. People call me "ma'am" instead of "miss." I've got crow's feet, a slower metabolism, less energy, and brand-new reading glasses. I'm not ready for these things, I tell ya!

However, I am experiencing a thing of beauty in growing older. My passion to bless others' lives has grown immensely. It isn't about me anymore. During my twenties and thirties, I felt a need to prove myself. As forty approached, I began to feel a stronger desire to make a difference beyond myself. I want to be a healer, a support, an encourager, someone who lives to make an improvement for others. And, oh my. That. Feels. Great. I feel as though Jesus is getting through to me.

At the end of my time on earth, I want to hear Jesus say that I've done what He created me to do, that I've put my all into loving Him and others, that I've taken hold of His joy and run with it, spreading it around wherever He carries me.

Give the rest of your days to Him with a sense of anticipation. Maybe this getting-old thing can be more than we bargained for—in a *good* way.

FAITH STEP: *Study Isaiah 46:4 and Romans 15:2–4 to build your faith in Jesus's presence with you and purpose for you as you live for Him throughout your life.*

—*Erin Keeley Marshall*

# FRIDAY, OCTOBER 17

*Jesus looked at them and said, "With man this is impossible, but with God all things are possible." Matthew 19:26 (NIV)*

I WAS HELPING MY SON, Jack, with his homework the other night.

Sixth-grade math is tougher than I remembered. But then again I was never great with pi, or any kind of geometry for that matter. As I was looking over the problem, Jack said, "Oh, never mind, Mom, I remember what I'm supposed to do." And I was thinking, *Thank You, Jesus!* Give me algebra any day. Start talking about circumference or radius or proofs and my brain starts hurting. My brain simply cannot wrap itself around the complexities of that type of math. I remember weeping over a geometry test in high school. It had me crying, "Uncle!"

It is the same when I look at the world's problems. They are too large. Too complex for me. I feel shut down by them and flattened by their enormity. I don't have the brain power to come up with solutions. That is where Jesus comes in. He is not daunted by the world's problems, by its tragedies, or its intricacies. There is no conundrum too large or no detail unimportant for Him to tackle.

I love that Jesus sees us for who we are. "Yes, if this is just about you solving this problem, you are right...it's impossible. But not with God...all things are possible with God." He is the Creator. He is the only One Who can put His creation to rights. And there is no situation that can shake Him. The word *impossible* is not in His vocabulary. When we hand our lives over to Him, too, the possibilities are endless.

FAITH STEP: *Think about the things in your life that feel impossible right now. Give them to Jesus in prayer and tell Him, "Jesus, I believe that with You nothing is impossible."*

—*Susanna Foth Aughtmon*

# SATURDAY, OCTOBER 18

*A joyful heart is good medicine, but a broken spirit dries up the bones. Proverbs 17:22 (HCS)*

SOME PEOPLE GET BORED WHEN they read the parts of the Old Testament (especially Leviticus) where God described the annual festivals that He wanted the Israelites to put on their calendars. Some of these observances were times of sober reflection and contemplation, but most of them were special days to rejoice in God's goodness and how He had provided for them. I love that He wanted His people to purposely schedule in times to be joyful and celebrate.

I used to get a sinking feeling the day after major holidays, especially Easter and Christmas. The fun and excitement had ended; it was time to get back to my ordinary life. Now I try to remember that the truth and reality of those holidays are a part of my life throughout the year. Plus, I have a personal relationship with the One Whom all the Old Testament joy-filled festivals pointed to. Do I need any more reason to celebrate every single day?

There are all sorts of ways that I can celebrate Jesus every day. I can sing praise and worship songs as I go about my chores. I can open the Bible and read words about Him or words He spoke. I can talk to Him in prayer or meditate on the new life and glorious future He made possible through His death and resurrection. I could do a kind deed in His name or make a list of things to thank Him for. Or I could commit to doing something that I've been struggling with, like forgiving someone who's hurt me or give up a habit that dishonors Him.

Building time into each day to celebrate Jesus takes some thought and commitment. But it pleases Him and helps my faith grow stronger. And an added bonus—it's good medicine for whatever ails me.

FAITH STEP: *In what ways will you celebrate Jesus today? Before going to sleep tonight, plan how you will schedule some time for rejoicing tomorrow.*

—*Dianne Neal Matthews*

# SUNDAY, OCTOBER 19

*Cast all your anxiety on him because he cares for you.* 1 Peter 5:7 (NIV)

OVER THE PAST FEW MONTHS, our family has been dealt our fair share of stress. The lease was expiring on the building for our business, and we didn't know where we would go. We had sold our house, and then the buyers decided not to purchase. Other minor stresses added to the major ones to overwhelm us and give us that sensation of drowning.

Then our preacher delivered a lesson that went straight to our hearts. Brother Dunaway started by asking, "Are you too blessed to be stressed? Or are you too stressed to know you're blessed?" We realized that in the past few weeks, our feeling stressed had outweighed our ability to feel blessed.

Christ told us not to be anxious about our life (Matthew 6:25). I need to recall this verse often, because I spend so much time lately being anxious. We are still working on a lease agreement for the building. The home is still for sale (in fact, we now have two for sale). And just today we are dealing with a potential theft at our business. So many things to be anxious about, and so many things to turn over to Christ.

Only with His help can I truly be too blessed to be stressed!

FAITH STEP: *Take a long, hot bath. Let yourself relax completely and remember that, with Christ, you are too blessed to be stressed.*

—*Renee Andrews*

# MONDAY, OCTOBER 20

*"I know your deeds. See, I have placed before you an open door that no one can shut. I know that you have little strength, yet you have kept my word and have not denied my name."*
*Revelation 3:8 (NIV)*

I CLUTCHED THE OPENING CHAPTER of my first novel in sweaty hands and listened to the swell of chatter around me. I was at my first writer's conference and felt like a minnow in a sea of majestic swordfish, jubilant dolphins, and even a few powerful sharks. The editors and agents here had the ability to open doors for my writing. My heart ached with longing to share my stories, but I felt overwhelmed and terrified. What if I said the wrong thing and ruined my career before it began? What if each professional who looked at my first chapter hid a grimace at the clumsy prose? I was convinced I'd be told, "Go home and learn how to write."

I picked up my name badge and information packet and scurried back to my room to hide. "Lord, why did You nudge me to come here? I don't belong. Do You *know* the odds against a new author getting published?"

As I prayed, peace slowly eased away my panic. "Lord, guide me through this experience. You know how weak and inadequate I feel. Give me a teachable heart. I trust You to open the right doors."

There have been times when I've tried to force my way forward and only proven my lack of strength. Other times I've tried to manipulate a lock and discovered my lack of cleverness. My human effort or schemes can't open every door. Although our culture tells us we can achieve anything we want, it's humbling to realize how small our plans, strength, and wisdom actually are. But Jesus has the power to open every door. Even better, He chooses the doors that will lead us to the greatest blessing.

**FAITH STEP:** *Have you been frustrated by a closed door in your path? Ask Jesus to open that door, or show you a new direction.*

—*Sharon Hinck*

# TUESDAY, OCTOBER 21

*But for those who are righteous, the path is not steep and rough. You are a God of justice, and you smooth out the road ahead of them. Isaiah 26:7 (NLT)*

I'LL ALWAYS REMEMBER THE FIRST time my husband and I rode a bus in Nepal. The vehicle sputtered to life and spewed diesel exhaust. It wound through the streets of Kathmandu and then climbed from the valley into mile-high hills and terraced rice fields. And that's when I learned how to pray.

The road was like none I'd ever experienced. Oncoming buses and cargo trucks passed us with nary an inch to spare. We dodged goats, cows, and people. We lumbered over landslides and lurched along mountain passes. Danger lurked at every curve and along every inch between. Honestly—I thought my time had come.

Sometimes life takes us down roads we'd rather not travel. We face disappointments and difficult relationships. We endure financial stress and health issues. We suffer tragedy. We experience loss. Uncertainty lurks at every corner, and sometimes we wonder whether we'll survive the ride.

The road may seem arduous or impassable at times, but God promises to go before us and make our way smooth. His presence and power travels with us. He will give us hope, peace, and wisdom no matter what we encounter on our journey.

Let's keep these promises in mind. And relax for the ride.

**FAITH STEP:** *Write a list of the tough stuff you're experiencing on your journey. Now write a prayer asking God to go before you and make the road smooth. Acknowledge your dependence on Him for wisdom, provision, and peace.*

*—Grace Fox*

# WEDNESDAY, OCTOBER 22

---

*Love is patient, love is kind. It does not envy, it does not boast, it is not proud. It is not rude, it is not, it is not self-seeking, it is not easily angered, it keeps no record of wrongs. Love does not delight in evil but rejoices with the truth. It always protects, always trusts, always hopes, always perseveres. 1 Corinthians 13:4–7 (NIV)*

---

SCOTT AND I GOT MARRIED on a bright cool day in October. I wore my mom's wedding dress and a wide, happy smile.

I was loved. It was that simple. All these long years I had longed for someone to know me and want me for his own. All my dreams had come true. Here I was, ready to join my life with the most amazing man I had ever met. And he was cute. That was a bonus.

But the real proof of his love has come over the coming years of marriage. Living with my inconsistencies and my weaknesses. Loving me in spite of the fact that I can be demanding and illogical on occasion. This has been no small task on his part. But just like that lovely day in October when he chose me, he chooses me still. There is a great comfort and joy in knowing that.

He reminds me of Someone Else who chose me. Even when I was in my mom's belly, He formed me. He has numbered my days and my nights, and He knows how many hairs I have on my head. He knows all my faults, my sins, and my failures. And yet, He still chooses to forgive me, to give me His grace and flood my life with His mercy.

When Jesus died on the cross, He showed us what real love looks like. It is the kind of love that opens doors and tears down walls and brings life. It is exactly the kind of love we need, and it is ours for the taking. And that is truly lovely.

---

**FAITH STEP:** *Draw a heart in your journal. Fill it with words that describe Jesus's love for you.*

—Susanna Foth Aughtmon

# THURSDAY, OCTOBER 23

---

*Even when I walk through the darkest valley, I will not be afraid, for you are close beside me. Your rod and your staff protect and comfort me. Psalm 23:4 (NLT)*

---

MY FRIEND JOYCE WORKS AT a school that has a dark stairway with an automatic light. The light only comes on when someone opens the door and walks over to the bottom of the stairs. This takes some getting used to. At first, people find it disconcerting to walk into a darkened stairwell, but eventually they learn to trust that the light will come on when they need it and illuminate the stairs so they can walk up.

Sometimes Jesus calls us to go down a path in life that looks dark and dangerous to us. Maybe we'd prefer not to take a step until He sheds some light on what lies ahead. Jesus wants us to respond the way His first disciples did. When Jesus walked by and invited them to follow Him, He didn't give an explanation. Nothing about the time frame involved or what they could expect from their experience as His disciples. Just a simple call to follow. Nevertheless, these fishermen left what they were doing and immediately followed Jesus.

When I sensed a calling to pursue writing for publication, I had no idea how that would play out. When my husband got a job on the other side of the country from our children and grandchildren, I wondered what that would look like. I've struggled with that same bewilderment during medical crises and family emergencies. And I've learned that during those times, Jesus wants me to demonstrate my belief in Him by taking a step of faith, even when the path ahead looks dark. Even when I don't know where it will take me. Jesus wants me to trust Him to give just enough light to follow Him day by day, step by step.

---

**FAITH STEP:** *Is Jesus calling you down a path that looks dark? Ask Him to strengthen your faith so you can follow Him as He lights your way.*

—*Dianne Neal Matthews*

# FRIDAY, OCTOBER 24

*"I have swept away your offenses like a cloud, your sins like the morning mist. Return to me, for I have redeemed you." Isaiah 44:22 (NIV)*

THE BOAT CUT THROUGH THE morning mist that hovered over the waves of Beaver Lake. As my husband steered around a bend, I turned to look where we'd been. The mist had immediately closed back over the landscape as if we hadn't just parted it.

I was tagging along on my first ever duck hunt, and as many Ozark mornings are at the lake, the air was shrouded in fog that made the journey difficult. The lake has many fingerlike coves and bends where it connects with the White River, plenty of places to veer off course or run aground on the shallow side. Fortunately the rising sun gradually burned off the fog, opening a clear view ahead so we could regain our course.

This verse reminds me of that day. Sin creates a fog in our life that makes it difficult to see Jesus's course for us. It clouds our spiritual vision, dulling its clarity with a hardened spirit or the temptation to rationalize our behavior. Pretty soon we become convinced that the direction we're headed is fine.

We need the light of Jesus the Son to burn away sin's lies so we can continue on His safe course. The world is full of ways to lose our vision of Him; in fact, the world is full of enemies that work hard to blind our view of His truth.

Jesus provides the light we need to burn off the fog so we can keep our focus on the end goal that means closeness to Him.

How clear is your vision on today's leg of the journey?

**FAITH STEP:** *Treat yourself to a decorative night-light to light a darkened space. As it glows each day, ask Jesus to burn off any fog of sin that may be clouding your vision.*

*—Erin Keeley Marshall*

# SATURDAY, OCTOBER 25

*O Lord, You have searched me and known me. You know when I sit down and when I rise up; You understand my thought from afar.* Psalm 139:1–2 (NAS)

*JESUS KNOWS ME, THIS I love.*

We were driving around looking for a famous BBQ place when I saw this on a sign in front of the First Christian Church of Hot Springs, Arkansas. At first I thought I read it wrong. Doing a double take, I realized it was a play on the words of the old children's hymn.

*Jesus loves me, this I know* were some of the first words I learned. My mother sang it while she rocked me as a baby. This was the air I breathed as I grew up in my home and church. They are simple words and proved formative during those simpler times of life. I'm forever grateful for their meaning and how it was engrained in me.

Especially now, when things are not quite as simple. It's a blessing to have that foundation—to navigate life as a grown-up knowing Jesus loves you. In fact, it's essential. But, as the sign suggested, it's also wonderful to be known and understood.

Psalm 139 says He is intimately acquainted with all of my ways. He sees my failures; He understands my limitations. He is deeply aware of everything I am—the good, the bad, the ugly. He knows. And yet, He loves me. What a Savior!

**FAITH STEP:** *Sing "Jesus Loves Me." Now thank Him that He knows all about you— and loves you anyway.*

*—Gwen Ford Faulkenberry*

# SUNDAY, OCTOBER 26

*"Go home to your family and tell them how much the Lord has done for you, and how he has had mercy on you." So the man went away and began to tell in Decapolis how much Jesus had done for him. And all the people were amazed. Mark 5:19–20 (NIV)*

SOME PEOPLE FEEL EVANGELISM IS best left to the so-called experts—pastors, career missionaries, and ministry leaders. We assume these experts know the right words to say—theological terms needed to convince people of their need for Jesus. That's a misconception. Ordinary people can become extraordinary evangelists simply by telling what Jesus has done for them.

Consider the Samaritan woman. After her life-changing conversation with Jesus, she returned to her townspeople and said, "Come, see a man who told me everything I ever did." As a result, "many of the Samaritans from that town believed in Him because of the woman's testimony."

Then a ripple effect took place. The Samaritans asked Jesus to stay there for two more days. He did. He taught. And many more people believed (John 4:29, 39–41).

Big religious words don't impress unbelievers experiencing life's pain. They're looking for answers. They want to find peace and forgiveness. They want to know how to keep their marriages intact and how to parent a difficult child or how to enhance their family life. They want to know someone cares about them and that their life has a purpose. They want hope.

A local businesswoman recently asked me, "Where do you find the strength to do what you do?" I told her my strength lies in having a relationship with Jesus Christ and explained what that meant. Within minutes she prayed to place her faith in Christ too.

Don't complicate evangelism. Don't use big words. Just tell your story—tell what Jesus has done for you.

FAITH STEP: *How has Jesus made a difference in your life? How can you explain this in words unbelievers can understand?*

—*Grace Fox*

# MONDAY, OCTOBER 27

---

*Some people brought children to Jesus so that he would place his hands on them and pray.*
Matthew 19:13 (CEB)

---

ONE OF THE DELIGHTS OF following Jesus is the endless stream of discovery—stumbling onto new connections in God's Word, seeing fresh applications of ancient yet relevant truths, finding a long-awaited answer right there in the pages before us.

We hold these truths to be evident, not from ourselves but from the Word of God:

- Jesus is ever interceding for His children.
- The angels are always before God's throne on behalf of children.
- People brought their children to Jesus to be blessed.

If Jesus is ever interceding, always praying to God the Father on our behalf—young and old—and if angels are always "in God's face" about the needs of the children, then what would Jesus have to say when the children were brought to Him for a blessing? Wasn't it already covered?

The Bible clearly shows the lesson He intended to teach the grown-ups gathered close that day. What lesson did the children gain? Was it important for their little ears to hear Jesus's own voice speaking a blessing over them? What kind of imprint might that have made on their young hearts? Even if they were too young to understand the words, to be touched by the Master had to have an effect.

Nothing He touched went away unchanged.

---

FAITH STEP: *How do you react to the statement that Jesus prays for you? How might it change your attitude toward the challenges you face today if you fully embrace that truth? Take a moment now to thank Him for that grace-gift.*

—*Cynthia Ruchti*

# TUESDAY, OCTOBER 28

*Then you will call upon me and come and pray to me, and I will listen to you. You will seek me and find me when you seek me with all your heart. Jeremiah 29:12–13 (NIV)*

MY THREE BOYS LOVE PLAYING hide-and-seek.

No hidey hole is off-limits. The hiders are extreme in their choices of concealment. They have been known to hide in the tiny cupboard under the sink. They shimmy into cracks under beds and conceal themselves behind curtains. They will lie as still as a rock hidden under a clump of blankets and pillows. I have found all of the towels taken out of the linen closet. As I yelled out, "Who left this mess?" a frantic voice whispered, "*Shhhhhh*, Mom! I'm hiding!" from behind the door.

And the seeker is equally as committed. The person whose turn it is to find the hiders will leave no throw pillow unturned and no closet unchecked. There is no such thing as giving up. The hiders will be found. The seeker is often calling out to them by name, "I am going to find you! Where are you? I can hear you . . . I'm getting closer!" I love the determination that they play with.

It reminds me of when Jesus talked about seeking the Kingdom of God. He said, "Ask. Seek. Knock!" He knew those who really wanted to find Him and the life He had for them would keep at it.

This is a theme that is mirrored throughout the Scriptures. Jesus isn't an absentee player when it comes to us. He wants to be found. He promises that when we seek Him with all our hearts, we will find Him. That is a promise I am banking on.

FAITH STEP: *Make it a point to seek Jesus today. Ask Him questions. Listen for Him as you pray. Read His words in Scripture and let Him know that you are looking for Him and long to be close to Him today.*

—*Susanna Foth Aughtmon*

# WEDNESDAY, OCTOBER 29

*"Roll the stone aside," Jesus told them. But Martha, the dead man's sister, protested, "Lord, he has been dead for four days. The smell will be terrible." Jesus responded, "Didn't I tell you that you would see God's glory if you believe?" John 11:39–40 (NLT)*

MARTHA KNEW THAT JESUS LOVED her brother. She had no doubt that Jesus would have healed Lazarus if He had arrived in time. But now it was too late; Lazarus had been dead four days. At least she and her sister had the comfort of Jesus's presence. She felt touched when He asked to see the tomb where His friend had been laid. She wasn't prepared for what He said next.

Jesus ordered the stone to be rolled away from the cave's entrance, but Martha objected. What good could that possibly do? By now the decaying process had begun; the odor would be horrible. Jesus gently urged Martha to trust Him and believe that she would see God's glory, so she relented. Moments later, she saw her beloved brother walking out of the tomb, fully alive.

When Martha balked at Jesus's instruction, she had no idea that she was getting in the way of one of His greatest miracles—one that would bring her great joy. That makes me wonder how often I hinder His work in my life by being reluctant to follow His leading. If I ignore His prompting to speak to that person, or balk at forgiving an enemy because it doesn't seem logical, I miss the joy of seeing Jesus at work.

At Jesus's urging, Martha trusted Him enough to give permission for the stone to be rolled away. When she did, she received more than she would have dared hope for. Why should I ever protest at a command from such an all-powerful and loving Savior Who also wants to do amazing things in my life?

FAITH STEP: *Have you ever objected to something Jesus asked you to do? Do you balk at following His clear commands from the Scriptures? Make a commitment to be more obedient and trusting.*

*—Dianne Neal Matthews*

# THURSDAY, OCTOBER 30

*Then Jesus asked them, "Didn't you ever read this in the Scriptures? 'The stone that the builders rejected has now become the cornerstone. This is the Lord's doing, and it is wonderful to see.'"*
Matthew 21:42 (NLT)

I HANDED MY SON A pail and shovel, and I showed him and his toddler sister how to fill it with moist sand, turn it over, and watch the pillar of the sand castle stand tall on the shoreline. Giggles poured from their lips and I helped them again. Soon they were forming the castles themselves as I watched from my perch on a nearby towel.

There are so many times in life I've tried to build my own destiny. I do the work, fill the buckets, set up my castles, and smile at the display. Tears come as my efforts crumble. I'm not sure why it surprises me every time.

My ideas—my work—are like temporary sand castles . . . if I'm lucky. Sometimes my efforts don't even get that far. They are like a handful of dry sand that slips through my fingers as I try to firm it up.

I'm so thankful that God doesn't expect us to build castles all alone. Our Lord is the Master Builder. He builds with stone and the foundation is His Son. God casts the vision of our lives and sets Christ as the cornerstone. To add to that, the quarry we mine from is of endless supply.

Do you have an area in your life where all your efforts are falling flat? Turn to God. Don't ask Him to help you work with your temporary sand. Instead, ask Him to point out where Christ is. Ask Him to help you build on the foundation His Son has already laid. And you will have a strong foundation indeed.

FAITH STEP: *Think of where you are putting your time and effort. Ask God to show you where you are building sand castles. Then take a moment to look around and see what God is doing. Finally, join Him in His work.*

—Tricia Goyer

# FRIDAY, OCTOBER 31

*"If anyone is thirsty, he should come to Me and drink! The one who believes in Me,
as the Scripture has said, will have streams of living water flow from deep within him."*
John 7:37–38 (HCS)

I ONCE HEARD A SPEAKER from the Cherokee Nation explain his belief system, which he said was more of a philosophy than a religion. He said his mother raised him with a concept called "Going to Water," which he still practices every day.

"When you go to water, you basically cleanse your face and hands with water, and as you do this you think of something of value that you can contribute to the world that day."

He went on to talk about the "White Path," which he said comes from the idea that you choose the path you take through the day. He chooses the white path—which means he chooses to have a good effect in someone's life that day.

I'm trying to teach my kids to "Go to Water," too. The girls about have it down, but Harper has yet to see the purpose of washing your face. Perhaps if I tell him Cherokee warriors do it, the concept will become more appealing.

I love the idea that as we wash our faces in the morning we are thinking of something valuable we might bring to the world that day. I also think it's biblical to acknowledge that we choose what path to take.

The beauty of both of these things for the Christian is that Jesus *is* the water. We draw from the source of Living Water and offer Him to the world. We can take His hand and know He walks with us, guiding our feet down the right path and helping us to do good in the lives of others every day.

FAITH STEP: *As you wash your face this morning, ask the Lord to show you someone who is thirsty today, that you may offer them a drink of Jesus.*

—*Gwen Ford Faulkenberry*

# SATURDAY, NOVEMBER 1

*Then John called two of his disciples and sent them to ask the Lord, "Are you the one who is coming, or should we look for someone else?" Luke 7:18–19 (GW)*

JOHN THE BAPTIST HAD FULFILLED his God-given assignment of preparing the way for the Messiah. He had boldly preached to crowds about the change that was coming. He had baptized Jesus while acknowledging Him as the Anointed One. Now John had been thrown in a dungeon; he knew he would likely be executed. He'd heard reports of the amazing things Jesus did, but perhaps he felt confused by commonly held beliefs about the Messiah. Wasn't He supposed to overthrow the Roman government and set Israel free?

John sent two of his disciples to ask Jesus if He was indeed the long-awaited Messiah. Instead of sending a rebuke to John for a lack of understanding or faith, Jesus told the messengers to describe to John what they had witnessed Jesus doing. John would understand the affirmative message that the Kingdom of God had come in full power. When John's disciples left, Jesus commended John for being a great man.

It doesn't take spending months in a dungeon for me to have moments of doubt. It's something I often wrestle with; maybe you can relate. I find Jesus's response to John's question comforting. It lets me know that I don't need to feel ashamed when I need some extra reassurance from Him. He understands my struggles and wants to help.

The first step to settling doubts and questions in my mind is to be totally honest about them. Why should I pretend they aren't there when Jesus already knows my thoughts? While I live on this earth, my faith will always be mixed with bouts of doubt. Jesus is not offended by those times. In fact, if I ask for His help, my doubts will help my faith grow stronger.

FAITH STEP: *Have you avoided talking to Jesus about doubts or questions that bother you? Spend some time in prayer honestly sharing your struggles. Allow quiet moments to listen for His reassurance.*

—*Dianne Neal Matthews*

# SUNDAY, NOVEMBER 2

*I love the Lord, for he heard my voice; he heard my cry for mercy. Because he turned his ear to me, I will call on him as long as I live. Psalm 116:1–2 (NIV)*

THIS PAST WEEK WE HAVE had the stomach flu at my house. There is nothing that I hate worse than stomach flu.

It is a steamroller of a flu that seems to flatten one family member at a time. When one of the boys starts feeling sick, the other boys cry. They know what's coming and it's not pretty. I cry a little too.

My son Will told Scott the other day, "Dad, Mom is the one who really takes care of us when we are sick." Scott is fine with that. He sleeps out on the couch, and we form a stomach flu colony with pallets and Tylenol in our bedroom.

The truth is, I love these guys. There is almost nothing that I wouldn't do for them. I administer medicine and put cool cloths on their foreheads. I rub backs and pray desperate prayers for calm stomachs. I hold hands and say soothing things like, "I'm so sorry you feel lousy." During the night I listen for their voices, making sure they are okay.

Even more so, Jesus has his ear tuned in to our voices. He knows that we cannot make it on our own without Him. We are desperate for His attention. He has not left us alone in our sickness, our sin, our pain. He has come to show us His great mercy and His unfailing love at every turn. Jesus wants to heal us and set us free.

No matter where we are at, we can know that His ear is turned to us and He is on our side.

FAITH STEP: *Write out a list of your needs in your journal. Offer them up to Jesus in prayer. Know that He hears your every cry and He is ready to answer with His mercy.*

—*Susanna Foth Aughtmon*

# MONDAY, NOVEMBER 3

*Cease striving and know that I am God. Psalm 46:10 (NAS)*

SOMETIMES I PUSH TOO HARD. I'm guilty of this faux pas in many areas, whether it's pushing my life to fit some ideal or pushing myself and others toward perfection. Sometimes I push my will with Jesus instead of resting and moving in step with His gentle guidance. Pushing is exhausting.

Recently I got to spend time with my sister, who lives several hundred miles away from me. As we shared a rare in-person conversation, we talked of deeper things going on in our lives and how Jesus was working in us. I remember telling her that I'd been feeling Jesus leading me to simply be. "I'm just tired of pushing," I admitted.

I also remember her wise reply: "I don't think much good ever comes from pushing."

Assertiveness and endurance have their place for sure; they're vital to keep us going in faith, to help us run the race Jesus sets before us. Yet pushing, as in striving or forcing, is not the Lord's way for us. He's the Shepherd Who leads us beside quiet waters and restores our soul (Psalm 23). He guides us on the right path, without us needing to force our way on it.

In her book *The Hiding Place*, Corrie ten Boom quotes her own wise sister, Betsie, who prayed, "Where You come, Lord, the spirit of strife cannot exist." If you know their story, you know Betsie spoke those words from inside Ravensbruck Concentration Camp during the Holocaust. Endurance was vital for survival; pushing could have been deadly. But somehow Jesus came into that hell on earth and set Betsie at rest from trying to push her way against impossible circumstances. She discovered the unearthly fulfillment of simply being with Jesus.

Enjoy Jesus's freedom from pushing today.

FAITH STEP: *Spend ten minutes in quiet with Jesus. Listen for His gentle presence.*

—*Erin Keeley Marshall*

# TUESDAY, NOVEMBER 4

*Then he said to his disciples, "The harvest is plentiful but the workers are few. Ask the Lord of the harvest, therefore, to send out workers into his harvest field." Jesus called his twelve disciples to him and gave them authority to drive out impure spirits and to heal every disease and sickness.*
Matthew 9:37–10:1 (NIV)

A FRIEND SENT ME A video of a multinational dance group based in Hong Kong. At the time, I was a choreographer interested in how the arts are effective in worship and evangelism. This group's message of love for Jesus was evident in their pieces. But I also noticed that some of the dancers didn't have the training and technique that could strengthen the artistry. The call to excellence is one of my deep passions—truly offering Jesus our best in the arts.

"Lord, bless their work," I prayed. "Thank You for the innovative ways they are finding to share Your love around the world in a way that crosses language barriers. But I also ask that You send them the training they need to grow in technique and dance skill."

A few weeks later a letter arrived. The Hong Kong company had heard about my work and invited me to be a guest teacher and choreographer. I'd never imagined traveling across the globe, and a million objections jumped to mind. But how could I refuse when I'd prayed that Jesus would send the group a teacher? For the next three years, I spent a few weeks each winter working with the team.

I see the same pattern in Matthew. Chapter 9 ends with Jesus telling the disciples to pray for workers. Chapter 10 opens with Jesus commissioning those disciples to be the workers they had prayed for. I've learned that when I notice a need in His Kingdom, it's time to ask Him to send help—and also listen carefully in case His plan includes sending me.

FAITH STEP: *Have you noticed needs around you? Ask Jesus to send the aid that is needed, and be ready to be part of His answer.*

—*Sharon Hinck*

# WEDNESDAY, NOVEMBER 5

*Blessed (happy, fortunate, prosperous, and enviable) is the man who walks and lives not in the counsel of the ungodly [following their advice, their plans and purposes], nor stands [submissive and inactive] in the path where sinners walk, nor sits down [to relax and rest] where the scornful [and the mockers] gather. Psalm 1:1 (AMP)*

WHEN I WAS IN HIGH school, a band called RUN DMC sang a song called "Walk This Way" (which I later learned was a remake of the song by Aerosmith). This song is about a pretty girl leading a guy into temptation, and he (of course) follows. During those high school years, I found myself following suit.

At first listening to the ungodly does seem okay, because our emotions seem to be in tune. And soon the godly path isn't even in the same neighborhood. Heartbreak and painful consequences follow. And it all started with listening to the wrong advice.

Whom have you been listening to lately? Most likely your friends today aren't trying to lead you into the same temptations as in high school, but have you been listening to other voices that equally promote ungodliness? Have you been listening to news reports that promote fear and confusion? Even a caring friend can speak bad advice, spurring from their own opinions and emotions rather than Scripture. I know I've given advice that came from me, rather from God, to others.

If you don't want to walk, or stand, or sit among the ungodly, then the first manner of business is shutting your ears to their words. Listen to another voice instead. In Mark 1:17 (NLT), we read: "Jesus called out to them, 'Come, follow me, and I will show you how to fish for people!'"

Jesus said "walk this way" long before Run DMC or even Aerosmith. And only Jesus will lead you along the right path.

**FAITH STEP:** *Next time someone offers you advice, pause and ask, "Jesus, is this what You are saying too?"*

*—Tricia Goyer*

# THURSDAY, NOVEMBER 6

---

*"Let your light shine before others, that they may see your good deeds and glorify your Father in heaven." Matthew 5:16 (NIV)*

---

WHEN MY FAMILY MOVED INTO our current neighborhood, we noticed several of the homes had dogs. Dogs in this neighborhood roam and aren't contained to their yards. One family, the Dixons, had a small cream-colored dog that was often playing in the front yard as we would come and go.

We hadn't been living in the neighborhood long when we passed their house and saw the dog on its back, feet straight up in the air. I gasped and pointed to the dog, then told my husband we needed to do something so the children wouldn't arrive home from school to find their dog dead in the front yard. We turned around and entered the Dixons' driveway, and the dog flipped over and came to greet us. Turns out, *that's* the way he sleeps!

Thinking about that dog, I wonder if that's the way we are sometimes perceived as Christians. We're just sleeping, looking rather dead, and then it's time for church on Sunday morning, and we pop to life again. I heard a preacher once say that Sunday morning is merely the pep rally to get you ready for playing the game that week. People should be able to look at us through the week and know that Christ is alive within us (Galatians 2:20). As you go through the week, think about how you perceive others, and then—more importantly—consider how you are perceived. If Christ is living in you, others should be able to see Him, see the peace He instills, the joy only He can provide. You will not be dead, but alive—alive in Christ!

---

FAITH STEP: *Look for a sleeping dog today (if you live in a town like mine, you won't have to look far). Remind yourself not to sleep through the day, not to let Sunday morning be the only time your light shines. Wake up, and be alive for Christ.*

—*Renee Andrews*

# FRIDAY, NOVEMBER 7

*My heart has heard you say, "Come and talk with me." And my heart responds, "Lord, I am coming." Psalm 27:8 (NLT)*

MARTHA FUMED AS SHE PREPARED dinner for Jesus and His disciples. It irritated her to slave in the kitchen while her sister, Mary, sat at Jesus's feet, absorbing every word He spoke.

Finally Martha interrupted the conversation: "Lord, doesn't it seem unfair to you that my sister just sits here while I do all the work?"

Jesus replied, "My dear Martha, you are so upset over all these details! There is really only one thing worth being concerned about. Mary has discovered it—and I won't take it away from her" (see Luke 10:39–42).

Jesus's response didn't belittle Martha's work or feelings. It did, however, imply that she'd allowed unnecessary details to take priority over time in His presence.

I understand Martha. Years ago, I served my family by packing amazing picnic lunches for day trips. That meant rising early to prepare. My quiet time with the Lord fell by the wayside.

As much as I thought I was showing love to my family, I stressed over my workload as Martha did. One day my husband suggested peanut butter and jelly sandwiches for picnics. Relaxing my standards freed me from unnecessary work and allowed me to start my day right—with alone time with Jesus. My whole family benefited.

The only thing worth being concerned about is our relationship with Jesus. If we're too busy for Him, then we're too busy.

FAITH STEP: *Have you allowed your work to overrule your time spent in activities that grow your faith? Studies, perhaps? Volunteerism? Ministry? If so, ask God for help realigning your priorities to reflect His heart.*

—*Grace Fox*

# SATURDAY, NOVEMBER 8

*Whatever you ask in My name, I will do it so that the Father may be glorified in the Son.*
*John 14:13 (HCS)*

A WOMAN SAT IN THE shade of her garage, watching as all the *unnecessaries* of her life were scrutinized, handled, and either rejected or purchased for mere pennies at her yard sale. A couple lingered over the mantel clock she'd found in the attic when she'd moved into the house forty years earlier. Tired of dusting it, she'd included it in the yard sale. "How much are you asking for this clock?"

The woman didn't want to seem greedy. "Fifty dollars?"

"Lady, we're not going to give you fifty dollars for this clock. You don't realize what you have here. It's worth so much more than that. In good conscience, we can't take advantage of you no matter how much we love a bargain. We were prepared to pay up to a thousand dollars for it."

What would happen if people expected as much from Jesus as He can offer?

Two blind men sat along the road and heard from the crowd that Jesus was passing by. They shouted out to Him, crying for mercy. The crowd told them to hush up. Jesus stopped in His tracks, the Bible tells us, and called back, "What do you want Me to do for you?"

They answered, "Lord, we want to see" (Matthew 20:33, CEB). Jesus touched their eyes and healed their blindness.

The last verse of that passage tells us that after they gained their sight, they immediately followed Jesus. Can't you imagine the conversations that ensued once they realized how much more they should have asked?

FAITH STEP: *What have you requested from Jesus? Are you asking big enough? Before you go further into your day, try asking for something only He can do. Be prepared to record the moment when that answer arrives.*

—*Cynthia Ruchti*

# SUNDAY, NOVEMBER 9

*If the Lord delights in a man's way, he makes his steps firm; though he stumble, he will not fall, for the Lord upholds him with his hand. Psalm 37:24–25 (NIV)*

WHEN I WAS PREGNANT WITH my first son, Jack, I was quite nauseous...for months. I had to keep a little food in my stomach at all times or the morning sickness could get the better of me. The only way I could make it through a church service was by slipping out to have a snack midway through.

One Sunday morning, I was exiting the pew for my mid-sermon apple when the toe of my shoe got caught on the carpet. The extra weight of my pregnant belly threw me off balance and I was sent catapulting down the aisle, arms windmilling wildly about. Our small church let out a collective gasp.

I reached out to steady myself, only to find myself grabbing a lady instead of a nearby pew. As I gripped both her arms in an effort to right myself, I found myself looking into the eyes of stranger...a poor hapless visitor. A sigh of relief was issued from the congregation as I tried to regain my dignity with a "So sorry!" and escaped into the lobby.

There was a moment during my fall when I thought, *Sweet mercy, I am going down!* And another moment when I thought, *Thank You, Jesus, for the stranger that I landed on.*

It seems that Jesus is always there for me when I am just about to fall. Even when I am out of control, full of fear, and losing my bearings, He seems to guide me to where I need to be. Even when I am doubting or struggling or tripping over myself, He is faithful to keep me upright. He loves me and He holds me in His palm. And I am extremely grateful for that.

FAITH STEP: *Go for a long walk. As you take each step, recognize that Jesus is with you, keeping your feet firmly planted on the ground, safe from harm.*

—*Susanna Foth Aughtmon*

# MONDAY, NOVEMBER 10

*Then when you call, the Lord will answer. 'Yes, I am here,' he will quickly reply. Isaiah 58:9 (NLT)*

I CAN'T IMAGINE GOING THROUGH a day without prayer, without turning to God. But what happens when we pray and it seems as if God doesn't answer? Our words seem to be going up on a helium balloon—floating into nowhere. Our heart aches, but still there is only silence.

"I wish God would answer and answer quickly," a friend told me. She felt dejected and alone. "Twenty years is a very long time to wait for answers to prayer. I'm beyond waiting. Heartbroken doesn't come close to put into words how I feel. I'm only just holding myself together. If only He would answer . . ."

Maybe you feel like that. You've prayed for something for years with seemingly no answer. But take a look at the verse above. His answer is "Yes, I am here." Too often we've been missing the answer! The answer is not a solution to a problem. The answer is Him!

Solutions only last so long. Resources run out. People will disappoint, but God's presence changes everything. Psalm 20:6 (NIV) says, "Now I know that the LORD saves his anointed; he answers him from his holy heaven with the saving power of his right hand."

God answers with His saving power. He answers with His right hand. We want a solution or a person or a new situation, but God gives us Himself. He knows that we need Him more than we need any *thing*.

Do you have a prayer that you've been waiting to have answered? Close your eyes and realize that the answer has already come. Can you feel God's Spirit descending on you? Can you hear His voice? *I am here.*

*Yes, I am here.*

**FAITH STEP:** *Take three Post-it Notes and write out three prayer concerns. Then fold them in half and write on the blank flap, "Yes, I am here. Love, God."*

—*Tricia Goyer*

# TUESDAY, NOVEMBER 11

*The earnest prayer of a righteous person has great power and produces wonderful results.*
*James 5:16 (NLT)*

THE LOCAL FOOTBALL TEAM HAS a former attorney for a coach. It turns out that this man wanted to touch the lives of teens, to be a godly example and help them be successful, and he chose to do that with the best way he knew to relate to them: football.

I've seen a change in this team since they've gained Coach Ozmint. He is their supporter both on and off the field, but he is also their guide, steering them in the right direction and admonishing accordingly when they head down the wrong path, both on and off the field. Coach Ozmint also allowed and encouraged a group of parents and local citizens who wanted to have a spiritual impact in the athletes' lives to start a "Praying Moms" group.

Have the spiritual coach and the praying moms caused the team to automatically win every game on the field? Of course not. (But wouldn't that be nice?) As Christians, we aren't promised that we will always receive a "yes" to our requests. We are promised, however, that if we ask anything according to His will, He hears us (1 John 5:14).

Those athletes step on the field each night knowing that their coach has prayed for them, knowing that the community is praying for them, and ready to face whatever obstacle is ahead, both on that field and off. How awesome is that power of prayer!

FAITH STEP: *Form a "Praying Moms," "Praying Dads," or "Praying Fans" group in your local community. Watch the bond form in athletes and community with the awesome power of prayer.*

—*Renee Andrews*

# WEDNESDAY, NOVEMBER 12

*"In the morning you will be filled with bread. Then you will know that I am the Lord your God."*
Exodus 16:12 (NIV)

FOR THE SECOND TIME IN a month I found myself asking a group of women to pray for something I felt burdened with but uncertain how it could affect the future. I wanted to be open to the possibility that Jesus could change my family's course in a certain way, but the idea of being shifted from the status quo was daunting.

How taxing would it be for our day-to-day lives if He brought the change I questioned? How much would it shake our family, and what fallout or blessings might we expect? What if our whole family wasn't on board? I tried to remember that the future in Jesus's will is exactly where we needed to head, regardless of some extra challenges and adjustments.

On one particular day when I was asking these very questions, a sense of peace came over me, along with the memory of manna, specifically how the Lord provides for His own. Back in Exodus when the Israelites were wandering homeless in the desert, He sent them miraculous manna. It appeared on the ground each morning, and the people had instructions to gather only what their families needed for the day, no hoarding more just in case. The extra they tried to keep went sour—an intended blessing spoiled by their lack of faith.

One truth stands out: Jesus does not give tomorrow's manna today. Therefore, it is often impossible to know how we will handle what's up ahead because we haven't received that day's manna. That means we can rely on Jesus's lead for today, stepping out in faith with Him as He leads us toward daily newness tomorrow too.

FAITH STEP: *In what area(s) are you relying on Jesus for day-to-day provision? Thank Him for teaching you that lesson.*

—*Erin Keeley Marshall*

# THURSDAY, NOVEMBER 13

*Jesus replied, "If you only knew the gift God has for you and who you are speaking to, you would ask me, and I would give you living water." John 4:10 (NLT)*

AFTER JESUS CONFRONTED THE WOMAN of Samaria one day, she faced a decision. She had been trying to meet her own needs in all the wrong ways and in all the wrong places. When Jesus asked her to call her husband, she denied having one. Jesus, Who sees and knows all things, told her the truth: She had had five husbands, and she was not married to her current partner.

How many years had this lonely woman been avoiding the eyes of others, seeking intimacy with lovers but finding only heartache? How long had she been trying to patch up the holes in her soul with Band-Aids that only hide, not heal the real wounds? This man knew her past and could give her "living water"? At first, she assumed Jesus was a prophet (John 4:19).

Even as believers, we may misunderstand Who Jesus is and what He really wants. Maybe we thought "no more thirsting" meant no more hurting or no more disappointment. But Jesus's purposes go deeper. He knows that intimacy with Him will always cost something. We don't understand that the things He allows into our lives will make us hunger and thirst for Him even more. But that enables Him to fill us up repeatedly with Himself—the Living Water—all the time taking us deeper into the relationship, deeper into intimacy with Him.

Jesus is like the prince waiting with a glass slipper pleading with the woman: "It will fit. Just put it on. You will never regret being part of My Kingdom!"

To her credit, the woman "tried on the slipper." And it fit.

FAITH STEP: *What does "living water" mean to you? As a symbolic reminder, place an empty pitcher on your kitchen cabinet, by your bedside, or on a nearby shelf. Ask Jesus to fill you daily with His living water.*

—*Rebecca Barlow Jordan*

# FRIDAY, NOVEMBER 14

---

*"Enter through the narrow gate. For wide is the gate and broad is the road that leads to destruction, and many enter through it. But small is the gate and narrow the road that leads to life, and only a few find it." Matthew 7:13–14 (NIV)*

---

I LOOKED FORWARD TO VISITING my extended family in west Tennessee with my husband and young children. But after several hours of barreling down the interstate, all I wanted was a little space and quiet. We'd just bypassed a city, which meant heavy traffic and bright signs everywhere, promising to meet our every need and desire. As we neared our destination, we had to pay closer attention to the signs. It would be easy to just go along with the traffic and miss our intended exit.

Later that week we hiked down a narrow wooded path that led to the site of a Civil War battle. The markers were difficult to spot, and with all the trees and foliage we didn't have a clear idea of the way ahead. The path led us through some rugged terrain that slowed us down. But when we finally reached the end, the rewards made the trip worthwhile. Besides getting to explore the remains of a fort, we had a beautiful hilltop view of a river and woods that stretched for miles.

Jesus talked about two roads that are very different. He referred to salvation and the Christian life as the small gate and narrow road that lead to eternal life. Sadly, He said that the majority of people choose the easy, popular route: the wide gate and broad road that lead to separation from God. In contrast, fewer people decide to take the less popular road that leads to a relationship with Jesus.

The going may not be easy on the narrow path of the Christian life, but when we reach the end of it, just imagine what a heavenly view will be waiting for us!

---

**FAITH STEP:** *Think about which road you are traveling down: the narrow path that represents the only way to God, or the wide road that leads to a dead end?*

—*Dianne Neal Matthews*

# SATURDAY, NOVEMBER 15

*But now, Lord, you are our father. We are the clay, and you are our potter.*
*All of us are the work of your hand. Isaiah 64:8 (CEB)*

MY TASTES IN DECOR HAVE morphed over the years. They change from morning to afternoon some days. When I flip through magazines with pictures of primitive seventeenth-century homes, I think, *Oh, I'd love to live in a house like that. All the history! How charming!*

Then I'll turn the page and see a crisp, all-white beach cottage and long to live there.

At one time, my family room looked like a country store—wooden barrels, country crafts, shadow boxes of miniatures with an antique thrown in here and there. Right now it has a north woods lodge feel, of necessity. My husband is an avid fisherman and hunter. So, it's canoe paddles and moose-shadow lampshades.

But one piece of decor survived both the country-era and the north woods look—a child-sized bent willow love seat from my sister-in-law.

It still fascinates me that straight branches with the thickness of ski poles can be bent into such graceful curves and arches. According to willow artists, it's done with water and heat, sometimes steam, and gentle, increasing pressure until the wood conforms to the desired shape.

I trace the arch of the love seat's back and ponder if Jesus runs His holy hand over my character in the same way. Is He pleased by how the steam and pressure of life's circumstances are shaping me? Am I conforming to a shape that resembles Him?

No matter what the "decor" of my life, anything that looks like Jesus can't help but enhance the picture.

FAITH STEP: *Are you yielding to or resisting His efforts to mold you into something beautiful? Lean in to the pressure of His hand today, and watch the art He can produce in you.*

—*Cynthia Ruchti*

# SUNDAY, NOVEMBER 16

*Therefore confess your sins to each other and pray for each other so that you may be healed. James 5:16 (NIV)*

I WAS A HOMESCHOOLING, CHRISTIAN mom who attended parenting classes, adored my husband, and hung out with good, Bible-believing friends. No one would have guessed that my heart was chained and locked tight. Even though I smiled on the outside, I rarely let anyone in. Why? I'd had an abortion as a teen. I took my child's life—my great, secret sin. I was sure that if anyone knew, they'd hate me. And the truth of total forgiveness didn't come through the Word of God and prayer alone. It came when I confessed to others—when I shared my deepest sins and listened to theirs.

The problem with a fortress is that the princess is lonely inside the cold walls. I was God's princess, and I was locked away by my own hand. In my self-protection, I blocked out sunshine, joy, happiness, peace, friendship, companionship. Yet confession opened the doors and let people in. Being transparent with my life helped me to see that others were hurting and locked away just like I was.

As I shared about my abortion, I felt broken, undone, naked, and ashamed. But those feelings only lasted for a moment, and when I saw the love and compassion in others' faces, the chains unlocked and the burdens lifted. When I opened the doors to my heart, not only did others enter, but I stepped out and was better able to enjoy the life God had given me. My emotions were no longer numb. I felt the sunshine and the rain, the heat and the cold.

There is a reason that God asks us to confess our sins to one another. It's not to shame us. God knows that when we confess, walls crumble. We also let others know they can be real with us. We can be real together.

**FAITH STEP:** *Do you have a sin you've been hiding? It may be a great, secret sin or something small. Follow in obedience to God and share it with someone trustworthy today.*

—*Tricia Goyer*

# MONDAY, NOVEMBER 17

*You are the temple of the living God. As God has said: "I will dwell in them and walk among them. I will be their God, and they shall be My people." Therefore "Come out from among them and be separate," says the Lord. 2 Corinthians 6:16–17 (NKJV)*

AT DINNERTIME IN OUR HOUSE, we play this game called "High/Low." Everyone goes around one by one and tells the rest of the family what the best thing about his or her day was, and what was the worst.

When it was Grace's turn, her high was that she made one hundred on her sixth-grade math test. The low was a lot bigger deal.

"Some of my friends were talking about having parties when we become teenagers. They said they were going to get drunk!"

"Which friends? What did you say?" my husband, Stone, and I said at the same time, seemingly sharing a brain.

Grace went on to explain how she asked if they meant what they were saying, and why they would want to start drinking.

"All teenagers do it," one of them answered. Another said, "It's no big deal. Normal teenage stuff."

Grace's face would not unfrown itself.

"I said it doesn't have to be normal teenage stuff and I'm not doing it."

How I pray she sticks to her guns. As a Christian, I tend to focus more on the things we have in common with others, and how to relate to them, than the calling to be separate. I teach my kids to be the same way.

However, there are times when we have to separate ourselves from the crowd in order to walk with Jesus. His Spirit helps us discern when those times are, and also provides the courage we need to do it.

**FAITH STEP:** *Is there some way God is calling you to be separate for the sake of walking with Jesus? Step out on faith today.*

*—Gwen Ford Faulkenberry*

# TUESDAY, NOVEMBER 18

*Praise the Lord, O my soul; all my inmost being, praise his holy name. Psalm 103:1 (NIV)*

MY TWO OLDEST SONS, JACK and Will, have been playing basketball for the past three months. It has been a joyful and nerve-racking experience all at the same time. I find myself filled with pride and anxiety as they weave their way down the court and try to score. Heart palpitations are often involved.

And then there is the yelling. I can't seem to contain myself and I give a running commentary as they play, calling out, "Get that ball!" and "Nice try!" and "Look for those rebounds!" They don't really appreciate my input. But they also know that they can count on me to cheer the loudest when they score.

A few weeks ago, there was a mad scramble for the ball at the end of the game. A teammate passed the ball to Jack, and as the buzzer sounded, Jack's shot circled the rim several times and then dropped in. His team swarmed him, patting his back and high-fiving. And I found myself standing, both arms thrust into the air, fist-pumping in victory, shouting, "Way to go, Jack!"

It was a full-body experience. This may have surprised the other parents since we didn't actually win the game. But I could not have cared less. I was so pleased with Jack and what he had done, I couldn't contain it, win or no win.

I think that when we consider all that Jesus has done for us, with all His mercy, His grace, and His forgiveness, He can expect no less from us. A full-body praise experience. Arms flung to the heavens. Shouts of joy on our lips. Fist-pumping the sky, not caring about what anyone else thinks about us. Praising Him with all our inmost being. Because of Who He is and how He has triumphed in our lives. It's exciting stuff!

FAITH STEP: *Turn on your favorite fast worship song. Do a dance of joy like King David! Go all-out and feel yourself come alive as you praise Jesus, jumping, hopping, and fist-pumping in celebration of who He is.*

—*Susanna Foth Aughtmon*

# WEDNESDAY, NOVEMBER 19

*So then, just as you received Christ Jesus as Lord, continue to live in him, rooted and built up in him, strengthened in the faith as you were taught, and overflowing with thankfulness. Colossians 2:6–7 (NIV)*

I FELT LIKE CRYING EVERY time I looked out my kitchen window. Just a few weeks earlier, our maple trees had been covered with golden leaves that glowed in the morning sun. Now the leaves had fallen, and the stark, bare branches showed the severe damage from an ice storm four years earlier. Heavy ice had accumulated on the trees that February, eventually snapping off about a third of the top branches. Seeing the broken tops of the trees made me feel hurt.

At least the maples still stood, lifting their branches toward heaven as if in praise to their Creator. As I thought about how deep and strong the trees' roots must be to withstand winds and winter ice storms, I remembered reading an article about a giant redwood tree in California. Despite its huge size, the tree had been knocked over by wind. The article explained that although giant redwoods can reach heights of more than three hundred feet, they have shallow root systems. That got me thinking about my own "root system."

Jesus doesn't want His followers to stop at receiving Him as Savior and Lord. He wants us to sink our roots down deep into Him so we can grow up spiritually strong and healthy. I can help my faith develop deeper roots by nurturing my relationship with Jesus through Bible study, prayer, and obedience to His commands, service, and fellowship with other believers.

If my root system is shallow, I'll be in danger of being knocked down by the slightest winds of adversity or suffering. But when my roots go down deep into Christ, He will help me grow up straight and tall. I can lift my "branches" to Him in praise and thanks, no matter how storm-damaged they are.

FAITH STEP: *What are you doing to help your roots sink down deeper in Jesus and His Word?*

—*Dianne Neal Matthews*

# THURSDAY, NOVEMBER 20

*Be patient, then, brothers, until the Lord's coming. See how the farmer waits*
*for the land to yield its valuable crop and how patient he is for the autumn and*
*spring rains. You too, be patient and stand firm, because the Lord's coming is near.*
James 5:7–8 (NIV)

A WHILE AGO MY THREE boys and I took a trip to see their cousins who live an
hour and a half away. It is a short little trip that is easily done in a morning.

You would have thought that we were making a ten-hour drive to Oregon.
"When are we going to get there?" "How much longer?" "How many more
minutes?" "This is taking *foreeeeeever*!"

I will not lie. I was frazzled by the time we arrived. It was a mighty long
hour and a half. My children are not schooled in the art of patience.

But if I am honest, I am not, either. I have an extremely difficult time waiting for things to happen in the course of life. I am not like the farmer who
knows how to wait. I am more like my kids.

When it comes to the dreams that Jesus has placed in my heart, I often say
things like, "How much longer?" and "This is taking *foreeeeeever*!" I find it
difficult to stand firm and say, "Okay, Lord, I am waiting for Your timing,
for Your wisdom, and for Your presence to reveal itself in this situation." But
in reality, it is always better when I stand firm and wait on His timing, than
when I go off willy-nilly and try to make life happen the way I want it to.

So I am going to take a deep breath and remember that the Lord's coming
is near. That is good to know.

FAITH STEP: *Take a moment to slow down. Sit quietly and meditate on the verse, "Be*
*patient and stand firm because the Lord's coming is near." Ask Jesus to help you be patient*
*as He continues His work in your life.*

—*Susanna Foth Aughtmon*

# FRIDAY, NOVEMBER 21

*Make sure that no one misses out on God's grace. Make sure that no root of bitterness grows up that might cause trouble and pollute many people. Hebrews 12:15 (CEB)*

THE BIBLE'S HEZEKIAH SOUNDS A lot like a man I met on a plane. The traveler couldn't bring himself to be civil to the airline agent who failed to find him a seat on the flight he wanted. The flight was full. He'd opted to fly standby, which to me means you take the chance of not getting on the flight.

For some reason, the traveler assumed otherwise. To his way of thinking, the fact that he *wanted* to get on the flight meant he *deserved* to get on that flight. He voiced his disapproval with the *oomph* of an opera baritone and with words as caustic as battery acid.

He and Hezekiah could have shared a journal. King Hezekiah wrote: "I will wander my whole life with a bitter spirit" (Isaiah 38:15, CEB).

I wonder if that traveler—that wanderer in the airport—knows he doesn't have to stay that way. Hezekiah knew. He called out to God. The bitter spirit verse is immediately followed by, "The Lord Most High is the one who gives life to every heart, who gives life to the spirit! Look, he indeed exchanged my bitterness for wholeness!" (Isaiah 38:16–17, CEB).

Bittersweet without the bitter.

Now, that's a testimony!

I don't know what made the traveler so disdaining about life. Could be plain arrogance. But I do hope he gets introduced to Jesus and discovers he can be whole.

FAITH STEP: *Have you considered that the opposite of bitter is whole? What's missing in your life, eaten away by the vitriol of bitterness? It's time to move past the "bitter spirit" verse to the divine exchange.*

*—Cynthia Ruchti*

# SATURDAY, NOVEMBER 22

*Jesus came and touched them and said, "Arise, and do not be afraid."*
*When they had lifted up their eyes, they saw no one but Jesus only.*
*Matthew 17:7–8 (NKJV)*

THE CONTEXT OF THIS VERSE is the Mount of Transfiguration. Jesus is glowing, Elijah and Moses appear, "talking with Him," and to top it off, God the Father speaks. "This is My beloved Son in Whom I am well-pleased. Hear Him!"

At this point the disciples are overcome. The Bible says they "fell on their faces and were greatly afraid" (verse 6, NKJV).

The experience must have been completely amazing. I wish I could have been there. Imagine! Dead people are alive, Jesus "shines like the sun," and God is speaking in an audible voice that probably sounds like James Earl Jones. But as I read these verses, something jumps out at me that is even more amazing than all of this: Jesus's response to their fear.

He comes to them. Touches them. "Stand up," He urges. And He tells them not to be afraid.

The next verse says that when the disciples opened their eyes, they saw no one else but Jesus. I know on one level that means Elijah and Moses were gone. But in my heart it holds significance beyond their absence.

When we are afraid and on our faces, Jesus's response to us is the same as it was with His disciples: compassion…a hand up…His peace. And in the light of Him, everything else fades into insignificance.

FAITH STEP: *Are you troubled? Afraid? As the hymn says, "Turn your eyes upon Jesus. Look full in His wonderful face. And the things of earth will grow strangely dim, in the light of His glory and grace."*

—*Gwen Ford Faulkenberry*

# SUNDAY, NOVEMBER 23

---

*Remember what it says: "Today when you hear his voice, don't harden your hearts as Israel did when they rebelled." Hebrews 3:15* (NLT)

---

ONE WOULD HAVE TO BE crazy to allow someone to set an alarm clock for 3:30 AM two feet away from the crib of a toddler, yet that's exactly the setup in our daughters' room. While I long for the little one, Alyssa, to get as much sleep as possible, it's her twenty-year-old sister, Leslie, who needs to get up so early for work. Since she's also a sleep-deprived college student, Leslie's cell phone alarm wasn't sufficient for waking her. The only solution was the high-pitched screaming of the alarm. And amazingly the toddler sleeps.

The first week or so that wasn't the case. The toddler woke up, wanted Mommy, and it took a while to get her back to sleep. And just when this tired mommy was about to demand a different solution, the next morning the toddler slept through the alarm. In fact, she hardly stirs as it blares not far from her head.

This makes me consider the alarms that sound in our lives. The Holy Spirit is quick to sound an alarm in our lives. We feel the inner tension. Scripture we have read comes to mind. Something within tells us there is a problem. Yet if we ignore the first warning—and the second, third, and fourth—our minds get used to blocking it out. Our hearts harden, and we no longer pay attention to God's truth. When that happens, we often end up where we don't want to go.

Alarms only work if you've committed in your mind to pay attention. Even the most blaring warnings become background noise if you don't force yourself awake to their interruption.

---

FAITH STEP: *Think back to a moment when God's Spirit spoke strongly to you about an unhealthy situation. Did you heed the warnings? If not, confess your hardened heart and tell God you're willing to listen today.*

—*Tricia Goyer*

# MONDAY, NOVEMBER 24

*Now therefore, give me this mountain of which the Lord spoke in that day;*
*for you heard in that day how the Anakim were there, and that the cities were great and*
*fortified. It may be that the Lord will be with me, and I shall be able to drive them*
*out as the Lord said. Joshua 14:12 (NKJV)*

WE'VE ALL FACED SEEMINGLY UNCONQUERABLE giants at times. So did Caleb. But this senior had a track record of faithfulness like few others. When God told Moses to send twelve spies into the land of Canaan to surmise their chances of conquest—and survival—Caleb and Joshua brought the only positive reports: "We can do it! Let's go in!" (Numbers 13:30).

The people wouldn't believe the two. Inevitably, they were the only Hebrews God allowed to cross into Canaan, forty years after wandering in the wilderness. Caleb, now eighty-five, still wore his running shoes, ready to tackle his world. "I am still as strong today as the day Moses sent me out," boasted the spunky senior (Joshua 13:11, NIV). Was he really that strong? *Real* giants ruled those mountains, not the animated superhero variety.

Regardless of how you view physical age and its limitations, one thing rings true here. Both Caleb's strength *and* his faith were still intact and well-seasoned. With God's help and a few others, Caleb took that mountain and defeated those giants.

Some of us may still be standing at the foot of a mountain wondering if we can conquer our giants. Fears of past failures or the negative voices of others can convince us to surrender without a fight. But Jesus offers us divine encouragement, no matter what our age. With only a "kernel of faith," Jesus will help us tackle anything!

**FAITH STEP:** *What giants are you facing? Ask Jesus to help you conquer those today.*

*—Rebecca Barlow Jordan*

# TUESDAY, NOVEMBER 25

*When the Sabbath came, he began to teach in the synagogue, and many who heard him were amazed. "Where did this man get these things?" they asked. "What's this wisdom that has been given him? What are these remarkable miracles he is performing? Isn't this the carpenter? Isn't this Mary's son and the brother of James, Joseph, Judas and Simon? Aren't his sisters here with us?" And they took offense at him. Mark 6:2–3 (NIV)*

As I'm writing this, the sound of a power sander carries up from the basement. My husband is doing the finish work on a desk he built for us. Our home is full of his handiwork. Our books rest on shelves he made with his father when he was still in high school. He built a dollhouse for our daughters, remodeled our kitchen, and every night we sleep on a beautiful bed that he built. By observing my husband and his projects, I've learned a bit about the patience and care that go into carpentry work.

The Bible tells us that Jesus was a carpenter. He could have chosen any family, any career, any sort of work during His time on the earth. His choice warms my heart. A carpenter cares about each detail of the project, uses the best materials, and chooses the right tools.

As I picture Jesus constructing our lives, shaping us into the works of art He intends to create, I'm reassured by the image of the caring carpenter skillfully fitting together the joints and dovetails of our life experiences, patiently sanding away rough edges in our character, and lovingly buffing a sheen onto our souls. One way He shows us how much He loves us, is by the time, care, and patience He invests in completing us.

**FAITH STEP:** *Study a piece of furniture today. Look at the complexity and detail that the carpenter put into the work. Thank Jesus for being the carpenter of our lives.*

—*Sharon Hinck*

# WEDNESDAY, NOVEMBER 26

*God has given us everything we need for living a godly life. We have
received all of this by coming to know him, the one who called us to himself.*
2 Peter 1:3 (NLT)

THIS ISN'T THE FIRST TIME I've written about my blender troubles, but I'm
hopeful it'll be the last. My husband and I finally caved and splurged on a
really good one, having gotten sick of replacing our mid-range models every
couple of years. We're pretty fond of breakfast smoothies, what can I say?

Anyway, I now feel that I have the tools needed to make mornings more
successful and less stressful. That same husband, my one and only, is fond of
saying, "It's all about the right tools." He was very supportive of the purchase
because he said it was downright painful to watch me holding back curses
for the old blenders as they refused to bully their way through anything I'd
throw in the pitcher. (Grace comes in the morning, but my output of grace
flows a little later.)

Even when we feel lacking and frustrations seem to bring out the worst in
us, Jesus is ready with the tools we need to succeed in living to honor Him.
What exactly are those tools?

Jesus's followers have His spiritual armor, which defends and empowers us
against onslaughts we can't handle with human strength—as long as we put it
on, that is. In Ephesians 6:10–18 we learn about the belt of truth that bolsters
our core; the breastplate of righteousness that guards our heart; shoes made of
the peace from the Good News, which helps us run with endurance; the shield
of faith that fends off the enemy's lies; the helmet of salvation that covers our
minds; and the sword of Jesus's Spirit, which is His Word, the Bible.

Jesus fits each of these tools perfectly and individually. With them He read-
ies you, no matter what the blender of life throws up today.

FAITH STEP: *Consider the difficulties you'd face without your favorite tool. Consider the
greater difficulties you'd face without Jesus's tools for you.*

—*Erin Keeley Marshall*

# THURSDAY, NOVEMBER 27

*"What should we do then?" the crowd asked. John answered,*
*"Anyone who has two shirts should share with the one who has none,*
*and anyone who has food should do the same." Luke 3:10–11 (NIV)*

GROWING UP, MY THANKSGIVINGS IN Alabama involved eating and visiting with family, napping, and then watching football and eating leftovers on Friday. When I married, I became part of a large Cajun family with slightly different Thanksgiving traditions. Cajuns know how to cook, and they know how to shop; therefore, shopping on Black Friday is part of their Thanksgiving ritual.

One Thanksgiving, I had my husband's entire family at our home in Atlanta. I'm not all that big on shopping, but I wanted to participate in their Thanksgiving tradition. To make the shopping trip meaningful, we obtained a "family list" from the DHS Family and Children Services. The sheet had an entire family's Christmas list, from things they needed to things the children wanted.

On Thanksgiving, we located the desired items in the sale papers and circled the things we'd purchase the next morning. We all woke predawn and got in line with the masses at the stores, with all of our shopping going toward the family's Christmas. Excitedly, we purchased every item on their list. I haven't had another Thanksgiving where I felt so blessed, so grateful for what I had, and so thankful for the desire God gives us to help others. The verses in Luke 3 tell us what we should do regarding helping others, and if we follow through with the command, we also see the beauty in Acts 20:35 (NIV), when Jesus Himself said, "It is more blessed to give than to receive."

FAITH STEP: *Call your local DHS and obtain a family's Christmas list. Make Black Friday plans this year to shop for them and feel the blessing of giving.*

*—Renee Andrews*

# FRIDAY, NOVEMBER 28

*Speak to one another with psalms, hymns and spiritual songs. Sing and make music in your heart to the Lord, always giving thanks to God the Father for everything, in the name of our Lord Jesus Christ. Ephesians 5:19–20 (NIV)*

MY YOUNGEST DAUGHTER WAS COMING home from college for Thanksgiving, so I decided to make Granny's meatballs and gravy as a special treat for the after-turkey days. Soon my eyes were tearing up, and it wasn't just because I was grating onions. Working on Granny's recipe startled me with a pang of grief. Even after many years, I missed her, especially at holidays. Memories flowed past of other family and friends who've gone ahead to heaven. The reunion one day will be glorious, but my sojourn here is lonelier without them.

As I patted the meatballs into shape, I thought how much my boys would enjoy them if they were here—but they both had commitments across the country and couldn't come home for Thanksgiving. Again. Another wave of sadness hit me.

I wanted to focus on gratitude, and I had every reason to be thankful, but as I set the table, more tears threatened. "Lord, transform these feelings of longing and loss," I whispered.

Jesus stirred a gentle reminder in my thoughts. The reason my heart ached from missing my children was because God gave me a wonderful privilege by placing them in my life in the first place. The reason I grieved family and friends in heaven was because He had granted me the gift of treasuring precious relationships while they were here. As I saw my life through His eyes, gratitude welled up. As the verse in Ephesians encourages, I was able to give thanks for everything.

FAITH STEP: *Write down any hurts or longings that make it difficult to be thankful. Do some of these exist because of a greater blessing? Write down any reasons for gratitude that come to mind next to each item on your list. Talk to Jesus about it, and ask Him to transform your feelings.*

—*Sharon Hinck*

# SATURDAY, NOVEMBER 29

*Let them give thanks to the Lord for his unfailing love and his wonderful deeds for mankind,*
*for he satisfies the thirsty and fills the hungry with good things. Psalm 107:8–9 (NIV)*

I DRINK A LOT OF water, and by a lot I mean several glasses through the day and around three glasses through the night. Yes, I wake up, drink my fill, and then go back to sleep several times through the night. I find that I crave water, and I've craved it even more since I donated a kidney two years ago. So, when I met with the surgeon for my annual checkup, I asked if giving up a kidney made me crave even more water than before. He laughed and told me that losing a kidney had nothing to do with my craving for water; however, he said that I may crave water because I know that it's better for my kidney if I drink plenty.

When I read the psalm above, I thought of my craving for water and how He satisfies the thirsty. Christ supplies my every need. And because of that— if I truly believe that verse—then I should crave Christ the way I crave those glasses of water each day, as though I can't live without it, as though I can't live without Him. And I can't.

I need water to survive (maybe not as much as I consume, but a human can't live more than a few days without water); likewise, my soul can't survive without Christ. In fact, I need Christ to thrive forever, for eternity.

FAITH STEP: *Drink at least three full glasses of water today. With each glass, give thanks to the Lord for satisfying the thirsty and ask Him to make you equally thirsty for His Word.*

—*Renee Andrews*

# SUNDAY, NOVEMBER 30

*Do not be overcome by evil, but overcome evil with good. Romans 12:21 (NIV)*

MY HUSBAND AND I WERE playing a board game with our son and his family. On one round, my son played a card that caused me to lose points.

"I don't get mad; I get even," I said to him with mock seriousness.

Our five-year-old granddaughter, Anna, overheard. She looked directly in my face and said, "Grandma—getting even isn't right. You must overcome evil with good. That's what Jesus said, so that's the only thing that works."

Wisdom from the mouth of babes. Wisdom from the heart of Christ.

When someone hurts us, our human tendency often wants to get even. But Jesus says not to take revenge. He tells us to treat the offender with respect. If he's hungry, feed him. If he's thirsty, give him a drink. As far as it depends on us, we're to live at peace with everyone (Romans 12:17–20).

Having this attitude isn't difficult—it's downright impossible in our own strength. But the Holy Spirit living in us reminds us of the truth and enables us to obey. Often that means making a deliberate choice to do what we know is right even though our emotions scream otherwise.

Perhaps someone has mistreated you. Ask the Lord for a creative way to demonstrate goodness toward the offender. Don't let evil overcome you, but overcome evil with good.

**FAITH STEP:** *Pray this prayer if someone has hurt you: "Father, help me see this person through Your eyes. Treating him with goodness is impossible in my own strength, so I trust You to empower me to respond in a way that honors You. Amen."*

*—Grace Fox*

# MONDAY, DECEMBER 1

*"Behold, you will conceive in your womb and bring forth a Son, and shall call His name JESUS. He will be great, and will be called the Son of the Highest; and the Lord God will give Him the throne of His father David. And He will reign over the house of Jacob forever, and of His kingdom there will be no end." Luke 1:31–33 (NKJV)*

WHEN I WAS A TEENAGER I read *Two from Galilee* by Marjorie Holmes. It made a huge impression on me because of how Mary was portrayed. Instead of the larger-than-life character she becomes in so many of our nativity narratives, Holmes imagined her as just a girl. She was special, yes. But mostly she was a normal teenager, like I was at the time.

Mary must have felt overwhelmed by the charge the angel gave her. Even though it was the honor of the ages, it was also the ultimate responsibility. How did she know she could do it? Further, what would make the hardships of her situation worth it?

I believe Mary grasped a concept that eludes many during the Christmas season, represented by the first candle of Advent: hope. As a Hebrew child she would have been taught to look for the Messiah, to place her hope in the promise of His coming. The angel offered the fulfillment of that promise, and a chance for Mary to participate in it.

When the hardships of your situation seem impossible, how do you know you can do it? Our hope is the same as Mary's. Jesus the Messiah, Hope of the entire world. When we allow Him to be born in us, we participate in the first miracle of Christmas. The miracle of hope.

**FAITH STEP:** *Is your hope in the Messiah today? Make a list of situations you see that look hopeless. Pray for Jesus to breathe hope into them, and to show you how you might participate.*

—Gwen Ford Faulkenberry

# TUESDAY, DECEMBER 2

*So you see, the Lord knows how to rescue godly people from their trials.*
*2 Peter 2:9 (NLT)*

GRACE IS AN AMAZING THING. God's grace saved our souls for eternity, but God often shows up with daily graces too. The important thing is having a soft heart and attentive spirit to see them. Grace is God doing for us what we could never do ourselves. It's preparing for our rescue.

Our family witnessed God's grace this year by providing a house. We moved from the Northwest to the South three years ago, and the hardest part has been settling down. The first condo we rented—sight unseen—was old and moldy. We moved into a nice apartment after that, but when my grandmother decided to move back in with us, we didn't have enough room, so we chose to move. After that we found a large, spacious house, but it was old, drafty, and expensive to heat and cool. I was thankful, but my heart hadn't settled. There were many wonderful houses in the area, but with my husband's new ministry position the cost was out of reach. So I started praying.

The answer came in an unexpected way. I offered a book to a new friend. When she came by to get it, I asked if she happened to know of a house that would fit our large family. Not only did she know of one, she owned one! Because of her husband's job they had to move across town. The house was a perfect fit and the right price. And our presence there was an answer to her prayers for good renters too.

Are you facing a trial today? God not only knows how to rescue you, but He has a plan for that very thing. The rescue may look different than you imagine, but His way is perfect. Trust Him in that.

FAITH STEP: *Create a small "rescue" journal. Start today by writing down how God shows up and answers your prayers. Every day add to your journal. Each page—each entry—will increase your faith!*

—*Tricia Goyer*

# WEDNESDAY, DECEMBER 3

*Blessed are the peacemakers: for they shall be called the children of God.*
Matthew 5:9 (KJV)

THE MOVIE *MUNICH*, DIRECTED BY Stephen Spielberg, is based on the massacre of eleven Israeli athletes by a Palestinian terrorist group who broke into the 1972 Olympic Games in Munich, Germany. After this atrocity, Prime Minister Golda Meir decided to send out teams of Special Forces to find and kill the perpetrators. "Operation Wrath of God" lasted some twenty years. In the movie, the main Special Forces character ends up asking himself deep questions about the futility of revenge, as he kills one terrorist only to see another rise up in his/her place. Almost every retaliation on Israel's part is answered by another violent killing of Jews in places around the world.

Watching the movie caused me to ask my own deep questions about what it means to live like Jesus in the world. I don't know if the same thing applies to whole countries, but I know in my relationships, someone has to be the first to say "I'm sorry" and attempt to be the peacemaker. I never want to be first, but I've started a little competition with my husband that he doesn't know about. In it, whoever apologizes first, wins. So far we're tied.

It's not easy to be a peacemaker, especially when you aren't sure how the other side will respond. You have to risk some things—mainly, pride. But Jesus said the risk is worth it regardless of how people respond. Peacemakers get to be called children of God.

FAITH STEP: *Is there a situation in which you are called to be a peacemaker today? Go for it, regardless of doubts about how someone will respond. Remember, the risk is worth the reward—you're a child of the King!*

—*Gwen Ford Faulkenberry*

# THURSDAY, DECEMBER 4

---

*"Men and women look at the face; GOD looks into the heart." 1 Samuel 16:7 (MSG)*

---

SOMEONE ONCE SAID THAT WOMEN will check out their reflections in almost any shiny surface: mirrors, spoons, store windows, even the bald man's head in front of them. Most of us spend large sums of money and time, both to cover up our flaws and to accent our good features. We follow the trends, color hair, paint our nails and even our toes. Some of us have those magnifying mirrors perched on our bathroom cabinets in case we miss something. (If you do, throw them away. Trust me. You really don't want to see that closeup. They're only good for magnifying our flaws.)

But both men and women can emphasize the outer appearance too much. When Samuel obeyed God and searched for a replacement for King Saul, the prophet looked for the most likely candidate according to his physical characteristics: good-looking, tall, strong build. But God reminded Samuel that His eyes see things differently. He takes X-ray pictures of the heart and holds them up to His own. Hmm.

Samuel discovered that God had selected David to be king on the basis of his own heart reflection: a young, runty shepherd boy who would one day become a "man whose heart beats to my heart" (Acts 13:22, MSG).

There's nothing wrong with trying to improve our outer appearance. But God is more concerned with what's on the inside. The question is not, "Mirror mirror on the wall, who's the fairest [most beautiful, handsome] of them all? Instead we should be asking, "Whose reflection do we see: ours or Jesus's?" Because that's what really matters to Him.

---

FAITH STEP: *Time yourself. How much attention do you give to your outer appearance? This week, spend more time on improving your heart, and ask Jesus to help you reflect Him daily.*

—*Rebecca Barlow Jordan*

# FRIDAY, DECEMBER 5

*"If the world hates you, remember that it hated me first. The world would love you as one of its own if you belonged to it, but you are no longer part of the world. I chose you to come out of the world, so it hates you." John 15:18–19 (NLT)*

I HAVE A FILE FOLDER that contains notes and copies of e-mails from readers of my devotional books. These messages thank me for writing and usually share how a particular devotion or book has helped them in their spiritual walk. But behind this folder is another one that has a single sheet of paper. Several years ago, a young man sent me a long message through my Web site—a message so filled with hate and viciousness that it took my breath away when I first read it.

The man had read my first book and called it trash. He referred to me and to Christians in general in the most insulting terms. He urged me to stop lying to people and then closed by saying he hoped I would die soon. Maybe you're wondering why I would hang on to such a nasty note. I do it because it reminds me of something important.

Jesus warned that those who follow Him can't expect to win a popularity contest. Since the world hated Him and His message, why should we be surprised when it feels that way about us? Those who reject Jesus will likely be offended when we share the truth of Who He is. But that doesn't let us off the hook. I can't stop writing about the Scriptures just because that angers some people.

Jesus commands me to love my enemies; that includes anyone who hates me or persecutes me for my beliefs. Rather than being intimidated, I can pray for that man who wrote me. And with Jesus's help, I can keep on speaking the truth in love.

**FAITH STEP:** *Have you recently experienced hostility, discrimination, or even hatred for your belief in Jesus? Ask Him to help you respond in a loving but truthful way.*

*—Dianne Neal Matthews*

# SATURDAY, DECEMBER 6

*God is good, a hiding place in tough times. He recognizes and welcomes anyone looking for help, no matter how desperate the trouble. But cozy islands of escape He wipes right off the map.*
*Nahum 1:7–8 (MSG)*

WHEN I WAS IN JUNIOR high, one of my favorite things to do was to dream about my future life. I pictured a great husband, a grand house, and a houseful of loving kids. I saw promise, not problems. I pictured possibilities, not pain. A few decades later, I have all the things I dreamed of, but it looks different in real life.

It seems *cozy islands of escape* have always been part of my plan. Teaching Sunday school to three-year-olds was the type of ministry that seemed right up my alley. Toddlers are cute, and how could I mess up telling the story of Joshua and the battle of Jericho with a stack of cardboard blocks? That's where I started when I first became a Christian. It was a ministry that I could be a part of with little effort and lots of rewards. But in the way God works, that's not where He let me stay. God led me to people with real hurts. He led me to starting ministries when I had no clue where to start.

Looking back, a close walk with Jesus didn't make the top of the list when it came to my future plans, but now that I'm here, I couldn't imagine doing it without Him. God leads me down paths where I need Him, and then He shows up and reveals Himself as He walks by my side.

FAITH STEP: *We all want an easy life. In what ways do you yearn for and seek out cozy islands of escape rather than turning to the true hiding place? Thank God that He's with you every step of the way. Tell Him you'd rather be with Him than on a cozy, meaningless island of escape without Him.*

—*Tricia Goyer*

# SUNDAY, DECEMBER 7

*Rejoice always, pray continually, give thanks in all circumstances; for this is God's will for you in Christ Jesus. 1 Thessalonians 5:16–18 (NIV)*

RECENTLY I WROTE A STORY about a young girl at our gym named Kathryn. Not long after she learned about the story and her mother read it to her, my husband came home from work with a card for me. The outside of the card had, in adorable block letters, *Mrs. J.R.*

The mere way that she addressed the envelope made me smile, but when I opened it, the message on her card melted me. It read, "Thanks for making me feel so loved." It was signed Kathryn and then followed with a big smiley face.

Too often I have someone do something kind for me, and I forget to let them know how much I appreciate their thoughtfulness. Kathryn didn't forget. She didn't have to make that card for me, but her effort and the sweet message inside gave me much joy.

Paul tells us in the verse above that we are to give thanks in all circumstances. Obviously Kathryn is taking that verse to heart. I plan to do a better job of following through with that command and look for each and every opportunity to say thanks.

---

**FAITH STEP:** *Buy a pack of eight thank-you notes today. Then strive to send them all within the next eight weeks.*

—*Renee Andrews*

# MONDAY, DECEMBER 8

---

*Therefore the Lord Himself will give you a sign: Behold, the virgin shall conceive and bear a Son, and shall call His name Immanuel. Isaiah 7:14 (NKJV)*

---

IN OUR CHURCH ON THE second Sunday of Advent, we light a candle to symbolize faith. Like early believers, who clung to the prophets' promises of a coming Messiah, we testify to our faith that He is here. He is with us when things are good, and He is with us when we suffer loss. Through the long, dark days of winter, faith in Jesus means we trust that spring will come again.

Because of this outlook, I often have people tell me I'm an optimist. But being a Christian really means so much more. Did optimism sustain the prophets of old through persecution? Was it optimism that drove Joseph to Bethlehem? Was it the reason the wise men followed that star?

By definition, an optimist looks for the good in all things. Surely that's a Christian's duty. But where we find that good is what it means to have faith. Faith doesn't turn a blind eye to what's difficult, ugly, or even impossible. Faith accepts those things straight-on—and then looks deeper. Like the shepherds who witnessed the poverty of Mary and Joseph, smelling the stench of the stable, they chose to kneel before the manger. They did this in faith, believing what the angels told them, that here—in this place, of all places—a Savior was born.

---

**FAITH STEP:** *Immanuel has come. God is with us. Let that truth be the gift your heart receives this Christmas season, and look for ways to share it with others.*

*—Gwen Ford Faulkenberry*

# TUESDAY, DECEMBER 9

---

*All Scripture is inspired by God and is useful to teach us what is true and to make us realize what is wrong in our lives. It corrects us when we are wrong and teaches us to do what is right. God uses it to prepare and equip his people to do every good work.* 2 Timothy 3:16–17 (NLT)

---

MY HUSBAND AND SON HAVE bad allergies, so we invested in a cleaning system that's a vacuum-and-then-some. It inhales dust and debris into a percolating water tank and doubles as an air purifier. The salesman actually told us not to call it a vacuum, ever. Yes, sir.

It really is quite gross what it pulls out of our year-old carpet on a weekly basis. We're not overly dirty people, honest. And we have no pets. It's just normal grime and dust, but wow, it's revolting.

Anyway, that may be TMI, but while I was cleaning it out after using it today, I saw that dirt had collected underneath the canister. I wished I'd discovered it earlier when it would have been easier to get rid of.

Sinful habits are like hidden dirt. When we overlook them, they grow and become tough to eliminate. A little resentment can fester into full-blown bitterness. A tendency toward impatience can turn into downright rudeness or unkindness.

Spending time with Jesus in prayer and reading His Word are the ever-faithful cleanup techniques for the dirt clogs of our character. Those negative habits and tendencies don't simply stay the same. We either go to Jesus to help clean them up, or eventually they cause malfunctions in our lives. We can't reflect Jesus's love as well through a mess of sin. And you know what? Given time, our human nature always, always acts as a dirt collector when we don't live with the filter of Jesus's Spirit.

---

**FAITH STEP:** *Memorize 2 Timothy 3:16–17, then ask Jesus to reveal areas in need of cleanup in you.*

—*Erin Keeley Marshall*

# WEDNESDAY, DECEMBER 10

*A certain ruler asked him, "Good teacher, what must I do to inherit eternal life?"*
*"Why do you call me good?" Jesus answered. "No one is good—except God alone.*
*You know the commandments: 'You shall not commit adultery, you shall not murder,*
*you shall not steal, you shall not give false testimony, honor your father and mother.'"*
*"All these I have kept since I was a boy," he said. Luke 18:18–21 (NIV)*

MY HUSBAND, DAUGHTER, AND I went to see a recent movie version of *Les Miserables*. We've seen various live performances and movies of Victor Hugo's powerful story. Each time I see it, I marvel at the biblical example of grace shown by the priest who offers forgiveness to Jean Valjean, and how that grace takes root and helps his life transform.

I also grieve every time I see Javert's despair. He has based his life on the law. Like the ruler who told Jesus, "I keep all the commandments," Javert is determined to earn God's favor through scrupulous obedience. But the law's purpose isn't to save us. The law shows us how much we need a Savior, and how impossible it is to reach the standards of holiness apart from Jesus standing in our place.

Even though I can spot Javert's mistake, I still slip into that way of thinking. *Lord, I tithed and worked hard, so why have You given more financial blessings to a person who was wasteful and selfish in their choices? I poured my heart into serving Your church, so when I needed a job, why didn't You open a door for me? I ate a healthy diet and exercised. It's not fair that I'm sick.* Whenever I demand some sort of "justice" based on my virtues (which are pretty slim virtues anyway), I'm forgetting that Jesus offers something much better. He pours blessings into my life out of His grace—undeserved, unearned, startling, and transformative love, freely given.

FAITH STEP: *Have you been tempted to tell Jesus how well you've been keeping all the commandments? Instead, confess your desperate need of His mercy, and thank Him for His startling and unearned grace.*

—*Sharon Hinck*

# THURSDAY, DECEMBER 11

*Jesus turned to Peter and said, "Get away from me, Satan! You are a dangerous trap to me. You are seeing things merely from a human point of view, not from God's." Matthew 16:23 (NLT)*

ONE MINISTRY IN WHICH MY husband and I were involved for more than a decade was particularly difficult. Personality conflicts, financial concerns, and fatigue due to long work stretches without breaks caused a lot of stress.

On one occasion, I spoke with a trusted friend about our experience. "Would you please pray for wisdom and strength for us?" I asked.

"Why?" she asked. "If I were you, I'd just quit."

My friend meant well, but her words floored me. God had led my husband and me to that ministry in a very obvious way, and we'd committed to staying until He said, "Go." Leaving because the work was difficult was not optional. We trusted in God's sovereignty and believed He had an eternal purpose to accomplish in and through us. If that purpose involved pain, so be it.

Jesus's ministry involved pain too. When He told His disciples about His upcoming death, Peter said, "No! Heaven forbid these things should happen to You."

Peter meant well, but his viewpoint was faulty. Pain was part of God's plan for Jesus, and seeking to escape it would mean Jesus's purpose for coming to earth would not be fulfilled.

Jesus rebuked Peter for his attitude. He called him Satan and told him that he was a dangerous trap for seeing things merely from a human perspective and not from God's. Strong words.

Let's take those words to heart when we face tough experiences. God has eternal purposes that we may not understand. Human nature wants to avoid pain, but God's perspective differs, and that's the one we must embrace.

FAITH STEP: *Pray, "God, give me Your perspective when Your purpose for my life involves pain. In Jesus's name, amen."*

—*Grace Fox*

# FRIDAY, DECEMBER 12

---

*For I am convinced that neither death nor life, neither angels nor demons, neither the present nor the future, nor any powers, neither height nor depth, nor anything else in all creation, will be able to separate us from the love of God that is in Christ Jesus our Lord. Romans 8:38–39 (NIV)*

---

KARI JOBE HAS A SONG I love called "Joyfully." My favorite lines are these:

"I will sing on the mountains high,

I will sing from the valleys low,

I will sing…"

I love it because it's a song of will. When I sing it I'm making a declaration: I will sing of His love forever. No matter what, no matter where.

It's easy, isn't it, to sing on the mountains. One time I was in the Swiss Alps and I burst out in the praise song, "Majesty! Worship His majesty!" I surprised myself as much as the people around me. I guess I was having a Maria moment—think *The Sound of Music*—as I listened to the goats' bells clanging and gazed down on the pristine lakes and storybook chalets dotting the landscape below me. That's a literal example of how I feel when everything in life is at its prettiest.

But valleys are also a part of our experience as humans. The ugly part. The good news is that Jesus's love is just as real in those places as on the heights, maybe even more so. We can choose, as an act of will, to trust in the promise that nothing can separate us from His love.

---

FAITH STEP: *What do you do when you are in the valley? Will yourself to sing of Jesus's love wherever you find yourself today, because the Bible promises He is with you.*

*—Gwen Ford Faulkenberry*

# SATURDAY, DECEMBER 13

*I have said these things to you so that my joy will be in you and your joy will be complete.*
*John 15:11 (CEB)*

WITH A CONFERENCE IN FULL swing and a break before the next workshop, I looked forward to the lunch hour during which conferees and speakers sat together and shared their projects and goals, about where they were in life and where they wanted to be.

After most of the tablemates had discussed their dreams and goals, a sweet-faced woman in her early twenties was next in line to share her story. She whispered something none of us at the table could hear. We all leaned toward her.

"You know those folded-up fine-print information sheets that come inside the boxes with over-the-counter or prescription medications?"

"Uh-huh." We nodded.

"I write those," she said, her facial expression revealing an almost apologetic quirkiness.

No one said anything for a long moment until I asked, "You write fine print?"

"That's me. Eight hours a day, five days a week. Dosing instructions, contraindications, side effects . . . That would be me."

I silently thanked the Lord for not giving me her job, then asked, "How do you do that? A creative writer whose day job is writing fine print?"

She smiled. "I apply myself to excellence while I'm at work. Then, when I get home, working on my novel is my joy time."

Jesus said, "My food (work) is to do the will of My Father who sent Me." But He also called it joy. "These things have I told you that your joy might be full." Not fine print, but bold print, splashed across the sky: There is a Redeemer!

**FAITH STEP:** *Have you read the fine print? In the Word God gave us, it isn't fine as in tiny. It's fine as in excellent, priceless, glorious. If you've fallen behind in your determination to immerse yourself in God's Word—the Living Word—find a quiet corner today and reacquaint yourself with the words that can make your joy full.*

—*Cynthia Ruchti*

# SUNDAY, DECEMBER 14

*We love because he first loved us. 1 John 4:19 (NIV)*

WHEN MY FIRST SON, JACK, was born I was completely unprepared for how much I would love him.

His wide blue eyes. His round cheeks. The small man-wig that was his hair. I loved everything about him. It was overwhelming. My husband, Scott, and I both wept when the doctor handed him to me. It is hard to hold that much joy in.

We couldn't take our eyes off of him. When my two younger sons, Will and Addison, were born, we felt the same way. The love seemed to multiply. We couldn't get enough of these three boys. In return, they loved us back. We loved being the ones that these three small people wanted to be with most of all.

In fact, Addison spent a good deal of the first three years of his life firmly attached to my knees. I was good with that. He felt safe with me. He wasn't letting go. It made walking a challenge, but I didn't complain. Mostly, I scooped him up in my arms and covered his sweet face with kisses.

Love is like that. It is the same with Jesus. He set the precedent of love in our relationship. He loved us first. He loved us most. He loved us best of all. When someone lives his life in a way that says, "I will do anything and everything for you. I will give My life so that you can have life," it is hard not to respond to that.

When we realize how much Jesus loves us, what He sacrificed for us, we are often like Addison. We want to grab Him and hold Him and not let go. We want to love Him back with everything that is in us. And the best part is? He is good with that.

FAITH STEP: *Make two columns in your journal. In the first column write all the ways that Jesus loved you first. In the second column write all the ways that you love Him back.*

—*Susanna Foth Aughtmon*

# MONDAY, DECEMBER 15

*When they saw the star, they rejoiced with exceedingly great joy. And when they had come into the house, they saw the young Child with Mary His mother, and fell down and worshiped Him. And when they had opened their treasures, they presented gifts to Him: gold, frankincense, and myrrh. Matthew 2:10—11 (NKJV)*

EXCEEDINGLY GREAT JOY. WORSHIP. GIFTS. It's interesting to me to note the progression in these verses as the wise men move closer to Jesus. First, they see the star. Like the sun, it beams joy into their hearts. Joy that their journey is not in vain—they will find what they are seeking. And what about when they reach their destination? The Bible says when they see Jesus, they fall down on their faces and worship, presenting Him with gifts.

In the Church Age it's easy for us to lose the wonder—the joy—of seeing Him. We have crosses on our walls, light-up Nativity scenes, paintings; Adelaide's Sunday school class even has a flannel-graph Jesus. Maybe there was magic when we first received Him into our hearts, but sometimes He becomes too comfortable. We're used to Him. He's a fixture in our lives we take for granted.

There's a beauty in being so secure, so familiar, that we're comfortable with Jesus. I believe on some level He wants us to feel that way. But there's also a lesson for us in the story of the wise men. As we recognize the reward for seeking Him, may our hearts be filled with joy. And as we move closer to the Babe in the manger, let's remember the majesty clothed in His humanity and worship Him. Bring Him our gifts, whatever they may be, that He may use us to build His Kingdom on the earth.

FAITH STEP: *Christina Rosetti writes, "What can I give Him, poor as I am? If I were a shepherd, I would bring a lamb. If I were a wise man, I would do my part. But, what can I give Him? Give Him my heart." Give Jesus your heart today.*

—*Gwen Ford Faulkenberry*

# TUESDAY, DECEMBER 16

---

*I will instruct you and teach you in the way you should go. Psalm 32:8 (NKJV)*

---

I LOVE HEARING HOW OTHERS determined their life's work. Did Jesus hand them a pre-written plan? Did they stumble onto something they truly enjoyed? Or did they discover God's will through trial and error?

I've always read the Bible avidly and listened to Jesus's teachings. Early on, I chose to follow Him with all my heart. But it seems like most of my life sort of happened and fell into place as I stumbled along. I knew God created me as one of a kind, and He undoubtedly designed a precise plan for my life, long before I was born (Psalm 139). But just how it unfolded is sometimes still a mystery.

The other day I was thinking about my early college days years ago when I was searching for God's will for my life. It wasn't until I married that Jesus laid a dream on my heart to write. But He used even basic college classes to prepare me for the future: For example, English nurtured my love and creativity for words. Bible classes increased my love for His precious Word.

Choir furthered my love of music and praise, and psychology helped me understand both those irregular people in our church ministry—and how Jesus could use my weaknesses for His glory. Speech class taught me that Jesus could bless a timid preacher's kid behind a podium, and missions involvement revealed a world beyond me. My husband and children showed me what's really important—and how much I needed Jesus's daily guidance.

Each year through every experience, Jesus has taught me more. You see, whether we think we know the direction of our future, or haven't a clue, Jesus knows. And if we will listen, He will lead us, one step at a time.

---

**FAITH STEP:** *How did God reveal His life plan to you? What is He teaching you right now?*

—*Rebecca Barlow Jordan*

# WEDNESDAY, DECEMBER 17

---

*He replied to him, "Who is my mother, and who are my brothers?" Pointing to his disciples, he said, "Here are my mother and my brothers. For whoever does the will of my Father in heaven is my brother and sister and mother." Matthew 12:48–50 (NIV)*

---

I PLAYED THE MELODY OF a Christmas carol on the piano, and sighed. When the children were young, a large part of our Christmas tradition included making music together. I'd always visualized that when they grew up they'd come home on holidays, bringing spouses and grandbabies, and we'd continue our traditions. Instead, our adult children and our grandchild were scattered across the country, and other commitments kept most of them far from us. Our gathering would be tiny again this year, and my heart ached from missing my children and also from letting go of my vision of how Christmas would be from now on.

When television commercials show touching scenes of family gatherings, many people feel the ache of a picture that doesn't match their reality. Sometimes family is absent because of geographic challenges. Sometimes family is fragmented by conflict and emotional distance. Sometimes the people under our roof whom we long to be close to feel like strangers.

That's why I'm comforted by Jesus's declaration that He is our family. Longing for a perfect family is a core desire. Finding it on earth is impossible. Jesus can bring healing and more closeness to our imperfect families, but He also envelops us in His love and welcomes us into the only perfect family of our heavenly Father.

---

**FAITH STEP:** *Look at some family photos and ask Jesus to help you show His love to your family. Also thank Him for being your family.*

—*Sharon Hinck*

# THURSDAY, DECEMBER 18

---

*Flee the evil desires of youth and pursue righteousness, faith, love and peace, along with those who call on the Lord out of a pure heart.* 2 Timothy 2:22 (NIV)

---

I THOUGHT I WAS DOING the right thing by signing my son up for the kid's basketball league. He was a quiet boy, and I hoped he'd make a few friends and learn to work within a team. I was eager to hear about how everything went after the first practice. Nathan sulked as he walked to the car.

"Everyone else has already been playing for three years. I was the only one who didn't know the plays."

How could that be possible? My son was in third grade.

Sure enough, Nathan was behind the curve when it came to playing with the team. Even worse was when the other kids teased him about it.

As a mom I considered how I should handle the situation. Should I talk to the other parents? Should I make him stick it out? Should we seek outside coaching to catch him up? In the end, I asked Nathan if he'd like to drop the team. Relief flooded his face.

In all our lives we have hard situations that we face, but there are times when walking away is the best choice. We are told to love our enemies, but that doesn't mean we need to hang out with them.

Instead of spending time with members of his basketball team, Nathan instead got involved with other kids in our church's children's program. His relationships flourished, and he benefited from the interaction. Seeing that made me consider my own relationships. We will benefit emotionally and spiritually when we connect with those who build us up, rather than tear us down—and as a result our own faith, love, and peace grow!

---

**FAITH STEP:** *Do you have a difficult relationship that you're wondering how to handle? Bring it before Jesus. He might ask you to press through, but He also might want you to step back, for your own peace in your heart.*

—*Tricia Goyer*

# FRIDAY, DECEMBER 19

*"If you abide in my word, you are truly my disciples, and you will know the truth, and the truth will set you free." John 8:31–32 (ESV)*

ONE DECEMBER AFTERNOON, I HUNCHED in the backseat of our overloaded car between my two youngest children. We were driving four hundred miles to spend Christmas with extended family. When we stopped for dinner at a restaurant, the server seated us in an open area surrounded by elderly couples. I couldn't help noticing how they enjoyed watching us. *They probably enjoy seeing my cute kids and remembering when their own were young,* I thought.

Later, I took my toddler daughter to the bathroom. When I sat back down, one grinning couple came toward me. Expecting some compliment on my family, I tilted my ear upward as the wife sweetly whispered, "Dear, you have a candy cane stuck to the seat of your pants." My face turned as red as the stripes on the "accessory" I had worn into the restaurant. But it was a truth I needed to hear.

When Jesus lived on earth, He always spoke the exact words people needed. Sometimes those words were unexpected or hard to listen to. When the rich young ruler claimed to have kept all the commandments, Jesus told him to sell all his possessions. The young man didn't see that coming. When the woman at the well told Jesus she had no husband, He told her she'd had five husbands, and was living with a man to whom she wasn't married.

When I read Jesus's words in the Bible, I often have a similar experience. His teaching on forgiveness might expose a grudge I'm nursing. His admonition to seek His Kingdom above all else can reveal how off-kilter my priorities are. What I read may sometimes be hard to take, but it's always what I need to hear. Jesus does more than let me know what's stuck to my pants; He shows me what's deep in my heart.

FAITH STEP: *The next time you open your Bible, invite Jesus to direct you to the truth you need to hear.*

—*Dianne Neal Matthews*

# SATURDAY, DECEMBER 20

*And Mary said: "My soul glorifies the Lord and my spirit rejoices in God my Savior, for he has been mindful of the humble state of his servant. From now on all generations will call me blessed, for the Mighty One has done great things for me—holy is his name." Luke 1:46–49 (NIV)*

I HAVE BEEN THINKING ABOUT the hard scrabble life of Mary, Jesus's mom. A teenager. An unwed mom. Donkey rider. Survivor. A refugee. A social outcast. Beloved and highly favored by God. Believer. Visionary. Joy bearer. World changer. That Mary.

Sometimes when I don't understand what is going on in life, I want to go into hiding and lick my wounds. But when Mary is faced with the impossibility of presenting her fiancé with a baby that is clearly not his and a life that is sure to be fraught with misunderstanding and heartache, she throws back her head... and sings.

She sings about how God is mighty and merciful and holy. She sings of blessing and how God has done great things for her. Even in the midst of the harsh realities of her life, she is still holding on to hope. With one hand on her belly and one hand in Joseph's, she believes that even though life isn't easy, it is about to get good. That Jesus is getting ready to pierce the sky with His unshakable goodness and pour out His love on humanity. Light is going to crack the darkness. Wrongs are going to be righted. Love is going to save the day.

And she is going get to be a part of it. There is no wound licking or hiding for Mary. She is all-in. And I want to be just like her. I want to find her song in my mouth... her hope in my heart... her resolve in my gut.

In the face of impossible odds and tenuous circumstances, I want to throw back my head and unleash a volley of praise into the heavens about how very good God is to me. Because... He is.

**FAITH STEP:** *Put on your favorite worship song. Sing a song to the Lord of His goodness, His love, and His faithfulness. Praise Him for all that He has done in your life.*

—*Susanna Foth Aughtmon*

# SUNDAY, DECEMBER 21

*Jesus replied, "It's written, 'People won't live only by bread, but by every word spoken by God.'"*
*Matthew 4:4 (CEB)*

A FRIEND SERVES AS A bell ringer each year for a charitable organization that provides food and shelter for the needy. With his white hair and beard, his red coat and faux ermine–trimmed red hat, he looks just like what we imagine Santa Claus should.

His bell ringing nets some exceptional donations and even more exceptional stories.

One year as he was *ho-ho-ho*-ing, ringing the bell with gusto, nudging shoppers toward the slot at the top of the red kettle, I stopped, ready to make a donation, and started a conversation, friend to friend.

He asked if I'd heard about another of the members of our life group. Despite his recent faith growth spurt, the young man had broken probation and was spending time in the county jail. It was surreal having that discussion with a bell ringer who looked just like Santa Claus.

Jesus stayed on the alert for those who needed His help, God's help. If they'd had them at the time, He might have volunteered to ring a seasonal bell to raise funds to feed the hungry. But, like my friend the bell ringer, Jesus also used every opportunity to show that heart-hunger trumps stomach-hunger.

"Man does not live by food pantry alone," Jesus might have reworded His famous speech for a twenty-first-century crowd, "but by every word that comes from the mouth of God."

FAITH STEP: *Consider in what ways you can couple a financial contribution with an in-person act of service that shows the love of Jesus to those in need.*

*—Cynthia Ruchti*

# MONDAY, DECEMBER 22

---

*"Come to me, all you that are weary and are carrying heavy burdens, and I will give you rest. Take my yoke upon you, and learn from me; for I am gentle and humble in heart, and you will find rest for your souls. For my yoke is easy, and my burden is light." Matthew 11:28–30 (NRSV)*

---

IN THE CHRISTMAS CAROL "IT Came Upon a Midnight Clear," there is a little-known verse that contains this phrase: "Oh, hush the noise, ye men of strife, and hear the angels." The idea is that there is so much noise in our lives, and especially at Christmastime, that we may miss the message the angels brought to the shepherds and to us down through the ages—the good news for all people, that Jesus is born.

I like to sing this verse on the last Sunday of Advent, when Christmas festivities seem to ramp up at their most frenetic pace. It's a great reminder, and a great admonition. Noise doesn't hush on its own. We have to be deliberate about hushing it. Will we be carried away by the rolling tide of a modern consumer Christmas? Once again, our source of strength is silence and trust in Jesus.

The invitation always stands: *Come to Me. Rest.*

In Him we find the power to hush the noise. The wisdom to discern when and how and even whom to hush that the angels' message can be heard in our hearts: Peace . . . Goodwill . . . A Savior is born.

---

**FAITH STEP:** *Take a few moments to "hush the noise" in your life today, and listen to the voice of Jesus inviting you into His rest.*

*—Gwen Ford Faulkenberry*

# TUESDAY, DECEMBER 23

---

*"See, I will create new heavens and a new earth. The former things will not be remembered, nor will they come to mind." Isaiah 65:17 (NIV)*

---

DURING MY TEEN YEARS, I spent one Christmas with my friend Ann's family. She'd just turned sixteen, and when she was handed a small box as a gift I thought she'd received a piece of jewelry. Instead, inside there was a key, and attached to the key was a string. Ann began following the string, and I was right on her heels. We went through the living room, into the kitchen, outside, back inside, and finally to the garage where a small convertible waited. I was shocked! The gift was more wonderful, more extravagant than anything I imagined . . . and it all began with a key.

At Christmas the birth of Christ is the key to eternity. Through Jesus's life, His work on earth was the string. And when we accept the gift, and follow the string, we are led straight to heaven.

Yes, Jesus is the reason for the season. We give gifts to symbolize our greatest gift . . . our Savior. But the gift didn't end there. And we need to remember that. As 1 Corinthians 2:9 (NLT) says, "That is what the Scriptures mean when they say, 'No eye has seen, no ear has heard, and no mind has imagined what God has prepared for those who love him.'"

When we come to the end of the string that links our lives to eternity, we'll discover the gift of heaven to be more wonderful, more extravagant than we can ever imagine. And it's offered by the greatest gift of all, Jesus.

---

FAITH STEP: *Find or buy a simple key to keep in your change purse or on your bathroom vanity. Use it to remind you that you've been given a great gift in Christ, and the rest of the gift is still coming in eternity!*

*—Tricia Goyer*

# WEDNESDAY, DECEMBER 24

*For unto us a child is born, unto us a son is given: and the government shall be upon his shoulder: and his name shall be called Wonderful, Counsellor, The mighty God, The everlasting Father, The Prince of Peace. Isaiah 9:6 (KJV)*

WE WERE GATHERED WITH MY husband's family one Christmas when our first child was just a toddler. We had placed a baby crib in the bedroom where we slept, thinking our child would fall asleep quickly. We were mistaken! Our daughter was so excited and filled with the "wonder" of Christmas that she refused to go to sleep. Finally around three or four in the morning, she whimpered her last objections and settled in for a short winter's nap.

I love how children view Christmas. In fact, a child's life is usually wonder-full. How different our lives would be if we saw life through the lens of a child.

We could start by realizing how God created us. Psalm 139:14 (KJV) says "we are fearfully and wonder-fully (my own spelling) made." Not only that, we can observe how our world is filled with the wonders God has done. Psalm 40:5 says there are too many to declare!

But we celebrate the most wonder-full thing of all at Christmas. Prophesied by Isaiah, he said the child to be born would be called "Wonderful." Jesus, the Son of God, born in a tiny manger!

When I think about the wonder of that first Christmas—the glory of it all—and how thoroughly God prepared for that event, I'm tempted to lose a little sleep myself, especially on the eve of His birthday.

This year, I'm reminding myself at Christmas—and all year long—that life with Jesus is indeed wonder-full. And I'm praying God will give me childlike eyes to always keep it that way.

**FAITH STEP:** *On Christmas Eve this year, take turns sharing some of the wonder-full names for Jesus you can find in this passage from Isaiah—and throughout the Bible.*

—*Rebecca Barlow Jordan*

# THURSDAY, DECEMBER 25

*So the Lord himself will give you this sign: A virgin will become pregnant and give birth to a son, and she will name him Immanuel [God Is With Us]. Isaiah 7:14 (GW)*

SOME OF MY FAVORITE THINGS about Christmas are the cherished traditions. Decorating my house for family to enjoy. Getting one of my children to help me hang ornaments on the tree while we reminisce. Baking cookies with my granddaughter. Having our children and grandchildren come over to our house for a big home-cooked Christmas dinner, complete with three kinds of pies. Unfortunately, those are all things I don't get to enjoy anymore. Not since my husband and I moved 1,500 miles away.

Having everyone come to our house is out of the question because of work schedules and the cost of airline tickets. The past two years we've gathered at my daughter's house on Christmas Eve, but she and her family recently moved. So last year my husband and I flew into Illinois and stayed in a hotel room. When we visited with our sons, and with our daughter's family when they arrived in town, we ate at restaurants. On Christmas Eve, our family gathered in the house that our younger son rents. We sat down to a dinner composed mostly from premade foods from the store.

We had a different kind of Christmas last year, not the ideal picture I carry in my mind from past years. But this stripped-down version forced me to be thankful for the blessing of simply being with loved ones. It also helped me focus on the one truth that's the whole point of celebrating: Immanuel, God is with us. I may not have a decorated tree or a house full of people, but Jesus will always be with me.

**FAITH STEP:** *During this busy season, do you need to strip away some of the trimmings from your Christmas celebration so you can focus more on Jesus? Schedule some time to sit quietly and read the Scriptures related to Christ's birth. End by singing a favorite carol or two.*

—*Dianne Neal Matthews*

# FRIDAY, DECEMBER 26

---

*Above all, you must live as citizens of heaven, conducting yourselves in a manner worthy of the Good News about Christ. Philippians 1:27 (NLT)*

---

ONE OF MY FAVORITE MEMORIES with my son, Paxton, happened on Christmas Day several years ago. Overnight our Arkansas land was blessedly dumped on by nearly two feet of snow, and we woke to a winter wonderland that filled this Chicago native's heart. That afternoon our family of four bundled up and went sledding down our sloped backyard. If we doubled up and got going fast enough we could careen nearly down to the lake several hundred yards below.

Energized and warmed by the climb back up, Paxton and I had nearly reached the top when we both dropped to the snow and rolled on our backs to look at the white sky. How still and beautiful it was, and what a precious memory those moments are, sharing the wonder with him. I love looking at the sky and marveling about heaven and wondering what it, my true home, will be like. This verse fascinates me because it commands us to live as if we're already citizens of heaven. What does that encompass?

Well, since heaven is the Lord's throne room, it is a place of royalty. And since Jesus conquered death, it is also a place of victory. Therefore, it seems to me that citizens of heaven ought to shine on this earth with the dignity of royalty and the assurance of winners.

Jesus's followers have the privilege of living confidently and with nothing to prove. Our victory in Him is certain; our place in His world is secure.

In the stillness of that wintery Christmas day, with my precious family having fun together and the scenery glittering like diamonds, I had a clearer vision of the glorious vista heaven will be as home one day and forever. I felt my spirit lift as a victorious daughter of the King.

---

FAITH STEP: *What in this world makes you think about heaven? How is your countenance affected as you live in the understanding that you have such a place awaiting you if you know Jesus as Savior?*

*—Erin Keeley Marshall*

# SATURDAY, DECEMBER 27

*For even the Son of Man came not to be served but to serve others and to give his life as a ransom for many. Matthew 20:28 (NLT)*

WHEN I WATCH TELEVISION PROGRAMS like *Iron Chef America*, I envision myself a pseudo-gourmet cook.

My pantry shelves hold vegetable oil, extra virgin olive oil, sesame oil, walnut oil, and hot chili oil. Yes, grapeseed oil is on my shopping list.

But nothing I've ever created in the kitchen could top the meal Jesus made for His disciples after the resurrection.

Such a small detail story in God's Word, but how significant! The gospel of John tells us that not long after Jesus rose from the dead, some of His disciples were fishing at the Sea of Tiberius. In the morning, a voice called from shore. "Have you caught anything?" The men answered back that they had not.

The Voice said, "Try casting your net on the right side of the boat rather than the left."

The unusual instruction revealed Who was talking to them. Jesus! They obeyed Him and found their nets so full of large fish they couldn't pull the net into the boat. They had to drag it to shore.

On shore, breakfast waited for them. Jesus had built a fire and made them fish and bread.

The hands so recently pierced, kneaded bread. They gutted fish. They collected firewood and laid a fire. The symbolism is so beautiful.

Jesus still served, after all He'd been through, after all He'd endured, including the betrayal of these very men. An ordinary breakfast of ordinary food. But what an extraordinary act!

FAITH STEP: *What moment of Jesus interacting with His followers most tugs at your heart? Why? Can you find a way to express that to someone else before this day is over?*

*—Cynthia Ruchti*

# SUNDAY, DECEMBER 28

*Form your purpose by asking for counsel, then carry it out using all the help you can get.*
*Proverbs 20:18 (MSG)*

THE END OF THE YEAR was approaching, and with it came the freedom to start planning my goals for the coming year. I love to plan! I love to cross off my to-do list and inhale great gulps of satisfaction over finishing something. In all honesty, this thrill has been compounded (and exacerbated!) in the past handful of years since having children because it's rare that I'm able to finish any task in one uninterrupted try.

I had several goals in mind for my writing life, but they were all swirling around in my head with no clear direction for making them happen. One thing I've learned to do over the years is to seek advice. I love wise advice about as much as planning.

After a couple of phone calls and a few one-on-one conversations, I felt like I had a much better handle on my next steps.

Good advice brings freedom to soar. None of us has all the answers, and the first bit of advice is to *ask for advice.*

Throughout the New Testament, Jesus offers a great deal of direction for our personal life, faith, relationships, money management, church organization and growth, weathering life's storms, and making the most of our days while we wait for His return.

Whose advice are you relying on today? Your own can be helpful to some degree, but the good Lord placed a bunch of us on earth together. He knows a whole lot about that thing or two we can learn from others.

FAITH STEP: *Give yourself the gift of not needing to have all the answers on your own. Consider a decision you're facing, and seek wise counsel. Consider yourself armed with more clarity to make the best choice.*

—*Erin Keeley Marshall*

# MONDAY, DECEMBER 29

*He is before all things, and in Him all things hold together. Colossians 1:17 (NAS)*

ADELAIDE TURNED ON THE STEREO—LOUD. As Selena Gomez alternated songs with Alvin and the Chipmunks, my five-year-old danced around the great room in her pink and brown piggy pajamas. It looked like so much fun I dropped my dishrag in the sink, ran over to her, and started cutting a rug myself. Pretty soon Adelaide was laughing.

"Mom. Stop. I need to show you some moves."

"What's wrong with my moves?"

"Um. Well, just let me show you." She never wants to hurt my feelings. "I know some really good ones."

For the next song, which happened to be the Chipmunks crooning "You spin me 'round, 'round, baby, 'round, 'round!" we performed Adelaide's "moves." This basically meant I spun her around in circles till we were both dizzy.

Stomachs churning, we stopped, but the room didn't. It seemed to keep spinning 'round and 'round, even with us standing still. She buried her face in my housecoat and I hugged her to me. We clung to each other to keep from falling down.

It was such a great feeling, having that little hand to hold on to. What a blessing it is to have loved ones who give us their hands and help us to stand.

Even more than that, though, Jesus is the peaceful place where we can be safe when our world spins out of control. His is the hand we can hold on to—the One who keeps us from falling. In Him we hold together. In Him, we are strong.

**FAITH STEP:** *Do you ever feel like you may fall apart? Reach for the hand of Jesus. He'll hold you up, and help you hold things together.*

—*Gwen Ford Faulkenberry*

# TUESDAY, DECEMBER 30

*"I've told you all this so that trusting me, you will be unshakable and assured, deeply at peace."*
John 16:33 (MSG)

ALTHOUGH THE HOLIDAYS RECENTLY PASSED, this morning I found myself slipping a Christmas CD into the player. I'm sort of a Christmas carol fanatic, as evidenced by my collection of twenty-five holiday CDs. I grew up on Bing, Perry, and Nat every December, and my heart feels all cozy and peaceful whenever I hear them sing.

As determined as I was last month not to get caught up in the hoopla (aka crazy busyness disguised as holiday cheer), I lived through my share of moments feeling swamped beneath the glittery decor overtaking my house when I wondered if I was missing the best parts of what Jesus wants to share with me during His birthday month.

What things might those be? Love, joy, hope. All favorites. But the one I like best when I'm feeling overwhelmed is peace. Peace. Say it out loud. Isn't it wonderful? It even sounds calming. The first song that rang from my CD this morning was "Silent Night," which embodies the peace that enveloped the land surrounding the manger where the Conqueror and King of the world came to us as a tender, vulnerable baby.

I know Jesus loves peace. He says quite a bit about it. He says in John 14:27 (NIV), "Peace I leave with you; my peace I give you. I do not give to you as the world gives. Do not let your hearts be troubled and do not be afraid." He offered His frightened disciples peace in John 20:19–20, and He readily doles it out to us today.

We need peace in ceaseless, flowing amounts. Trouble is here to stay until Jesus demolishes it forever. His peace reigns over all that. Ask Him for peace today, and enjoy His love, hope, and joy that fill your heart along with it.

FAITH STEP: *Look up these verses next time you need a reminder of the peace Jesus offers you: Acts 10:36; Romans 1:7; Romans 5:1; Romans 16:20; 1 Corinthians 1:3.*

—*Erin Keeley Marshall*

# WEDNESDAY, DECEMBER 31

---

*Truly, O God of Israel, our Savior, you work in mysterious ways.*
Isaiah 45:15 (NLT)

---

ON NEW YEAR'S EVE, J.R. and I spent the evening visiting with church friends. We wanted to be off the road before midnight, so we left at 10:30 PM, but I forgot my purse, and we went back to get it. Then the church youth group needed blankets at their lock-in, so we went home for blankets and delivered them to the group. By the time that was done, it was midnight.

On the way home, we saw a teenaged girl standing beside a car on the side of the road and stopped to help. She had run out of gas and was scared and trembling. We drove her to a gas station, where two employees were locking up. After telling them what happened, they opened the station and helped.

Driving home, I couldn't help but run through the "What ifs." What if I hadn't left my purse? What if the kids hadn't needed more blankets? What if we'd made it home by midnight like I wanted? What if someone else had seen that girl on the side of the road—someone who wasn't intending to help her at all?

I don't know about you, but I believe God indeed works in mysterious ways. He put each of those events in place and allowed us to start the New Year showing His love to someone who needed help. I pray that God continues to show us—to show all of us—ways to share His love in this New Year.

---

FAITH STEP: *Christ told of a Good Samaritan who stopped to help. I believe He gives all of us opportunities. Start the New Year showing His love to someone needing help.*

*—Renee Andrews*

# ABOUT THE AUTHORS

RENEE ANDREWS spends a lot of time in the gym. No, she isn't working out. Her husband, a former All-American gymnast, co-owns ACE Cheer Company, an all-star cheerleading company. She is thankful the talented kids at the gym don't have a problem when she brings her laptop and writes while they sweat. When Renee isn't writing, she's typically traveling with her husband, bragging about their two sons, or spoiling their bulldog. Renee is a kidney donor and actively supports organ donation. She welcomes prayer requests and loves to hear from readers! Write to her at Renee@ReneeAndrews.com, find her at facebook.com/AuthorReneeAndrews.KelleyBowers Zeringue, or visit her at reneeandrews.com or twitter.com/reneeandrews.

SUSANNA FOTH AUGHTMON is the mother of eleven-year-old Jack, nine-year-old Will, six-year-old Addison, and the wife of Scott, lead pastor of Pathway Church in Palo Alto, California. Susanna loves to share the message of God's grace and love through her books and speaking. Using humor and everyday situations in her writing, she explores the life that God has for us as believers. She has written *All I Need Is Jesus and a Good Pair of Jeans: The Tired Supergirl's Search for Grace*, *My Bangs Look Good and Other Lies I Tell Myself: The Tired Supergirl's Search for Truth*, and *I Blame Eve: Freedom from Perfectionism, Control Issues and the Tendency to Listen to Talking Snakes*.

GWEN FORD FAULKENBERRY lives and writes in the mountains of Ozark, Arkansas, where she grew up and the school mascot is a hillbilly. Really. She and her husband, Stone, have four ornery yet adorable children. Gwen is a professor of English at Arkansas Tech University-Ozark Campus, where her students teach her a lot. She is also the author of three novels and three devotional books, as well as a book of prayers for couples. Gwen loves to connect with her readers, so check out her Facebook page at Gwendolann Adell Ford Faulkenberry or drop her an e-mail at gfaulkenberry@ hotmail.com.

GRACE FOX is best described as "deep, daring, and devoted" in her relationship with Jesus. Through speaking and writing, she encourages others to embrace the same characteristics in their spiritual lives. Grace has published magazine articles and six books, including *Peaceful Moments to Begin Your Day: Devotions for Busy Women* and *Morning Moments with God: Devotions for the Busy Woman*. She also produced the award-winning Bible study DVD *Moving from Fear to Freedom: A Woman-to-Woman Conversation*. Married to Gene for thirty-one years, they live near Vancouver, British Columbia, and have three children and five grandchildren. Connect with Grace by visiting gracefox.com or meet her at fb.com/gracefox.author and twitter.com/ gracelfox.

TRICIA GOYER is a best-selling and award-winning author and has written more than thirty books. Tricia's intention is to serve ordinary women by encouraging extraordinary things with God's help. In addition to writing, she enjoys sharing Jesus's love through volunteering as a mentor for teenage moms in her community and ministering in the Czech Republic on missions trips. Tricia and her husband, John, have four children and live in Arkansas. You can find out more about Tricia at triciagoyer.com.

SHARON HINCK is a wife and a mother of four, who lives in Bloomington, Minnesota. She loves spending mornings—and all day—with Jesus. Her novels explore ordinary women on extraordinary faith journeys, including her award-winning Sword of Lyric series and the recently released *Restorer's Son—Expanded Edition*. Sharon welcomes visitors at sharonhinck.com.

REBECCA BARLOW JORDAN is a best-selling author of eleven books and over 1,700 greeting cards, articles, and other inspirational pieces. Rebecca says there are few things she enjoys more than painting pictures with words and encouraging others to have a heart-to-heart with God's words. As a minister's wife, Rebecca has also been involved in women's ministry, discipleship, marriage enrichment, and teaching various Bible studies. She and her husband have two children and four grandchildren and live in East Texas. You can find her on Facebook and blogging on her Web site at rebeccabarlowjordan.com.

ERIN KEELEY MARSHALL is the author of *Navigating Route 20-Something* and *The Daily God Book*, and a contributor to *Mornings with Jesus 2012* and *2013*. Other projects include *Becoming 2* and *Becoming 2008*, *Revolve 2007*, and *Revolve Devotional Bible*. She writes and edits on a freelance basis from her home, while also enjoying family life with her husband, Steve, and their two children, Paxton and Calianne. You can find her on the Web at erinkeeleymarshall.com and on Facebook, LinkedIn, and Twitter @EKMarshall.

DIANNE NEAL MATTHEWS has published magazine articles, newspaper features, and four daily devotional books, including *The One Year Women of the Bible* and *Designed for Devotion*. She also contributes stories to compilation books, writes for several Web sites such as CBN.com and FindingGodDaily.com, and enjoys speaking and teaching at writers' conferences. Married to Richard for thirty-eight years, Dianne currently lives in Salt Lake City, Utah, where she monitors airline ticket prices in hopes of visiting their three children and two amazing grandchildren. Please visit her at diannenealmatthews.com.

CYNTHIA RUCHTI tells stories of hope-that-glows-in-the-dark through her novels, novellas, devotionals, and nonfiction, drawing on thirty-three years of experience as writer/producer of the radio broadcast "The Heartbeat of the Home." Her books have been honored by Reviewers' Choice, Family Fiction Readers' Choice, Retailers' Choice, Lime Awards, and the Gayle Wilson Award of Excellence, and her debut novel was nominated for an American Christian Fiction Writers' Carol Award. She and her plot-tweaking husband live in the heart of Wisconsin, within minutes of their three children and five grandchildren. She frequently speaks for women's events, retreats, and writers' events. Cynthia appreciates connecting with readers at cynthiaruchti.com and facebook.com/cynthiaruchtireaderpage.

# Scripture Reference Index

# TOPICAL INDEX

# A NOTE FROM THE EDITORS

*MORNINGS WITH JESUS* was created by the Books and Inspirational Media Division of Guideposts, a nonprofit organization that touches millions of lives every day through products and services that inspire, encourage and uplift. Our magazines, books, prayer network (OurPrayer.org), and other outreach programs help people connect their faith-filled values to daily life.

Your purchase of *Mornings with Jesus* makes a difference. When you buy Guideposts products, you're helping fund our work, which includes ministry to military personnel, prisons, hospitals, nursing homes and educational institutions. To learn more, visit GuidepostsFoundation.org.

To find out about our other publications and to enjoy free online resources such as inspirational newsletters, blogs, videos, Facebook and Twitter links, visit us at Guideposts.org.

To delve more deeply into *Mornings with Jesus*, visit Guideposts.org/MorningswithJesus.